The Meaning of 360 Zodiacal Degrees

The Meaning of the 360 Zodiacal Degrees
by Charubel, La Volasfera / Sepharial & Isidore Kozminsky

Lay-out: www.burokd.nl

ISBN 978-94-92355-68-3

VAMzzz Publishing
P.O. Box 3340
1001 AC Amsterdam
The Netherlands
www.vamzzz.com
vamzzz@protonmail.com

THE MEANING OF
THE 360 ZODIACAL DEGREES

by
Charubel, La Volasfera / Sepharial
& Isidore Kozminsky

contents

THE ZODIACAL DEGREES:
EXPLORING MEANING AND INDEXING ATTEMPTS

The zodiacal degrees, often considered as the building blocks of astrological interpretation, have intrigued mystics, astrologers, and scholars throughout history. These degrees, each representing a specific point along the zodiacal circle, are believed to carry unique symbolic meanings that influence personality traits, life events, and spiritual growth. Over the centuries, various astrologers and writers have attempted to index and unravel the profound meanings embedded in these degrees.

Early Pioneers and Their Contributions
In astrology, the zodiac is divided into 360 degrees, with each degree associated with a particular astrological sign and its corresponding attributes. The study of zodiacal degrees involves not only understanding the characteristics of each sign but also delving into the nuanced interpretations of 36 decans, 72 half-decans, and each individual degree within a sign. The exploration of these zodiacal degrees can be traced back to ancient civilizations, where early astrologers observed celestial movements and their impact on earthly affairs. In Vedic astrology, the zodiacal degrees hold great significance, as each separate degree is subdivided into 10 parts with different meanings, resulting in a total of 3600 symbolic descriptions. Claudius Ptolemy, a renowned astrologer in the 2nd century, made significant contributions by associating each zodiacal degree with specific planetary influences. However, it was during the Renaissance that a more detailed examination of degrees gained prominence.

Johannes Engel (2 March 1453 – 29 September 1512), also known as Johannes Angelus, was a distinguished physician, astronomer, and astrologer hailing from Aichach, situated near Augsburg, a Free Imperial City within the Holy Roman Empire during his era. He published a work on the decans and degrees of the zodiac, republished in translation by Raphael in 1879 as *A description of the Faces and Degrees of the Zodiac.* These descriptions were made long before the psychological orientated astrology arrived and can appear a bit outdated for the 21st century: *"The ninth degree of Taurus, ascends a man holding a whip in his hand, feeding sheep and goats in a field. The person under this degree will be a neatherd or shepherd."*

The early 20th century

In the early 20th century saw a revival of astrology in Europe, mainly because of Allan Leo, who turned astrology into a system for psychological mapping and insight. In this period the degree interpretations of Charubel, La Volasfera/Sepharial and Kozminsky, described in this book, are published. In 1925 the clairvoyant Elsie Wheeler and the astrologer Marc Edmund Jones collaborated to create the Sabian Symbols, a set of 360 symbolic images associated with each zodiacal degree, allegedly from an ancient Mesopotamian source. This innovative approach aimed to provide richer and more nuanced insights into the meaning of each degree. The Sabian Symbols became a valuable tool for astrologers seeking a deeper understanding of individual birth charts.

Dane Rudhyar and Humanistic Astrology

Dane Rudhyar, a prominent astrologer in the mid-20th century, further expanded the exploration of zodiacal degrees within the context of humanistic astrology. Rudhyar emphasized the psychological and spiritual dimensions of astrology, focusing on the individual's journey toward self-realization. His work laid the foundation for incorporating zodiacal degrees into a holistic framework of personal growth and transformation.

Contemporary Perspectives

In the contemporary era, astrologers continue to explore and reinterpret the meanings of zodiacal degrees. Modern techniques involve a synthesis of traditional symbolism, psychological insights, and intuitive understanding. The advent of digital tools has also facilitated data analysis, enabling astrologers to identify patterns and correlations associated with specific degrees.

Fixed stars and Zodiac Degrees

Fixed stars wield substantial influence within an astrological chart The also played a pivotal role in shaping the meanings associated with Moon-houses, decans, and half-decans. However, the term "fixed" stars is somewhat misleading, as they exhibit a gradual motion, covering approximately 4 arc-minutes every five years. This continuous movement implies that the influence of fixed stars and the nuances attributed to degree interpretations undergo periodic shifts.

Navigating the intricacies of fixed-star influences poses a challenge when seeking a definitive and unwavering interpretation of zodiacal degrees. Crafting an analysis that remains steadfast and independent of the ever-shifting positions of fixed stars proves to be a complex undertaking, given their dynamic nature. In this endeavor, comparing insights from various sources emerges as a valuable practice, providing a more comprehensive understanding of the intricate interplay between fixed stars and the symbolism associated with individual zodiacal degrees.

Benjamin Adamah,
December 6, 2023

PREFACE TO SECOND EDITION

This book, first published in 1898, has met with a very wide sale and hundreds of copies are in daily use by earnest students, all over the world. As to the manner in which the symbols on pp. 17 to 77 were obtained, it will be enough to quote from the Preface to the First Edition:

> 'The two writers whose work is here found have approached the subject from different points of view and each is responsible only for that portion of the book to which his name is attached. "Charubel," who is a born seer and normal clairvoyant, has used his psychic faculty to ascertain the nature and influence of each degree of the Zodiac, and the record is here presented for the use of the practical astrologer. Whatever credit is due for this belongs to "Charubel" alone, for he has attacked and accomplished his task unaided. What he has recorded is original with himself and is not copied from any author, ancient or modern.' *

Concerning the second set of symbols, pp. 83 to 199, we may refer readers to the Translator's Note on p. 79.

---

* It may be of interest to mention that "Charubel" was of the opinion that the Zodiac commenced at ♎25° and not at ♈1° as is usually considered the case. What reasons he had for this opinion we do not know. In a note appended to the first symbol (♎25°) in their original form he states:—"*The preceding fraction of a degree bears the nature of the next complete degree.*" We take this to mean that, for instance, from ♎24°1' to ♎24°59' is reckoned as ♎25°. Some writers have expressed the opinion, and we are inclined to agree with them, that the point (say) ♎25°0'0" should be regarded not as the beginning but as the centre of the 25th degree of Libra, and that this 25th degree consequently extends from ♎24°30'1" to ♎25°29'59"; the *point of maximum intensity,* so to speak, being ♎25°0'0". But there are many who strongly oppose this view, and each must use his own judgment in the application, either of these or of other symbolisations of the Zodiacal Degrees to actual nativities.

Why Two Series of Symbols?

In replying to the inevitable question why there should be two distinct series of symbols—and still more why they should be altogether out of agreement in some cases, as they assuredly are—and further why, that being the case, one only has not been selected and the other omitted—it will be sufficient to say they both have unmistakable value, and even where they differ, are not necessarily mutually exclusive.

As regards "Charubel's" symbols, many students have made a continuous study of them since 1899, and are convinced that whatever may have been the supernormal means by which they were obtained, they have a definite and a substantial basis which experience will justify.

The symbols translated from *La Volasfera* and their interpretions, on the other hand, have been highly thought of and constantly used by some who have unusual opportunities for testing them in their daily work.

In short, practical experience confirms the utility of both series, and this, we think, is sufficient justification, if justification be needed, for the additional symbols here given. As for discrepancies, to the very natural objection that two contradictory statements cannot possibly both be true of the same individual, it may be suggested that one description may apply to the bodily temperament and the other to the personal disposition.

Actual experimentation alone, rather than *à priori* reasoning, will enable one to come to definite conclusions regarding this and other points.

Those who will consult the Index in Vol. XIV. of *Modern Astrology* (Old Series), can find sufficient evidence of value in these symbolisations to reassure them should they be doubtful, but for the benefit of those who have not access thereto, the following from page 204 of the *Astrologer's Magazine* for April, 1893, where these symbols first appeared, will be appreciated:

We have from time to time received letters from correspondents as to the symbolification of the Zodiacal degrees that have appeared in our pages, asking "are they reliable?" It is impossible for us to say whether they all are, inasmuch as we have not a personal knowledge of 360 different persons born each under a different degree—yet we have applied them in many cases with gratifying and satisfactory results. We will give a few instances.

• The poet Shelley was born when 27° ♐ arose, the symbol "a beautiful star the colour and size of the planet Venus, situate about 50° from the mid-heaven, it shines brighter and brighter, then it suddenly disappears. A mighty genius, poet, painter or musician, promises great things, but dies before middle life." The reader is referred to "Sepharial's" able delineation of this horoscope in *Fate and Fortune*, and in the first volume of this magazine, and it is worthy of remark that in his death figure (*vide* March issue, p. 175), the 28° ♐ ascends, and the symbol gives "death through violent means, an accident, etc."

• Edison was born when 5° ♏ ascended, the symbol being "a trefoil; faith, hope and charity are the characteristics, a projector of new schemes for the benefit of the race." Is not this borne out?

• The late Prince Imperial had 10° ♑ ascending, symbol "a noble person, a true knight such will be; a defender of the defenceless, a benefactor of the poor and indigent." This was in keeping with his character.

• The late Princess Alice had 10° ♈ rising; the symbol denotes "a person who will occupy some singular position in life, one whose career will be remarkable, if not unique; noted for daring and hazardous exploits."

• "Sepharial" had 25° ♐ rising at birth; symbol, "a man in a balloon, with dark clouds beneath him. Denotes an experimentalist, an investigator of the imponderables, one whose life will abound with trials, but success will ultimately crown his labours."

14

From the foregoing examples it will be seen that there is verity in *some* at all events, and now the symbols of the 360 degrees are before them students will be afforded an opportunity of testing them individually.

A suggestion

It may be remembered that a brief delineation of each degree was given in Chapter XXIII. of *Astrology for All, Part I.* It will be found a fascinating study to take the nativity of any one who is thoroughly well known to the reader, and to examine step by step the degrees occupied by the Ascendant, Moon, Sun and ruling planet, by the aid of each one of the three series of delineations spoken of. The sidelights on character and temperament that will thus be obtained will be found fully to compensate for the slight trouble involved. *Experto crede.*

In some few instances it may be felt that there must be another and a more spiritual meaning appertaining to the symbol given than that deduced by the seer, or the translator; for example, ♈19°, ♈21° in the first series, ♎12° in the second. In such cases the intuition of the reader should be allowed full play; for it should be remembered that it is the symbol itself which is of deepest significance, and not the particular interpretation given, which is furnished rather as a hint or guide to the understanding than as a final pronouncement. For a further elucidation of this subject, students are recommended the study of zodiacal divisions, contained in *How to Judge a Nativity, Part II. (Synthesis).*

NOTE.
[In this Third Edition beyond a few trifling verbal emendations, no alterations has been made either in matter or arrangement.]

Charubel

ARIES

♈ 1°   *A man ploughing in the midst of a boundless plain.* This denotes one possessing a great amount of individuality and originality; ambitious of being the first in everything. Very jealous of a rival; not an agreeable companion.

♈ 2°   *A man in a very dark room, sitting at a table, with books, papers, and mathematical instruments distributed about him promiscuously.* It denotes one possessing great powers of concentration; a mind capable of great achievements in science, especially in mathematics; yet, owing to some peculiarity of temper, he will never benefit himself by his studies.

♈ 3°   *A man, rushing along on horseback, sword in hand, to meet a company of armed men.* It denotes a violent and fearless person, showing more courage than discretion. He will be liable to get into trouble through rash acts.

♈ 4°   *A man covered with decorations and ornaments of the most gorgeous kinds. He is standing in the midst of a garden abounding with fruit trees, flowers, and fountain. The Sun is shining brightly, and he appears to enjoy himself amazingly, with self-admiration.* A most fortunate degree; fortune smiles on the native, from first to last, by showering on him her choicest gifts. It will not, however, be the result of any particular merit on his part, but rather in the order of good luck. He, or she, will be as vain as a peacock.

♈ 5°   *A large iron cross lying on the ground. All looks dark, sad, and gloomy. There is perfect stillness in the scene; not a ruffle; not a sound of any kind.* This denotes much more than I am able to explain; but the main or leading points are these:—The native will be a sufferer through life. His, or her, cross will prove too heavy to carry. The distress will be of such a nature that it will be out of the power of another to help. It may be the native is born a cripple, or lacks some other important faculty, such as the eyesight, or some other sense; but, whatever it be, he will pass his days in gloom and darkness.

♈ 6° *I see green everywhere; every object is a dull green. At the same time everything is on the move.* The person born with this degree on the ascendant will never have rest, but will ever be on the move. He will ever be seeking rest, but will find none, and notwithstanding the changes be may make, he will find himself at the close as far off from the goal as ever. He may be a balloonist, or he may take a fancy to the study of what is termed the imponderable in nature.

♈ 7° *A large forest of big oaks; no underwood; all is clear beneath; hence a spacious vista presents itself, affording plenty of scope for wandering.* This denotes firmness of purpose; singleness of aim; a lover of rural life; a person holding conservative principles, and opposed to change, or what is called "reform." This person will prosper if allowed to go in his own groove. His chief amusement is the chase.

♈ 8° *I see the earth covered with a deep snow; not a vestige of vegetable or animal life to be seen.* This is a most cheerless degree, and the person so born will experience a most cheerless and uneventful life, and unless well born will be poor through life, as he, or she, will lack that native energy, so requisite to ensure success. I do not consider it possible for such an one to live beyond the prime of life. This person will be free from crime.

♈ 9° *A straight road, going in a direct line up to a point from which lead a number of branch roads, parting in four different directions. There is a finger-post which points but one way—the primal way, the direct one, alluded to.* This denotes one who will miss his way in life, but who will eventually recover, and will become a teacher of others, or may prove a reformer, either as a public speaker or writer.

♈ 10° *A large glass ball, or globe. It is capable of receiving the images of the stars in space, as well as reflecting the panorama of the earth.* The person here denoted will possess a mind open to receive truth and will reflect the truth in his or her daily life. Such will be scrupulously just and honourable. He, or she, may prove to be a great seer, or naturalist. Should this person be of humble origin, he will rise far above his birth.

♈ 11° *A man with a large telescope, which he employs chiefly in looking at things in his immediate surroundings, and what lies on the earth. The most remarkable thing is, that he is looking at the large end of the instrument.* This denotes an egotist, a boaster, a traducer and slanderer. He will never utter a good word for anyone, and will never acknowledge merit. There is no one so great as himself. Of course, a liberal education may tend to tone down much of these extravagances, yet it can never obliterate the whole.

♈ 12° *A labyrinth.* This denotes one who will prove very eccentric in his or her conduct through life. Will have a way and will of his own; and will find his way, if permitted to do so: but as the world is now governed, this person is likely to come into collision with the ruling powers, and thus be in danger. Be this as it may, he will not prosper in the world by following his own way.

♈ 13° *An inverted triangle immersed in a dark fog; slowly this fog clears away, and the triangle becomes a bright blue, imbedded in gold.* This is a most significant degree. It denotes great native powers or abilities which, by some occult power, bring about a host of heart-rending trials for the native during his earlier days. This may be noted in a number of instances, where there is a born genius; and it has proved a puzzle to the philosopher. The question has been asked again and again, "Why should such persons be the subjects of such trials? "The answer I give is that by virtue of pre-natal conditions, combined with the natal, the psychic nature of that person being more open to outside influence than the ordinary, there is a rush of the unfavourable and malignant powers to that sphere, with the object of extinguishing that luminary, or otherwise bringing on a total eclipse.

♈ 14° *A Sun rising in the south-east quarter of the heavens, a little further south than that point which the Sun occupies at the winter solstice.* This person will prove a true Solar man, destined to rule or command. Let such an one ever look towards the south-east of the place of his birth for success in all matters of a worldly nature.

♈ 15° *A black, or very dark, curtain, like a pall, which seems to defy my vision.* My impression is that this degree denotes an untimely or premature death in some terrible way which I am unable to explain. It is to be hoped that such an one may die in infancy.

♈ 16° *A man with a sheaf of corn under one arm, and a sickle under the other.* This denotes a hardworking person, one who will devote his energies to husbandry, and who will prosper by his labour. I advise those who may have this degree on the ascendant to keep to agriculture.

♈ 17°   *A ship in mid-ocean; a boundless expanse of water. It is a merchant ship.* The person of this degree will be a successful merchant. He may prove a great traveller or navigator, and may get a name that will be handed down in history.

♈ 18°   *A battle-field where two contending armies are engaged in deadly conflict.* This prefigures a life of conflict. Such an one can scarcely avoid being a military person. Should he pass through an engagement, he would be killed. If he does not become a soldier, he must be watchful over his own conduct, or he will come to grief. [SEE NOTE TO ♓ 12°.]

♈ 19°   *A country site at the foot of a mountain, with many small dwellings thereon. There are coal-pits in the locality. A poor wo-man is nursing a baby; she is weeping, having just been made a widow.* This denotes that the native will be engaged in mining operations, and will lose his life thereby.

♈ 20°   *A man on the ground with his throat cut.* This appears a bloody degree. Those who may have this degree ascending are advised to do all in their power to fortify the soul, and to pray to God for help and guidance.

♈ 21°   *A shovel standing near an open grave, in which I see a man digging.* This degree points to one who will be a sexton, an undertaker, or otherwise will have to do with the dead.

♈ 22°   *A place of amusement with music, dancing, and singing on the programme. A very large ball-room.* The person so born will take an active part in such a calling; yet will never become a great musician or actor, nor yet a great anything.

♈ 23°   *A comet with a very long tail, pointing towards the earth.* He, or she, will be a notorious character; and may become an in-strument in the bands of evil powers, so as to bring evil on this earth generally, as well as on individuals in particular. Such persons, if born in a high position, may become the scourge of nation. But whatever be their position, their influence will prove baneful to all with whom they may have to do.

♈ 24° *A green field surrounded by shrubberies; a nice villa on the north-east side of the field.* It is from the north-east point of the place of birth that persons born under this degree will derive all their good. It denotes one who will possess an adequacy to keep him; and with this he has the disposition to be content.

♈ 25° *An out-house with a dark loft, to which a ladder conducts the homeless ones.* Unless the person who has this degree be born rich, he, or she, will become a vagrant and beg.

♈ 26° *The person born with this degree ascending, will make a discovery; a new idea will dawn on the world through his agency.*

♈ 27° *A man in a garden, pruning some trees.* Denotes a lover of horticulture, and one who may prosper on those lines.

♈ 28° *A farmyard, with a lot of cows. A woman milking a cow.* A dairyman, or woman; a milk seller, or a dealer in such articles as milk, cheese, or butter.

♈ 29° *Two men engaged in a fight.* This denotes one who will ever be ready to oppose anything and everything; a pugnacious individual; if not respectably connected, may become a professional pugilist.

♈ 30° *A man wheeling a barrow load of earth over a hollow run.* This denotes that the person so born will be engaged through life in downright hard labour; and, although such an one may be born in different circumstances, yet he may be driven to poverty, through crime, or the force of circumstances. So this degree may safely be designated a hard degree.

TAURUS

♉ 1°   *A black, diamond-shaped figure.* Denotes a person of strong character; of a rather morose disposition, and possessing magical powers; one with strong will-power, very reserved, inclined to be cruel.

♉ 2°   *A large figure 2 comes before my vision.* Denotes that he, or she, born under this degree will live alone, isolated, mentally; not in sympathy with the present state of things.

♉ 3°   *A double cross; two lines parallel in the upright, and two parallel in the horizontal.* Strong sympathies, excessive sensibility, very impressionable and mediumistic.

♉ 4°   *A ram standing alone, looking towards a flock of sheep in the distance.* Denotes one in whom the male principle predominates *excessively*, the female being nearly nil, sympathies towards the opposite sex wanting. If a man he rarely ever marries, if a woman, she ought not to marry.

♉ 5°   *A boat on a large lake, it might be a big river; two men are rowing in it.* Denotes a person fond of company and of changes; a speculative bent of mind and fond of adventure.

♉ 6°   *A large elliptical figure on the ground, and a man standing upright within.* A person who loves passionately, one who is a great admirer of the opposite sex; a lover of the beautiful, in art, and in nature.

♉ 7°   *A horrid sight! a naked man suspended by the feet, to a cross-beam, mutilated, and the blood running down the body.* Denotes one liable to torture, in one form or another.

♉ 8°   *Two swords forming a cross lying on the ground, and a man standing on them with a sceptre pointing heavenward.*

A person of peace, one who confides in the higher power.

♉ 9° *A new Moon, on a very dark sky.* Denotes one who will have a very gloomy life and who is likely to die before he passes his prime.

♉ 10° *A large water-wheel attached to a corn mill.* This denotes a mind capable of many accomplishments, a person with a flexible mind; an excellent mathematician; much ingenuity.

♉ 11° *A scrawl or flourish of the pen.* This denotes one doomed to many disappointments through lack of judgment, incapable of adapting himself to conditions required of him, ever anticipating what be can never realise.

♉ 12° *A fork, resembling a farmyard implement, with four prongs.* A laborious person, very unambitious, a useful member of society, ever content with his present lot.

♉ 13° *An anchor unattached to any vessel's chain, but lying with its hook fast to a rock, the cable broken.* The native will be the subject of terrible trials, over which he will appear to possess little or no control; hence his end is very mysterious.

♉ 14° *A dark and sombre curtain hanging from a horizontal pole which covers the mouth of a dark cavern in a rock.* Denotes a recluse, a lover of solitude, a student of the mystical, a possessor of hidden knowledge.

♉ 15° *A natural well surrounded with moss, low shrubs, and briar's. The water is clear as crystal and cold as ice. The immediate locality is dry and barren.* A person possessing wonderful abilities, numerous accomplishments, and, above all, a revealer of secrets, much given to researches in nature.

♉ 16° *Two acute-angled isosceles triangles, the bases of which are attached to an upright, the triangles pointing to the left.* Denotes one who is a stranger to the public and not very popular among his friends; incapable of thinking on abstract truths.

♉ 17° *A very small cottage at the base of a very high mountain, where jutting rocks appear to overhang the cottage perpetually threatening its destruction.* A truly good person; one who has implicit faith in the Most High.

♉ 18° *A man beating an ass with a stick.* Denotes what it pictures; one of a low and savage nature, who, unless properly trained, will lead a criminal life.

♉ 19° *A large star in the western sky, half as large as the moon, but more brilliant. Its rays appear to be confined to one spot. The surrounding sky is dark.* This denotes a great genius. His home is, or will be, the western hemisphere.

♉ 20° *A large flag on a flag-staff, fixed on the top of a very high mountain.* Denotes one who will rise from a very low degree to eminence.

♉ 21° *A stile.* Denotes one having an analytical mind. He may succeed as a chemist, or where application to minute analytical effects is called for; a very sound reasoner.

♉ 22° *A pair of shears.* A most dexterous person at any handicraft; a -good artizan; an expert in surgery.

♉ 23° *A smelting furnace.* A large hearted persoa, but at the same time particularly sensitive to an imposition or a fraud. Such transactions rarely escape being detected. Soul force is great; whilst the intellectual powers may be but of moderate capacity.

♉ 24° *I seem to be above the earth; I see the sun ascending above the horizon, while it is yet dark on that hemisphere towards which it is approaching.* The signification of this strange phenomenon, in part, is: A man, yet one greater than a man!

His mission is a world mission, but present conditions will scarcely admit of such a development.

♉ 25° *A dark, moving column, it stands very high.* This denotes a very mysterious character. Whilst living among men, a stranger to men. He has a life of his own, a world of his own, he is content to live and die unknown.

♉ 26° *An elephant.* A person possessing much sagacity. A great amount of secrecy, and implicit confidence in his own strength.

♉ 27° *A dark cloud passing over a part of the earth. This cloud is charged with elemental shapes, most hideous and repulsive.* Such a person must beware, or he will be tempted to dabble in Black Magic, which would terminate in his utter ruin.

♉ 28° *A very straight road; an interminable perspective.* This denotes an evenly balanced mind, and a most uneventful life; a life that will be long and happy.

♉ 29° *A crucifix.* Be careful. A life full of strange events, and liable to grevious accidents.

♉ 30° A very rough sea, a wreck; the life-boat is despatched; all are finally rescued. Thou shalt save many, and thou shalt save thyself. An active philanthropist.

GEMINI

♊ 1°   *A white oval figure on a very black background. The background contains no forms or shapes of any kind.* This is an important degree; whoever may have this degree on his or her ascendant will be unfortunate through marriage. If a female, should she ever become a mother, the labour will be attended with much suffering, and possibly death. A very negative person, open to evil influences.

♊ 2°   *A narrow vista of considerable extent, resembling a square tube, the interior of which is luminous, rendered so by some means I do not understand.* Denotes much power of concentration. The native will discover some one thing, some force in nature, perhaps, according to the bent of his, or her, genius. It may be connected with optics or some new phase of electricity, or he may find his way in chemistry. It is possible that this may apply with equal truth to the metaphysical or the transcendental.

♊ 3°   *A tremendous Corinthian pillar, with a large amount of earth, buildings and rocky ramparts resting on it, and which appears to be the only support of the massive superstructure.* Denotes a strong character—strong in every way, both physically and psychically. Should this person be so circumstanced he may cut a prominent figure, as the founder and supporter of some gigantic scheme or organisation. As a rule such an one cannot fail to find his way into some very important position in life, attended with great responsibilities.

♊ 4°   *A profile, with only one eye in view.* Great powers of perception. An active, sharp intellect; an exact or accurate observer of men and things. He would make a good detective; a practical mind; no mere theoriser.

♊ 5° *A person of good proportions; fine dark eyes with arched eyebrows.* This is an all-round person. What ever he, or she, takes in hand will be accomplished most efficiently. Very neat in attire, orderly in business, and methodical in mental pursuits; a good reasoner; proud, and a little selfish.

♊ 6° *A promiscuous lot of creatures, consisting of cattle, sheep, pigs and poultry.* Denotes one given to domestic pursuits, and very partial to domestic animals, but more as pets than as a means of profit.

♊ 7° *There is NOTHING connected with this degree.* A blank. Some mystery here which I do not comprehend.

♊ 8° *A large office, and a man sitting at a desk, writing in a large book resembling a ledger.* A person having good practical abilities, especially adapted for commercial pursuits.

♊ 9° *A labyrinth, situated in the heavens, and a fine silver thread suspended from it to the earth.* Denotes a peculiarly constituted mind. He, or she, will engage to do what the majority of mankind would have no patience to do. A talent for propounding and solving conundrums; for solving enigmatical problems, or any given theorem requiring solution.

♊ 10° *A monster plant of the gourd tribe, arising spontaneously from beneath the soil; growth is in the act of taking place before my vision.* The native possesses mighty energies; his or her fortune in life is of rapid growth. Anything he may engage in will succeed as if propelled by magic power. In the meantime, I would advise such to temper their exuberance with cool and deliberate reflections.

♊ 11° *A triangle, whose base-line is three-fourths the length of one of its sides, having a small circular figure at the extremity of each of the angles.* This denotes an extraordinary character. He is one not easily understood. Outwardly, he appears destitute of that force which one would suppose he possessed. There is some defect in his outward organism, which impedes his development on the outer plane, in that force of character you may have been led to anticipate. Of this the native is conscious. He cannot, under these circumstances, avoid being a little deceptive, and is not free from duplicity. In the meantime, be will prove an eminent financier. He will have much of that shrewdness which is the leading trait in a man of the world. He will be lacking in the moral or religious principle.

♊ 12° *Two men turning a handle of a crane from the jib of which a large chain is suspended, attached by a hook to a large stone.* This denotes one devoted to the study of Mechanics, and he will be ever fond of experimenting in dynamics.

♊ 13° *Stairs, or a large step-ladder, with a landing, and a hand rail at the top, which leads to nowhere.* Denotes one having lofty aspirations, possessing, withal, superior abilities, but who, through a lack of fixedness of purpose, seldom performs anything of real benefit to himself or others, save affording himself a certain amount of self-amusement.

♊ 14° *I see a number of quadrangular figures, consisting of straight lines forming an oblong square, with two triangles on the top. It appears to assume the form of a cube.* This denotes a person possessing vast powers of intellect. An accurate reasoner; a profound philosopher; a person who will make an impression on the age in which he lives.

♊ 15° *A rapid inland stream which might be called a narrow river.* Denotes an active temperament, a restless disposition, self-willed, of a turbulent temper, a shallow thinker.

♊ 16° *A man on the roof of a building putting slates on it; and another carrying the slates up a long ladder.* This denotes one who is ever engaged in such deeds as tend to benefit the community. A lover of peace, and promoter of all good works.

♊ 17° *A square, containing twelve small squares, resembling the breast-plate of the Jewish high priest.* Denotes one of a reverential and devotional disposition. Very secretive, a student of the occult, and one capable of mighty deeds as a magician.

♊ 18° *The number 6 rules this degree.* Denotes a purely mercurial person; an expert in all mercurial employments.

♊ 19° *An empty space.* A person not disposed to settle down to any kind of work of a plodding nature. A very weak character, and one open to extraneous influences of any kind.

♊ 20° *A red tree covered with golden fruit.* A very noted degree. A person of a very positive nature, who, by dint of personal efforts and work, will produce something that will be a blessing to the race. No ordinary person, he or she will rise to eminence.

♊ 21° *A traveller struggling onward in the midst of a terrible snowstorm. He pushes forward in hope of finding a refuge, but the storm thickens, it grows darker and darker. The brave man is lost in the darkness.* This symbol must be its own interpreter. The sun that sets on one clime rises on another.

♊ 22° *I see the Sun rising in his brightness. It is on the horizon, but all the other part of the sky is covered with dark clouds, over which hang the shades of a lingering night. A noble nature.* This nature is stamped with a generous disposition. The native's early life is marked with promise but fate and fortune conspire against him. The winds are too cold for that sensitive soul. He is born out of time and place. His grand schemes prove failures. His sun sets under a cloud while it is as yet but morning.

♊ 23° *A man standing on a lonely plain, weeping.* This denotes one who is liable to give up in the struggle of life to despondency; very much wanting in energy, and destitute of moral courage.

♊ 24° *A deer.* A person of fine sensibilities; a lover of art; a student much given to scientific research.

♊ 25° *A balloon.* A person capable of performing remarkable feats, yet he will never succeed in any one great enterprise.

♊ 26° *A spacious room filled with expensive furniture, among which several mirrors are to be seen.* Denotes a strict conformist to conventional usages, and fashionable life; one who devotes much of his or her time to self-aggrandisement. In the meantime, he will possess artistic accomplishments and love for the fine arts in general.

♊ 27° *A large room, on the ceiling of which is a gilded star.* Denotes a superficial person, one who sees more to admire in decorative art than in Nature.

♊ 28° *A baronial mansion with spacious park abounding with gigantic trees.* Denotes a person not given to change, a student of antiquity, who takes but little interest in new inventions. A profound scholar, if circumstances permit, and possessing a sound judgment.

♊ 29° *A man flogging a boy with a horse whip.* A cruel person, a despot, one who may obtain some post of authority, where he will disgrace himself by exceeding his duties.

♊ 30° *An execution.* I would warn the native to be very careful as to the company he associates with, as he may have to suffer for what another may have done.

CANCER

♋ 1° *A large clock with weights in sight, suspended from a high place, on which I see a large dial-plate, with hours and hands complete.* This denotes a splendid timeist in music, and one who will delight in this study of dynamics, a shrewd observer in what pertains to cause and effect.

♋ 2° *A man in a green-house, with a watering-can, watering some flowering shrubs.* This denotes one whose delight will be in the study of the beautiful in Nature; who will devote time and energy to the development of the beautiful, more especially in the floral kingdom.

♋ 3° *A deep shaft descending into the earth, and right overhead a balloon.* This denotes an all-round person, one conversant with the different strata in the information of the crust of our globe. In the meantime the native will make himself familiar with those graduated densities in the atmosphere that are found at different altitudes. He will be a scientist of some note.

♋ 4° *I see that side of the Moon which is never seen by the inhabitants of this planet.* As this is a thing I dare not look at, inspection being dangerous, I will simply give the character it typifies. A strange character, one whom no one will ever understand. A person possessed of powers unknown to the present race, and who, unless the mind has been much distorted, will pursue studies with which the age is not conversant. He will not be tied down to any religious tenets, as he can never be brought to submit himself to any. He will be a magician, but not of any known type. Such an one may be called insane, whilst the brain and intellect generally are quite healthy. But the powers are what I call, *Moon-set!* That is, such a man is out of the ordinary groove of everyday life; but he is not insane. All that the average person may be taken up with, is uncongenial to him. There is ever a gulf between such a character and ordinary humanity.

♋ 5°   *A person holding up a scale in his hand, with even beam.* A just person, one whose mind will spontaneously detect a falsehood, or an injustice, or any wrong.

♋ 6°   *A large tract of land mapped out and enclosed with posts and rails, intended for a farm and homestead in the near future.* This denotes one possessed of boundless resources; an adventurer; a person who generally accomplishes what be purposes. His speculations are successful.

♋ 7°   *I see one large, ripe, nicely-tinted apple suspended from a bough.* There is but this one on the tree. This denotes one who will advance himself from comparative obscurity to a position where there will be no compeer to rival his excellencies.

♋ 8°   *A man pulling at a rope attached to a bell which is suspended near the top of a high tree.* A person who will take a delight in publishing what he knows about everybody. As the conductor of a newspaper he may be in his sphere; but it will be with difficulty that he will preserve himself from the crime of defamation of character.

♋ 9°   *A spider in the corner of a room intently watching the giddy dance of silly flies, as they heedlessly approach the confines of his dominions.* This denotes a student of law and order, a shrewd lawyer. He would make a good detective.

♋ 10°   *A bulbous plant, just pushing its way upward from beneath the sod, and beginning to unfold itself in order to show forth its beauties.* This denotes one possessed of a great amount of soul-force; in whom the principle of life is very strong. He will make a powerful magnetist, as he will have a strong will.

♋ 11° *A young girl playing on a lyre.* A gay person, fond of youth and youthful amusements; artistic and musical.

♋ 12° *A cypress tree.* A person of melancholy and fretful disposition, mournful and gloomy. He will suffer much through bereavement.

♋ 13° *A man, delving.* An industrious person; most particular in all small matters; ever partial to manual labour.

♋ 14° *A man, standing before an audience, with all the paraphernalia of a juggler.* This denotes one having allround accomplishments. He is never at a loss through lack of resources. He is capable of turning his band or his wits to anything.

♋ 15° *A pool of water.* An easy-going person, content with only a little. Poor abilities; rather unstable; fond of home.

♋ 16° *This is a blank degree.* What this implies I cannot say. There is some mystery about the number four and its square.

♋ 17° *An artificial globe.* This denotes one who will travel; a student; and one who may make many discoveries.

♋ 18° *A bull tossing a man with his horns.* This denotes a wilful person, one who will be always on the defensive, and too often on the aggressive. Personal property will have but little sacredness with him, his motto being, "What I can get is my own."

♋ 19° *A man with a very old-looking book before him. It has the appearance of some ancient record.* This denotes a studious person, a profound thinker, one capable of grappling with abstruse studies. He loves his books, and his studies are more for self-amusement than with the object of appearing in print. He is free from that craze.

♋ 20° *A large building with walls of granite, having a dull or sombre appearance.* This denotes something lasting. This person will do some great deed in life, which will be handed down to posterity. His chief characteristic is firmness, not ghoulish. He will live to a ripe old age.

♋ 21° *A king, an emperor, or commander on horse-back.* This is the degree of power, and should raise the native to some post of honour where he will be in a position to command rather than obey.

♋ 22° *A quantity of toys or common ornaments of glass and tinsel.* This denotes a proud person, fond of the artificial, and he is highly superficial; one of a fretful and peevish disposition, creating misery wherever he, or she, may reside.

♋ 23° *A burly man with an apron before him.* This degree governs work connected with catering for the public. It will answer for the manager of a restaurant, an inn-keeper, or a butcher.

♋ 24° *A small church, but highly ornate, having all the sacerdotal display usually met with in larger places of that class.* This denotes one who will be very religious, a strict observer of feasts, fasts, and festivals; but a very narrow-minded person, and a most intolerant bigot.

♋ 25° *A very lofty pine tree.* This denotes a noble person, one whose mind is fired with grand aspirations, and whose good influence will be felt beyond the limits of his own neighbourhood. His deeds will speak louder than words.

♋ 26° *A gentleman with a number of ladies in a carriage.* This denotes a good and kind disposition; a person very liberal with his presents, in whose nature benevolence bubbles, lacking in circumspection, a veritable "Timon of Athens."

♋ 27° *A pear tree, loaded with large ripe fruit.* This person abounds in goodness; his nature is charged (so to speak) with good influences, which flow from him spontaneously. He is a living talisman for the healing of discord and strife; a peace-maker.

♋ 28° *Heaps of gold and silver coin.* This person will grow rich, however poor or low his birth may have been; he will get money, and he will know how to look after it. He loves money for its own sake, hence becomes a miser.

♋ 29° *A man driving a bull, or an ox.* A person who will be fond of dealing in cattle, a cattle dealer; he will prosper by such means.

♋ 30° *An acute triangle with a cross on the top.* A person of particularly strong will, very lofty in his deportment, and commanding in appearance; he would succeed in some official capacity under Government.

LEO

♌ 1°   *An obelisk.* Denotes one who will suffer many and great trials, reverses of fortune, etc., but will, or *may*, leave behind him a name on the pages of history. Such a life may, for a time, be so much involved in the life of the nation, or people, among whom he may live and labour as to be lost sight of, but finally he mounts to the surface.

♌ 2°   *A rostrum.* This denotes one who may pass through the greater part of his life unconscious of those high abilities he possesses, abilities which might render him a very popular character and an important factor in the life and character of society. The rostrum is empty; he may therefore miss his calling.

♌ 3°   *A veiled statue.* The degree of mystery! Denotes the gradual unfoldment of the sublime and the glorious. The student of what is great and lofty; a vivid imagination; he is fired with enthusiasm, and liable to err through an excess of passion, but if all be well under control he will bless his race.

♌ 4°   *A carrier's waggon; one of those with the tarpaulin overhead.* Denotes an active person; one who is always on the move. In his case the saying is true: "The grass is not allowed to grow under his feet." A practical person, always engaged in what is useful to himself or others, A business man, he will at a glance take in what may be to his own advantage or otherwise.

♌ 5°   *Something like a forge beneath the surface of the earth. A number of men are working in an almost nude state, owing to the heat. It proves to be an engine room belonging to a large steamer.* This person will undergo much suffering.

He may leave his native land under very gloomy circumstances. I advise such an one to live very quietly, to get into some settled and uniform mode of living; to keep clear of all of a speculative character, and never to take on himself any office of trust, or where great responsibilities are involved.

♌ 6°   *A large ball of fire flying through the air.* Denotes one who has a special mission of an extraordinary character; and providing all be favourable as to birth and surroundings he cannot fail to become a ruler of men, and a gaint among men—intellectually or morally, if not physically.

♌ 7°   *A pyramidal figure with a Maltese cross at the top, or rather on the apex.* THIS IS POSSIBLY AS GLORIOUS A DEGREE AS ANY IN THE ZODIAC. This degree is impinged by a ray from a transcendental sun, one of those suns which with our sun revolves round the grand central sun. Denotes the greater good; the sublime; gives prophetic inspirations; rules the wonderful; and fills the soul with a flood of celestial glory. This degree throbs sympathetically with the seventh degree of Libra.

♌ 8°   *A hedgehog.* A person of harmless disposition; secretive, and he naturally shuns the public gaze. In the meantime he knows how to defend himself, hence he appears to be always on the defensive.

♌ 9°   *A bomb exploding in mid-air.* This is not a good degree. The fact is, it denotes what is very pernicious. Such a person, unless there be in his nativity some counter influence, will prove a pest to his generation. The astrologer will know how to balance such matters. This degree resembles a bad mixture of Saturn and Mars.

♌ 10°   *A shovel suspended in mid-air.* Denotes a would-be agriculturist, but he will devote much of his time and energy to what is impracticable and consequently profitless, as much so as digging the air and sowing to the wind.

♌ 11°   *A new Moon, but only the smallest portion of it to be seen in the western sky.* Denotes prematurity in all things. Such an one may give some promise of developing into a genius, as there will be much in early life calculated to inspire such hopes or anticipations; but nothing comes to maturity.

♌ 12°   *A sailing ship on a calm sea. The sails are all unreefed, and the masts are decorated with a profusion of bunting.* Denotes one who will experience much happiness in life. It may be safely said of such an one, "Whatsoever he doeth shall prosper." In whatever sphere of action he may be engaged, he will come out with honour. He will be popular, he will receive the plaudits of the age in which he lives; but such popularity will not long survive his demise.

♌ 13°   *The letter Q appears.* Denotes dissatisfaction. One who never takes anything for granted, or on trust. A sceptical person; a quibbler; hypercritical; one disposed to consider "all men liars" save himself; a most disagreeable, querulous, cantankerous, and quarrelsome person.

♌ 14°   *A large bubble floating on the water in which are seen all the colours blending.* Denotes an admirer of the sublime and the beautiful. An idealist; an occultist; a transcendentalist; in the meantime, a comparative stranger to the ordinary matters of every-day life.

♌ 15°   *A profile of the head and face of a man. His face is long, but inclined to the oval; the eyes are large, but somewhat expressionless; he is clean-shaven, save a very carefully cultivated moustache.* A veritable type of the ordinary man of the day; fond of pleasure, and enters heartily into the fashionable amusements of the age; a stickler for the conventional and the popular.

♌ 16°   *A giant amusing himself with a child's doll.* Denotes one who possesses great abilities; a mind, which, if rightly directed, could accomplish, or at least assist in bringing about, great and beneficial changes on the earth. But in place of this, he condescends to employ his time and his energies in the pursuit of what is childish, whimsical, and worthless; by which he not infrequently makes himself the laughing-stock of his contemporaries.

♌ 17°   *A wild boar.* Denotes one whom you may kill, but never conquer; nor will he be induced to adopt *willingly* the tricky policies of modern civilisation. He has a life of his own, a sphere of his own, and pleasures of his own. He may be designated coarse and impolite, but such epithets make little or no impression on him.

♌ 18°   *The Greek letter Lambda, λ.* This is no ordinary person; he or she may be born of humble parentage, but must eventually rise above the plane of his birth. This life is marked by sobriety, with a plodding disposition. He may not be noticed during his younger days and during his earlier efforts, but by virtue of that innate courage which he possesses he is bound to gain publicity.

♌ 19°   *A star surrounded with many rings.* It is a star outside the zodiac, and beyond the vision of the outer sense. It is one of those suns which revolve about the grand central sun. Its rays impinge this degree, and impart to it a virtue. The native who may have this degree on his or her ascendant never need be cast down. Thou wilt meet with trials, but fear not, "Thy bread shall be given thee, and thy water is sure."

♌ 20°   *A man, like the fabled "Sisyphus," rolling a stone up a hill, but who never gains the top.* Denotes a person whose life may appear a complete failure and whose energies appear to be expended on what produces nothing; consequently there is no apparent result. But do not despair, study your natal figure.

♌ 21°   *A high mountain having a plateau on the summit. In the centre of the plateau I see one of the ancient magi in the act of performing his matutinal devotions.* The lord of day ascends on the luminous horizon. This requires no interpretation beyond this: that he who may have this on his ascendant must become, to some extent at least, like the one I see in my vision.

♌ 22°   *A man with a long wand with a glass globe on the top. The globe is charged with aromatics. The bearer as he passes along fills the air with sweet odours.* This denotes one who feels most honoured when he most serves. To serve in his day some of the numerous wants of a suffering humanity is the end and aim of his life. A transcendental sun impinges this degree with its rays. Its nature is Mercurial.

♌ 23°   *A large undershot water-wheel.* Denotes one who will prove a leading character in some great movement, or he may be the founder of some society, or school of philosophy.

♌ 24°   *A farmhouse between high mountains. A yard about the house entered by a white gate.* Denotes one whose proclivities are towards a rustic country life. He will prosper if be deals in things or creatures of a white colour. When he moves, let him go south-west of the place of his birth.

♌ 25°   *An orange tree loaded with fruit.* Denotes one very fond of pleasure, and who indulges rather freely in luxuries. Let him beware! The sun does not always shine! The longest day ends in night! In the meantime, he is a person of fine tastes, and the possessor of many accomplishments.

♌ 26°   *A rock, and men getting large granite stones out of this rock.* Denotes one who will succeed with the most ordinary things of this world; yes, he will even become wealthy by means which other people would consider beneath their notice. This person must ever go north of the place of his birth.

♌ 27°   *A large stone falling on the head of a man.* The man is working in a very low place. Whoever may have this degree on his ascendant must avoid low places, such as cellars, or at the basement of buildings. He must keep on high ground, and sleep in the uppermost sleeping apartment. This person should move due south of the place of his birth.

♌ 28°   *A man descending a pit.* This person will do well by dealing with what lies deep in the earth. Let him, or her, never travel or move about, but ever remain at, or near, the place of his birth all his days.

♌ 29°   *A number of mathematical instruments on a table, with a large sheet of blank white paper.* Denotes one possessing mathematical abilities beyond the ordinary; but there is some room for doubt that he may fail to follow up such a noble exercise. His mind may be carried away into other pursuits, for which he is not at all adapted, and which in the end yield no satisfaction.

♌ 30°   *An old sage, sitting by his midnight lamp, studying some grand problem.* This denotes one who has a profound intellect; a gigantic will; a mature judgment. One who is a true magician.

VIRGO

♍ 1°   *A wolf carrying away a lamb.* Denotes deception, cunning, avarice, and cruelty. Such a degree, unless there be much to counteract it, would render the native liable to become a great criminal.

♍ 2°   *A man peeping around a corner at a company of armed men, who are in the act of reconnoitring.* Denotes a strategist; one well adapted for the army; or might succeed in almost any other department. In the meantime such proclivities might appear, at times, anything but enviable.

♍ 3°   *An elephant with his castle on his back.* Denotes strength, cool courage; a defender and helper of the weak; and one endowed with great sagacity.

♍ 4°   *A square patch of ground, resembling what might be set apart for lawn tennis; covered with red cloth, or what resembles such.* Whoever may have this degree on his ascendant is born for the enjoyment of the luxuries of this life; plenty follows him; but wilful waste, and useless expenditure on what pertains to matters conventional, superficial, and the artificial, these prove his leading characteristics. Whilst he is intensely devoted to art, he will ignore the beauties of nature.

♍ 5°   *A very long, straight road, the terminus of which I do not see.* This life is uneventful, there is little or no ambition, nor is there much in such a life to stimulate such a feeling. This life being uniformly even, there is but little calculated to put caution on the alert. Hence the native is liable, after the prime of life, to become poor, as adequate provision for future contingencies has not been thought of. Thus a quiet life is not always to be desired, where provision depends on one's own exertions.

♍ 6°   *A room full of machinery and jars of chemicals.* A scientist, a chemist, an inventor; an active person. Great power of perception; and a promising experimentalist.

♍ 7°   *A person with wig and gown.* The law is your sphere of action. You will excel in forensic science; and it is possible you may attain to eminence on these lines.

♍ 8°   *A coach heavily laden with passengers.* Denotes a public character; one who will do much for others, but liable to forget those duties he owes to himself, and to those who may be dependent on him. In the end he finds himself but poorly treated by those whom he devotedly served.

♍ 9°   *Four long posts at right angles forming a four square: and four rails fastened horizontally to the top of each. It looks like the rude framework of some temporary building, or "shanty."* An explorer; a discoverer; a traveller; one the history of whose life will be marked by more than one exploit.

♍ 10°   *The Mundane Cross,* ⊕. A student of Nature's mysteries; a lover of the sublime; an author, or revealer of the strange and the curious.

♍ 11°   *A pyramid of red, very conspicuously situated on a large open plane.* This denotes one of a strong character; much strength of will, great energy; he seldom fails to accomplish what he takes in hand to do. Strong animal passions; and these, unless well regulated, may occasion some trouble, This person will "never say die."

♍ 12°   *Several figures of eight in a row, thus: 8 8 8 8 8 8 8 8. Thus you see the square of eight.* Denotes a man, or woman, of mystery; a lover of the mystical; a student of the mystical; a secretive person; a profound understanding; he will leave for himself a name in history.

♍ 13° *A naked infant, exposed, sleeping alone in an open and dreary place. Around and above that helpless form are beasts and birds of prey. But, by some strange power, unseen, this embodied picture of innocence is protected.* Denotes a simple unassuming person; one who has been but little noticed; no special favourite of anyone. His parents were cruel, and ever since his birth, cruelty has dogged him. Yet, withal, he has some strange power about him, and whilst exposed to the plottings of enemies, be is saved from the power of their malice, and in every contest he comes off, eventually, the victor. "No weapon formed against him shall prosper."

♍ 14° *A fine horse, with curved neck and flowing mane, prancing in the pride of his strength.* A noble person; a generous person; a kind-hearted person; but a proud person.

♍ 15° *A man standing, resting lightly on the end of his bow, with his quiver full of arrows on his back.* A mind capable of grand achievements. A warrior, yet not exclusively such; a quick observer; a designer; a prompt and a skilful executant.

♍ 16° *A man wading through mud knee-deep. The opposite bank towards which he is struggling is enveloped in fog.* Denotes a hard life, a struggling life, a life bestrewn with the wrecks of perished hopes and abortive speculations, the final one of all being a plunge into the dark.

♍ 17° *A person being carried by four men in a sedan chair.* A favourite of fortune, he will have the good luck to accumulate wealth; will be endowed with good parts and possessed of numerous accomplishments. But his idleness and characteristic sloth may render him a useless member of society, and, as a consequence, self-indulgence may prove his ruin.

♍ 18° *An angle of 45 degrees, thus ∠.* Denotes a person possessed of good abilities; one scientifically inclined. Ever seeking public favors by pandering to the popular taste and supporting what are the views of the moment. He is nevertheless, one who will eventually suffer from the public, This person thinks but slightingly of his best friends, nor will he confide in them.

♍ 19° A strong farmer's cart, and a horse to match. The cart is loaded with farmyard manure. Denotes a frugal, industrious person. An agriculturist, and one who studies that branch scientifically.

♍ 20° *A lion whose head is the only part exposed.* Denotes one who is ever on the defensive, and being on the alert, is always prepared for any attack. One void of fear, ever living in the consciousness of his superior strength. Thus, instead of shunning an opponent, he prefers to wait, or rather to provoke the onslaught. He may not be the first in the arena but he will be the last to quit it.

♍ 21° *An ostrich.* Denotes a person of large build, lofty looks, and pompous in his general demeanour. In appearance, a gaint; in assumption, a hero; but when brought into close quarters, where his valour is put to the proof, a veritable "John Falstaff," one who despises the ideas of another and has none of his own. "A sounding brass and a tinkling cymbal."

♍ 22° *An extensive forest; in the distance, the sun just peeping above the horizon and flooding the tops of the trees with his glowing rays.* This denotes what the Greek cynic, Diogenes, was looking for with his lantern. *A man.* Yes, a man among men. One who will spontaneously elicit the goodwill and plaudits of his fellow-men. Thousands will look up to him for light and for guidance. It is possible he may initiate a new epoch, or prove himself the founder of a new philosophy.

♍ 23° *I see rings of light in the heavens; ring within ring, or zone within zone.* A mind not at all adapted for this day. He fails to fit in the general mould of modern ideas. He lives in a world of his own, nor will be be understood by the men of his age. He is the man for a far distant future.

♍ 24° *A large assembly room. A large audience and a man at the piano.* An artistic person, an eloquent person, a musician, a popular person.

♍ 25° *A golden ball suspended from the ceiling of a circular hall.* This is very mystical; there is something about this person that he never makes known. At the same time it is that which lends a charm to his life; it endows him with a power to fascinate those who may be favoured with his company.

♍ 26° *A man climbing a steep hill in the dark, allured by a light he sees illuminating the summit.* He succeeds in gaining the top, but instead of the sunrise it proves to be but a meteor. Such an one must avoid all things of a purely speculative character. His inspirations are misleading. Let him not believe every spirit but try the spirits.

♍ 27° *I see nothing but sunshine; all is bright—a cloudless sky.* Denotes a prosperous person; he is truly happy, being born under most favourable conditions.

♍ 28° *A man in his shirt sleeves turning a big wheel.* A laborious life; at the same time assisting in a work that is producing a mighty influence on the world.

♍ 29° *A bird perched on the top of a high tree, welcoming the day-dawn with its song.* Denotes a prophetic soul; a poetic mind; and one who is ever hopeful.

♍ 30° *A country scene; on the right hand a large tract of land enveloped in gloom and fog; on the left the scenery is all sunshine.* Denotes a person of a discriminative mind, very truthful, and very decided for the truth, and that exclusively.

LIBRA

♎ 1°   *A four-square figure, thus:* □. Denotes one who is scrupulously honest, and rigidly just in all transactions. A person of a sensitive nature; not happily disposed, as a rule, owing to the incompatibility of circumstances.

♎ 2°   *A man playing on a violin.* One possessing splendid abilities; of most refined taste; exquisite accomplishments; and a generous disposition. Much fineness of perception; and in whose higher nature the intuitional, abounds.

♎ 3°   *A long pole suspended horizontally in mid-air with a rope attached to each end connected with the earth.* Denotes one who may have a knowledge of a law in nature not popularly recognised, whose operations are as marvellous as that of the pole in mid-air. If such an one does not make his or her mark in his day, there must be some terrible power frustrating.

♎ 4°   *A man with a knife in his hand.* Denotes one having great dexterity in the use of edged tools. He is capable of great achievements as an artist or engraver as well as in the more humble departments, such as carving, etc. As a surgeon he would excel.

♎ 5°   *A man feeling his way over a bog, where he appears to be sinking at every step he takes.* Such a native would find it a difficult matter to make his way through this world, more especially after middle life.

♎ 6°   *An old-fashioned signboard suspended from the branch of a tree before an ancient looking wayside inn.* One of a very conservative disposition; one who reveres the usages and customs of by-gone days. An antiquarian and a relic-hunter.

50

♎ 7° *An angel standing in mid-air, with a long scroll in his hand, unfolded. This scroll is covered with writing.* This degree has been pointed out to me as the Messianic degree. At the same time, it does not follow that those having this degree on their ascendant are all Messiahs. But, should the native have the favourable aspects of the superior planets at his birth, he must be more than an ordinary person. NOTE.—LIBRA HAS THE LEAST SYMPATHY WITH THIS EARTH OF ANY OF THE SIGNS OF THE ZODIAC.

♎ 8° *A figure resembling what is called "the true lover's knot."* A person having strong sympathies; very affectionate; very confiding. In the meantime be or she may pass through this world unnoticed and with the finest feelings of the soul un-reciprocated.

♎ 9° *A man standing on the top of a high momitain; on the one side a perpendicular rock; he is standing near this precipice with a red flag in his hand, which he is waving by way of sig-nalling a promiscuous crowd, who appear to be rushing on horseback at a gallop towards this rock.* Denotes one who will be endowed with great powers of discernment, much fore-thought. One able to detect a fault where another would see nothing wrong. An excellent critic, and may become a proficient analyst.

♎ 10° *A lovely garden of flowers.* Denotes a person of good taste, fine sensibilities, and an admirer of nature in her most lovely garb; but unable to appreciate her in her ruder though more sublime grandeur. Thus, whilst admiring the tiny springs from the fountain on the lawn, he would be uneasy in the roar of Niagara.

♎ 11° *An ancient shepherd with crook in hand, standing in the midst of his flock.* Denotes one of great sagacity and who has an extraordinary love for rural life. This is the only degree in this sign that tends to adapt a person for this ordinary earth life, and which at the same times furnishes him with a large amount of this everyday world's wisdom. This person should reside amid mountain scenery, and should deal in sheep and cattle.

♎ 12° *A man with a bow in his hand; but he has no arrow.* A person of splendid parts and excellent abilities, but who is ever unfortunate in being deprived of the means of effecting his purpose. When an opportunity presents itself, he finds himself unable to turn it to advantage.

♎ 13° *A man with his arm in a sling, and his head bandaged.* Denotes one who is liable to accident, and is very unfortunate.

♎ 14° *An innocent-looking woman with fair hair; rather tall; she appears restless. I see a very dark-looking being behind her back.* This native will be liable to obsession. I would warn such to beware of mediumship, and would say "strengthen your system, and fortify yourself in every way."

♎ 15° *A fat pig lying down.* Denotes one who will ever appear to live for self. Hence all his or her study will be: "What shall I eat or what shall I drink?" At the same time a harmless person, one free from criminal acts. Being nearly destitute of ambition, he will care but little how the world goes on, so long as he gets his fill of his own desires.

♎ 16° *A soldier, going through his drill.* Denotes one who, although possessed of military proclivities and perhaps ambitious of military honours, will ever be unfortunate in that calling. And should he ever be engaged in active service he is nearly certain to be killed, or at the best, badly wounded.

♎ 17° *A horse saddled and bridled, and galloping away without a rider.* Let this native shun the hunting field and beware of all equestrian adventures. [Let him remember also that the horse is the symbol of the senses, and the rider of the mind.]

♎ 18° *A man at a desk writing all kinds of hands, from the largest hand to the most microscopic.* Denotes one who possesses some one special gift; a gift that is allied to the artistic. Not a mere painter in colours, but a painter in words. He can read a character quickly, but may indulge a little too freely on these lines, so as to render himself actionable for slander.

♎ 19° *A man on the tread-mill.* This does not imply criminality, but rather that this native will have a very hard and unsatisfactory life. He is compelled by the force of circumstances to labour hard, and will witness but little, if any, of the fruits of his labours.

♎ 20° *The sun shining brightly.* Denotes a great man; a public character; one who will be noted in his day, and whose presence among mankind will be considered essential. The world will ever appreciate the presence of such an one.

♎ 21° *A cross formed of darts, that is, having a barbed termination to each arm.* A very positive character. A person of strong will. He will never allow anyone to impose on him. He is ever on the defensive; one with magical abilities.

♎ 22° *The open Bible with a sword on it.* Denotes a truthful person, a good person and a just person. The judge who has this degree on his ascendant will give righteous judgment.

♎ 23° *The clear blue sky covered with stars.* Denotes one possessed of numerous gifts, and endowed with many accomplishments. He will never reside long in one place. A wanderer over the earth; an explorer; an astronomer; and one who will make great discoveries.

♎ 24° *A big man. He resembles a giant, but the lower limbs look black; this appears to creep upwards.* The one who has this degree will be the subject of many misfortunes, and liable to numerous losses. He possesses ambition and capacious desires. But whatever he speculates in will fail. In the meantime, let such an one examine his natal figure carefully, and it is possible by so doing that he may be able to master what some call destiny.

♎ 25° *A Welsh harp.* Denotes equanimity; evenness of temper, and great regularity of conduct; a degree of passivity; a lover of the harmonious, in all things.[*]

♎ 26° A heron. It denotes finesess of perception, one who very keenly appreciates what may be going on around him; he cannot be apathetic under any circumstances; a sensitive person, liable to be carried to extremes. This is a sensitive point of the Zodiac.

♎ 27° *A rhinoceros.* Denotes strength of body, calm courage; one who can stand unmoved on the battle-field simply because he is incapable of fear, or of realising danger, Such an one has but one object at a time, that absorbs him.

♎ 28° *A man with a crown on his head, and a spear in his hand.* Denotes dignity, valour, and humanity combined.

♎ 29° *A woman standing on the head of a serpent.* Denotes great sagacity, under the guise of feminine weakness; a person of great fascinating power.

♎ 30° A raven standing on a stone. Denotes individuality, moroseness; a person avaricious, destructive, or revengeful; secretive; a recluse; a misanthrope.

---

[*] "Charubel" was of opinion that the Zodiac commenced at this point. See Preface.—Ed.

SCORPIO

♏ 1°   *A heart.* Affectionate, confiding, unselfish; much influenced by others.

♏ 2°   *A human skull.* Mystical, fond of the occult; great depth of penetration; liable to melancholy.

♏ 3°   *A triangle.* Denotes a variety of gifts, much force of character; one who will make his mark in the world; a large brain, the moral and intellectual predominating; one who commands respect without assumption.

♏ 4°   The double triangle. Denotes great will power; a magician.

♏ 5°   *A trefoil.* Faith, Hope, and Charity are the characteristics: a projector of new schemes for the benefit of the race.

♏ 6°   *A monster with two faces, like the ancient Janus.* Denotes duplicity and deception; a slanderer.

♏ 7°   *A naked boy, a crown on his head, a sceptre in his hand.* Denotes innocency combined with great native dignity, and promise of future greatness.

♏ 8°   *A comet (like the one in 1882).* Denotes waywardness and eccentricity; but he will do some great deed in his life.

♏ 9°   *A sheaf of corn.* Denotes a practical benefactor of the race; a good member of society.

♏ 10°   *A mariner's compass.* Denotes one with great intuition; fond of secret studies; will make discoveries.

♏ 11°   *A lamb at a distance from its dam, but looking towards her.* Denotes one with strong filial affections; he cannot be happy without one to love or to cling to.

♏ 12°   *A bull pawing up the earth.* Denotes a person who will have his own way; his anger is lasting.

♏ 13° *A fox sitting on his haunches.* Denotes one who is ever on selfish ends; he makes a good strategist.

♏ 14° *A dove.* Innocent and harmless; much moral courage; one who thinks and acts from the heart more than from the head; a true friend; a constant lover.

♏ 15° *A round temple with pointed roof.* Denotes a person partial to the outward observances of religions rites; very superstitious regarding its mysteries.

♏ 16° *A red flame, ascending upward to a great height.* Denotes a person possessed with ardent desires; an enthusiast to the cause he espouses; a true friend and an open enemy.

♏ 17° *A female in a state of nudity.* Denotes a voluptuous person, liable to be carried away by the lower passions.

♏ 18° *A man holding a pair of scales in one hand and a sword in the other.* A just person, but prone to become too severe.

♏ 19° *A serpent with many heads, all in a circle, with fangs protuding.* Denotes one who may become a pest and a terror to society; unless overruled by benefics, will prove a curse to his relations and acquaintances. This is the cursed degree of the so-called cursed sign; yet even this may have its purposes.

♏ 20° *Two men fencing with swords.* A duellist; a pugilist, a gymnast; one who would not admit an equal; a very formidable kind of opponent.

♏ 21° *A man in the midst of a lot of children at play.* Great simplicity of manner; one fond of children and childish amusements.

♏ 22° *A man holding a fowl by the neck in the act of strangling it.* A cruel person and a coward; one who will take advantage of the weak and defenceless.

♏ 23° *The moon in her first quarter.* One fond of change; a speculator; one too sanguine in his or her expectations; yet, on the whole, fortunate.

♏ 24° *A woman sitting on a tombstone in the act of weeping.* One sensitive and sympathetic; destined to have much sorrow through the death of friends; a lover of the shady side of life more than the sunshine.

♏ 25° *A white flag unfurled, with a red Maltese cross on it.* A person of noble mind, pure intention; the subject of much suffering, but eventually triumphs over all obstacles, and vanquishes every puny foe.

♏ 26° *A mole.* Great individuality; very reserved; very determined; one who hates the public.

♏ 27° *** With this degree ascending at birth, and other testimonies good, the native will prove a very extraordinary person; one destined to take an active part in public life, and one who will exercise a great influence on mankind.

♏ 28° *A tiger crouching, ready for a spring on its prey.* A revengeful, treacherous and cruel person. This degree is an evil mixture of Saturn and Mars.

♏ 29° *A man with a bow and arrow in the act of taking aim at some object in the distance.* A good marksman; very expert; fond of the chase, yet noble and humane; generally prosperous in life.

♏ 30° *A man in full armour, with helmet on head and spear in hand.* One fond of military pursuits; will make a good soldier; generally of very good proportions.

SAGITTARIUS

♐ 1°   *A serpent in the shape of the letter S.* Denotes one very saga-
cious, sensitive and subtle; one who will not be imposed on ;
will readily see through a plot; would make a good detective.

♐ 2°   *A stupendous waterfall.* Fond of the wild and romantic in na-
ture and in art; the ordinary humdrum life is by far too tame for
such a nature, where the love of the marvellous superabounds.

♐ 3°   *A man at a table with drawing instruments and paper before
him.* Denotes one who is artistic; may make a good architect
or engineer; also a lover of the fine arts.

♐ 4°   *A man walking on the edge of a precipice.* A very reck-
less person; one who scarcely ever foresees danger until
overtaken by it; very sensitive; very impulsive; but also very
affectionate and honourable in all transactions.

♐ 5°   *A female with the lyre in her hand.* Denotes a person with
much musical talent; highly appreciative of the refined in
art, and of the sublime in nature; fickle and fond of change.

♐ 6°   *A man viewing himself in a looking-glass.* This degree de-
notes vanity; he who may have this degree ascending at
birth will be inclined to be vain of himself, or will devote his
energies to some vain pursuit or profitless calling.

♐ 7°   *A lady sitting on a divan fanning herself.* He or she having
this degree ascending will enjoy the good things of this life.
This is a fortunate degree, and always denotes prosperity.

♐ 8°   *A man, stripped to the shirt, with sleeves up, and wheeling
a barrow along a plank.* This denotes a servant of servants;
the slave, the toiler; he born with this ascending, if rich at
birth, is in danger of becoming poor late in life.

♐ 9°   *A man standing on a platform and an audience in front.* A public man, a lecturer, a politician; an orator in some line. It also denotes a literary person, or one fond of literature.

♐ 10°   *Cross-swords.* A person always at variance and involved in quarrels and broils.

♐ 11°   *A lion standing alone with tail erect and in the act of running towards a panther.* A person of noble disposition, high-minded, honourable, but bold, courageous and fearless of foes.

♐ 12°   *An apple tree whose boughs are bending with ripe fruit.* A person of fixed habits, fond of his home; an aflectionate husband or wife; a kind parent and a benevolent citizen.

♐ 13°   *Death, with a scythe in one hand, and a bag of money in the other.* A miser; one who will starve himself for gain; and one who would delight in slaughter and carnage if it would prove of some monetary advantage to himself.

♐ 14°   *A magician in his sacerdotal vestments, standing in a magic circle, performing some magic rites.* Denotes a person fond of "Art magic," one devoted to the ceremonial; very credulous and highly superstitious.

♐ 15°   *A large telescope pointing heavenwards.* Denotes a scientist and one gifted with clairvoyance; also a lover of sidereal studies.

♐ 16°   *A person about entering a dark tunnel.* He or she having this degree on the ascendant will go wrong in life if there be no saving influences in operation. A most unfortunate and hopeless degree this.

♐ 17°   *A little boy in a state of nudity blowing bubbles.* Much innocence, one who will live long, but one who will do but little good or harm; ever bent on personal amusement, and such as may be deemed worthless.

♐ 18° *A ploughman engaged in the act of ploughing.* Denotes one inclined to agricultural pursuits, and one who will prove a steady, industrious person; one content to live by hard labour; a plodder.

♐ 19° *A man in a boat on a lake.* A person fond of fishing and aquatic exercises; but in other respects indolent and partial to the joys of Bacchus.

♐ 20° *A man in the act of distributing papers among a multitude of people.* Denotes one who will be a person of a restless disposition; an enthusiast and a strong partizan; a reformer on a small scale, but very superficial.

♐ 21° *A wooden bridge over a chasm, a man at the end hesitating to trust himself on it.* One of a fearful disposition; very much inclined to doubt everything, and prone to suspect even his best friends.

♐ 22° A May-pole with a crown of flowers at the top, and a man climbing to procure it. Denotes one whose sole object in life is popularity, and in whose organism the love of approbation predominates.

♐ 23° *A person at the bottom of a deep ravine, with lamp in hand looking for something.* A mineralogist; a geologist; and one who will be fond of such researches as lie within the earth.

♐ 24° *A ship in full sail on the midst of the ocean.* Denotes one fond of change; will travel far from the land of his or her birth; may become a trader in foreign produce, but on the whole unstable and never settled.

♐ 25° *A man in a balloon with the dark clouds beneath him.* Denotes an experimentalist; an investigator of the imponderables; one whose life will abound with trials, but success will ultimately crown his labours.

♐ 26°   *A giant of monstrous dimensions.* Denotes one who will be a prodigy of some kind; maybe in stature or maybe in mind.

♐ 27°   *A beautiful star of the colour and size of the planet Venus, situated about 50° from the mid-heaven; it shines brighter and brighter, then suddenly disappears.* A mighty genius; a poet, a painter, or a musician; promises great things, but dies before middle life.

♐ 28°   *A funeral procession and an open grave, and a great concourse of people; great excitement.* This is a dangerous degree. The native having this on the ascendant will not die a natural death, but will die through violent means, an accident, etc.

♐ 29°   *A dissecting room, where are a number of medical men engaged in a post-mortem examination.* Denotes a student of human nature, an anatomist and physiologist; one who would succeed in surgery; a very dexterous person, and particular in details.

♐ 30°   *A man standing alone in a dark and gloomy valley, and a ray of brilliant light coming direct from the heavens on the crown of his head.* Denotes one who will have a mission to execute; a cyclic man, not a time man; one who lives a life beyond his day; not always understood, he suffers accordingly.

CAPRICORN

♑ 1° *A man standing on a rocky eminence with arms folded, in a contemplative mood.* Denotes one who is self possessed; has entire confidence in his own abilities, and in the cause he may have espoused. Generally, he is right.

♑ 2° *A lofty building, with nave and massive pillars on each hand.* Denotes a mind capable of appreciating the sublime in archi- tecture, and imbued with the deeper feelings of veneration for the sacred or antique.

♑ 3° *A gigantic "dragon tree " (known to botanists as Dracoena Draco) belonging to the Canary Islands.* This denotes one who is possessed of almost boundless resources of vitality; and, when brought low by illness, will very soon recuperate. Such are no common specimens of manhood, they generally live to be very old.

♑ 4° *The planet Venus (♀).* Denotes a person of much refinement; one partial to the ornamental, and enamoured of the beau- tiful, both in nature and art; delights in the company of the opposite sex far more than in his or her own.

♑ 5° *A very small unpretentious window in the wall of a mas- sive tower.* Denotes one whose native powers and mental resources are so great and abundant that the native will be independent of external aids, and will feel ever happy amid the offspring of his own genius. Further: such persons will never seek display; these are creators, not imitators.

♑ 6° *A butcher clothed in his working dress conducting a sheep into the slaughter-house.* A person of dangerous proclivities; unfortunate to those with whom he may have to do; selfish, crafty and cruel.

♑ 7° *A maze.* Denotes one fond of enigmas, who will spend his life in profitless researches; liable to be carried away by foolish whims; nevertheless, one possessing great ingenuity.

♑ 8° *A man desponding, standing on a barren plain with leaden coloured clouds overhead.* Denotes a gloomy and monotonous life; uneventful, and generally poor in worldly substance.

♑ 9° *A man climbing a steep hill, a road consisting of steps; an angel form at the top giving words of cheer with a golden crown awaiting him.* Denotes one who will be inspired to pursue an object worthy of his ambition, and one who will labour hard and suffer much in the fulfilment of his mission.

♑ 10° *A large encampment consisting of women, little children, old people and invalids; a man at the gate keeping guard.* Denotes a noble person; a true knight will such be; a defender of the defenceless, a benefactor of the poor and indigent.

♑ 11° *A man inspecting horses.* This denotes a horseman; one fond of horses, a good judge of such; fortunate as a horse dealer.

♑ 12° *A spacious park with a baronial mansion in the background.* This degree denotes much: the ancestors of the native must have been of a high order, whatever he or she may be to-day; there are large possessions belonging to such, and possibly others are enjoying it whilst the native lives in poverty. I advise those who may have this degree on their ascendant to look into this matter.

♑ 13° *An Eastern town (Constantinople).* Denotes one whose proclivities are eastward, and whose sympathies will be with Turkey and the Turkish dominion, and who may, eventually, have much to do with those climes.

♑ 14° *A vista extending to a great distance; on either hand are majestic trees covered with a profusion of foliage.* A person fond of landscape paintings; and one possessed of artistic gifts; open to enchanting visions. This is in a special way an idealistic degree.

♑ 15 *A lonely traveller in a solitary way, with a heavy burden on his back; he is assaulted by ruffians.* Denotes one most unfortunate; his whole life is one continued struggle, and that for a mere existence; always imposed on and wronged out of his hard-earned pittance; everything seems to be against him, and do what he may he cannot succeed.

♑ 16° *A man of stout make, good proportions, round, rosy features, looking very merry, dancing grotesquely.* Denotes one who lives to eat and enjoy himself; never troubles his mind with cares; seldom thinks of the future by way of providing for the same; the present is his all; his creed is, "Let me eat, drink and be merry, for to-morrow I may be dead and 'done for.'"

♑ 17° *A man with a large pair of scales in the act of weighing.* One who will have much to do with weights and measures; he will have a liking for such employment, and will be apt in matters of detail.

♑ 18° *A racecourse, the racers at full speed.* Denotes a gambler, a "bookmaker," a betting man; one who will devote his time and his money to such speculations.

♑ 19° *A coal pit, the machinery at a standstill, the whole of the plant in a dilapidated condition.* Denotes one who will have much to do with mining operations; if a miner, liable to suffer by accidents; if a proprietor, liable to become bankrupt by such pursuits.

64

♑ 20° *A person ascending a spiral staircase with sunshine at top, within a dark enclosure.* Denotes one who has to do much in life for very small returns; he may always appear busy, yet with but little to be seen for his labour; nevertheless, good luck falls to his lot at the end of his days.

♑ 21° *A ferry boat in the act of taking people across a wide deep stream.* Denotes one who will be a guide and a teacher of the public; he or she will prove of much service to others, far more than to himself.

♑ 22° *A spacious hall, like a museum, the walls of which are covered with symbols and hieroglyphics.* Denotes a student of the mystical, an antiquarian, a person given to curious studies.

♑ 23° *The sun shining brightly in a cloudless sky.* Denotes one who is liable to be carried away with brilliant anticipations, being too sanguine; he is ever liable to disappointment, and for as much as I see the Sun in the south-eastern quadrant, these anticipations will be more or less confined to early life.

♑ 24° *A man struggling in a lake; only the head out; sometimes the head appears to sink under, but it rises again and again until at last a lifebuoy is thrown to him by a person witnessing his position; finally he is saved.* Denotes one who will always be in trouble through debt; always involved; always on the verge of bankruptcy; finally by some unlooked for and unexpected "god-send," he or she is delivered.

♑ 25° *A field of ripe corn; the reapers are at work 'neat the beams of the Sun.* A very fortunate person, more especially about middle life, when fortune smiles on him, and an abundance is his lot.

♑ 26° *Too revolting to be given.* Whoever thou art who mayest have this degree on thy ascendant, keep out of bad company. Indulge not in stimulants; keep clear of the gambling hells, and seek to develop thy higher nature; by such a course thou mayest save thyself.

♑ 27° *Two men running a race.* Denotes a pedestrian, one fleet of foot, an adept at cricketing or any of the athletic sports.

♑ 28° *An indescribable scene; chaos, confusion, dissolving views.* Denotes one who is born with some very marked defect of intellect; or he may become insane after he has passed childhood. This degree gives weak intellect, generally idiocy.

♑ 29° *A man walking beside a cow, with his hand on her back, and bringing her home from the pasture at eventide.* Denotes one very fond of cattle, also one who will possess great control over the bovine species, and one who will prosper by a dairy farm.

♑ 30° *A shepherd on the mountain top with crook in hand, looking out for the locality of his sheep.* This symbol is more figurative than literal; it denotes one who, by reason of his superior powers and advantageous position in life, will be called to be a leader and a commander of a society, a community, or perchance a nation, in the capacity of president. This degree is pre-eminently the degree of rule, and that ruler who has this degree on his ascendant will be a ruler indeed.

AQUARIUS

♒ 1° *A man standing at the junction of cross roads, not knowing which way to go.* Denotes a weak character, one who will not make headway in the world through indecision.

♒ 2° *The trunk of a large tree covered with moss, and hollow.* A romantic degree this, one who will outlive the other members of his family; he will probably be the last of his race.

♒ 3° *A warrior in bright armour with drawn sword, pursuing a savage multitude.* One with great occult ability, and who has a mission to accomplish; a White Magician! Go and conquer.

♒ 4° *The letter T or the Tau.* One whose inner nature few understand, and who will never be popular in the nineteenth century; one outwardly a babe, but inwardly a giant—"of such is the kingdom of heaven."

♒ 5° *A cherry tree in full blossom.* One who is very precocious, with early promise of genius, but who rarely lives to maturity.

♒ 6° *Two bulls fighting.* A disagreeable, unsociable man, a fault-finder; one who cannot talk without argument, and who cannot argue without losing his temper; hypercritical.

♒ 7° *A crown and sceptre.* One who is entitled to more than he possesses, and who has powers of which he is unconscious.

♒ 8° *An astrological chart in square form.* One who is fond of Astrology; a just, kind person.

♒ 9° *A farmer's horse aud cart with man driving.* An unambitious person, one who is quite contented with his lot.

♒ 10° *A ruin consisting of the remains of an ancient massive wall, with an archway therein.* A lover of antiquity; an archæologist; one who finds more pleasure in the retrospective than in the prospective.

♒ 11°   *A monster rocket exploding in mid-air above a crowd.* One who will seek and attain ephemeral popularity, but it is soon over.

♒ 12°   *A sexton digging a grave.* A secretive, unsympathetic person, who takes pleasure in others' misery.

♒ 13°   *A tastfully furnished room, with a large wax candle on a round table in centre.* A lover of his home, a person of conventional proclivities who may be called a "house-proud" individual.

♒ 14°   *An oval-shaped mirror.* One with a very impressionable mind, who retains but little.

♒ 15°   *A beacon light on a high rock.* One with great intuition. Those having this degree should pay strict attention to those impressions which the world calls foolish, but which show the Divinity speaking through humanity.

♒ 16°   *A vessel rolling in the trough of a rough sea.* Denotes one who will ever live in a state of uncertainty, subject to many changes and severe trials; his career will be a struggle for existence.

♒ 17°   *A naked man, having a serpent coiled around the lower part of the body.* A vicious degree; denotes one subject to filthy habits and deeds; he that hath this degree on the ascendant should "Know himself" and seek to conquer his evil nature.

♒ 18°   *A man on crutches.* An unfortunate degree. Denotes one liable to infirmities and diseases of the legs and feet.

♒ 19°   *A man seated at a desk with account books before him. He has dark hair, projecting eyebrows, receding forehead, keen, dark eyes.* Denotes a business man, an expert accountant.

♒ 20°   *A man playing a violin.* Denotes a musician of no mean order; a brilliant violinist with musical ability.

♒ 21°   *A man in monkish dress, with long hair and flowing beard.* Denotes one fond of solitude and very reserved; a recluse; one naturally inclined to a religion of a severe type.

♒ 22°   *A lady with rounded features; fair skin, hair between auburn and brown, deep blue eyes; she is busy at her toilet.* This is the degree of beauty; those of either sex who have this ascending will be always admired.

♒ 23°   *Three men in a boat, two on one side, one on the other.* Denotes one who will meet with much rivalry and opposition in whatever he may engage in.

♒ 24°   *A man with arms folded, unmindful of danger; behind him an assassin with dagger about to stab him.* Denotes one who will ever be beset by secret enemies of the worst type, and may eventually be killed, although there may be no apparent reason for this.

♒ 25°   *An old fashioned wooden pump; a man in rustic garb at the handle, pumping for a crowd with vessels reaching forward for them to be filled.* Denotes one who, ostentatiously, will dispense much good by charitable deeds.

♒ 26°   *There is no symbol to this degree.* A degree of mystery. It is allied to the fourth dimensional space. Denotes one who has SOMETHING not in common with the rest of his race.

♒ 27°   *A Standard-bearer.* Denotes a leader of the multitude, a public character, or perhaps a reformer.

♒ 28°   *A neat little thatched cottage in an Alpine valley.* Denotes a true child of nature; one who will never conform to the ways of Society.

♒ 29°   *A man with open breast, showing enlarged heart overflowing with blood.* A degree of sorrow. Denotes one who will be subject to most harrowing trials through life, and who will die heartbroken.

♒ 30° *A man reclining on a rustic seat 'neath a shady tree; a ray of sunshine has fallen on him.* A degree of good fortune. He who has this will not have trouble; wealth flows to him, but he only lives for himself, and seldom benefits others.

PISCES

♓ 1° *A hand holding a roll of paper or parchment.* Denotes one devoted to the calling of a copyist, a lawyer, or one having much to do with documents of one kind or other, but chiefly connected with the public.

♓ 2° *A very long ladder, such as is used by fire brigades.* Denotes one possessed with a considerable amount of ambition. At the same time open to inspirations of a very lofty character. He or she will ever feel disposed to indulge mentally, if not actually, in speculations on a grand scale. A scholar and one who may do much in his day towards the elevation and salvation of mankind.

♓ 3° *A luminous cloud, one of the woolpack type, isolated and sailing slowly in the azure sky. The cloud suddenly opens and pours out on the earth an influence resembling a shower of pearls of variegated hue.* Whoever may have this degree on his or her ascendant will be the subject of numerous celestial gifts. He will prosper in matters temporal and spiritual, and that without apparent effort on his part. At the same time he will be liable to lose by recklessness, accompanied by a degree of prodigality.

♓ 4° *A man holding the end of a rope in his hand, the other end out of sight in the heavens.* Denotes one who will betimes develop a very peculiar psychological power, which will place him or her in the condition to procure esoteric truth at will consciously. This belongs to a class of mediumship of a very high power.

♓ 5° *A black pall suspended, and a man in a gloomy enclosure looking at it despairingly; finally he musters courage to lift the pall, and enters a dark passage, which, however, finally conducts him into the light of a glorious day.* Whosoever thou art with this degree on thy ascendant, be prepared for trials, but don't give up in despair; for ere thy fortieth year shall have expired, thy day will have dawned.

♓ 6° *A target.* Denotes one who is endowed with great powers of concentration, and in whom the spirit of rivalism abounds. A military man and a good marksman.

♓ 7° *An extensive plain on which a dense fog hangs, but the fog is low and there is sunshine above.* Denotes one ever liable to frustrations and confusion with worldly matters, and consequently ever liable to go wrong and come to losses; but in the meantime, he may have attained to great heights in matters spiritual and transcendental.

♓ 8° *The full Moon.* Denotes a practical business person, one who readily allies himself with the world's ways, and with ordinary matters in general. One never short of expedients. A little cantankerous and not one of the pleasantest companions.

♓ 9° *A deep red star, a star of the first magnitude, on the ascendant; but a very short interval elapses between its rising and its setting. But when set, I see a pale golden light succeeding.* This is a virulent degree. If this be thy ascendant beware! Do not follow the dictates of passion, nor yield to the desires of thy lower nature. If thou dost, a short and wretched life is thy lot; thou wilt die before thy prime is passed. But if by virtue of a firm resolve thou art able to overcome those elemental promptings, then thou wilt pass through the evil crisis, and thereby ensure a long, useful, prosperous, and happy life.

♓ 10°   *A fixed star. A transcendental Sun. It sheds a halo of supernatural glory on the ascendant.* The person having this degree will have much psychic power. There will be much in his or her life not capable of explanation in the light of Astrology. He will possess most brilliant gifts, but at the same time will not be appreciated by the present day world, simply because it will not understand him. His life will be long on the earth, and his influence will extend to future generations.

♓ 11°   *The ascendant enveloped in gloom and blackness.* This is the degree of death. I think few live, or come to maturity, who have this ascendant. If they do, their life will be a misery so far as this world is concerned. I advise such to devote their energies to the spiritual side of their nature. Here they may find comfort, even when walking through the way where the shades of death abound.

♓ 12°   *A very large disk consisting of circles of light with dark grey interspaces. These circles resemble wheels within wheels, which I find on closer examination to be spiral, all revolving.* This symbol contains far more than I am able to express in words. First of all, this native cannot live and have his being upon those ordinary lines along which the multitude are eagerly rushing. Secondly, his or her early life will be passed amid considerable confusion, attended with much apparent contradiction. He may seek to do as others do, but it will not answer. Next, he is inclined to give up in despair, but just at that critical moment an inspiration fires his inner self, a new light develops, he gets out of those dark interspaces where possibly he may have been floundering about for years, on to the circle of revolving light. Henceforth he is on his groove and is carried onward and upward. His path is the path of the just that "shines brighter and brighter unto the perfect day."

[NOTE.—The Zodiac of the Constellations commences at about ♈ 18°*hence the Vernal Equinox or First Point of Aries (from which the Zodiac of the Signs is reckoned) is situated in or near the twelfth degree of the *Constellation Pisces*. As the two Zodiacs have a mutually sympathetic relationship, the above delineation obtains an added significance from this fact—especially the allusion to "wheels within wheels." See also delineation of ♈ 18°.—ED.]

♓ 13°   *There is no symbol to this degree.* But I perceive that this degree is charged with evil, and wickedness of the most diabolical nature belongs to this degree, or is denoted by it. This nature will be subtle but plausible in appearance. Destitute of one spark of REAL sympathy. One who will ever prove treacherous to those who take him into their confidence. He is reserved, he is studious, but his favourite pursuit is black magic. Much of this is liable to modification, providing a benefic be on the ascendant or aspecting the same; but under the most favourable circumstances such a person will find very strong leanings to injure his fellow men rather than do them good.

♓ 14°   *A field of ripe corn ready for the sickle. A cloudless sky and brilliant sunshine.* A most fortunate degree for all mundane matters. Health of body, peace of mind, a most happy disposition, prosperous in all worldly transactions.

♓ 15°   A hand with a sword in it. Just rising in the ascendant, a halo of golden light envelopes it. That sword is not for indiscriminate slaughter. It is to defend the right. Whosoever thou

---

*   See *The Hindu Zodiac,* by G. E. Sutcliffe, 1s. 6d post free.

art, thou hast a mission to accomplish, and thou wilt be armed with the necessary power and authority to execute that mission. Thou art a child of the sun. Thy pedigree must be looked for in the archives of the solar world. But the poor worldlings, the inhabitants of this red planet, will not see thee as thou art seen by thy compeers.

♓ 16° Two swords crossing each other. Denotes one nearly always involved in litigations and quarrels. A person of a repellent disposition.

♓ 17° *A man with two hourses ploughing.* This is not to be taken literally, but psychically or spiritually. The field denotes this world of mankind, and as the plough is the first instrument employed by way of preparing the earth for the reception of the precious seed, this native will be a pioneer, or forerunner, to prepare the way for a higher manifestation.

♓ 18° A military officer mounted on a fine-looking charger, with sword in hand, on the top of a hill as if on the look-out. This degree denotes a strategist, one competent to organise a multitude or an army, and will possess abilities for commanding the same. This symbol is capable of two applications, the one temporal and the other spiritual.

♓ 19° *A man lying in a bed, a grey dark cloud cloud hanging over him. His chamber is also dark and gloomy. Yet the horizon looks bright.* This denotes one who will be the subject of some heavy affliction during his younger days, but whose latter days bring health and other comforts.

♓ 20° *An angel blowing trumpet.* Denotes one whose office will be to publish to the world some important message: a message having a bearing on the social or spiritual condition of mankind. A preacher, a lecturer, or some popular person.

♓ 21° *A man walking in darkness with an old-fashioned lantern in his hand.* Denotes one who possesses much individuality; very conservative in his predilections; one who will experience much adversity; at the same time one who will find his way out of every difficulty, ever guided by a divine instinct, having an implicit faith in those religious truths as taught and practised by his forefathers.

♓ 22° *A man sitting at a table with a carving knife in hand, about to carve a round of beef which lies before him.* An epicure, or one particularly fond of good living, but harmless, and as a rule fortunate in the things of the world.

♓ 23° *A column of smoke ascending on a gigantic scale, followed by a terrible burst of flame. The phenomenon partakes of the character of an explosion.* This degree is subtle; its events are sudden, always falling out unexpectedly, and generally disastrously. He or she having this degree ascending should exercise caution in every undertaking, as such persons will be in danger of sudden losses in life, and a sad death.
NOTE.—THIS IS NOT FATE, but there will ever be a tendency in the direction already mentioned.

♓ 24° * * *. One not capable of being described in words, but the signification is a person who will possess great magnetic powers; also, one who will, in his day, do much by way of destroying popularised evils—a reformer, a healer, and a philanthropist.

♓ 25° *A very large field of corn; a great number of reapers, but a very few sheaves.* Denotes one whose aspirations are high and whose motives are good, but who will labour much without adequate results.

♓ 26° *A very high flagstaff, with a red flag floating on the top.*

An agitator, a person of great organising abilities, a person of radical notions, a revolutionist.

♓ 27° * * *. *This is an occult degree.* The person born with this degree on the ascendant is *sure* to be possessed with strange influences. He or she will have a familiar or a spirit companion and will be liable to obsession, the nature of which will be determined by his character.

♓ 28° *A triangle with a round hole in the centre.* A person possessing good and amiable qualities and many gifts, but who will fail to bring anything to perfection owing to some defect in his body or his mind. Such are generally possessed of some secret notions, which, being false, render all their other good intensions abortive.

♓ 29° *An old-fashioned clock.* Denotes a person of very exact habits, very particular in matters of detail, will follow rules to the letter, a good disciplinarian, has no inventive powers, never brings out anything new, but give him a system and he will follow it—a truly mechanical mind.

♓ 30° *Two men striving to hold a mad bull with ropes about his head.* Denotes a very self-willed person, one who will have his way and who is possessed with strong passions. This degree is in sympathy with the sign Taurus.

La Volasfera / Sepharial

INTRODUCTORY NOTE BY THE TRANSLATOR

AMONG the many methods by which the student of astrological science has endeavoured to refine and enlarge his knowledge of sidereal influences, the study of the special attributes or qualities attaching to the various degrees of the Zodiac is, perhaps, the most important.

In India this particular line of research has long since been carried out to a condition bordering upon perfection. It is to be found embodied in the famous nadigranthams, such as the S'ukranâdi and others of equal repute. In these kadjans, which consist of original or copied writings executed on palmyra leaves by means of the stylus, the influence and nature of the various degrees are given with great precision, separate *phalam* being given for every tenth part of a degree, or six minutes of space measured on the Ecliptic.

In the West, however, the subject has not received the same amount of study, nor has it reached the same degree of perfection. So far as I am aware, there are at the present time only three statements of this gradual influence of the Zodiac in existence.

The first of these is the Theban Calendar, attributed to P. Christian, a man of singular occult attainments closely associated with the work of Eliphas Levi, the Abbé Constant.* The second is that of John Angel (Johannes Angelos) who wrote about the sixteenth century, and whose work is to be found embodied in the Faces and Degrees of the Zodiac, reprinted by "Raphael." The third is that very luminous series of readings rendered by a writer under the name of "Charubel" which forms the earlier part of this present book.

---

* No modern version of this work is extant, so far as we are aware.—Ed

In view of so much that is already effected, and with such diversity and contradiction, one would hesitate to add another series to the number already furnished for the bewildering of students, save that there is some spark of virtue in the old saying: In the multitude of counsellors there is wisdom. For this reason alone I put these interpretations forward and design that they shall occupy the cardinal point in astrological literature which is found to be vacant. Thereafter the student may range the whole circle of the Zodiac from four separate points of view, and make his own selection in conformity with experience.

A word or two is necessary in regard to the character of the work now presented. In the original of Sig. Anton. Borelli, the symbols and natures of the separate degrees (indicated respectively by *italics* and *capitals*) are alone given, and in the present work the interpretations included between these are my own. It is therefore obvious that with the symbol before him the reader may attempt his own interpretation and prefer it, if he will, to that which he finds here. It will be seen upon comparison of the four systems which by this publication are rendered accessible to the student of Astrology, that three of them give the symbol, one gives the interpretation without the symbol, and that the present system gives the symbol and character of the degree, which I have extended in the interpretation.

As to the use of these researches the reader will form his own opinion on the evidence before him. It is certainly the fact that our knowledge of celestial influences would be enormously extended were we able to define the natures of the several degrees of the Zodiac with the same rule-of-thumb precision that attaches to the influence of the Signs and Planets, the Houses and other factors of modern astrological science. Possibly we may have to wait for a translation of one of the Indian nadigranthams before we can determine the methods by which western writers have affixed specific symbols and influences to the degrees, and it is even possible that with such material before us we could afford to dispense altogether with the symbols, retaining only the record of influences and characteristics attaching to the degrees themselves. Yet while these sources of information are in private custody and so jealously guarded, the symbols are the only material to which we can revert.

I have purposely left out of account the Star-points of the Hermetic circle contained in my *Birthday Book of Destiny*, because they attach only to the influence of the Constellations and parts of Constellations with which the Sun comes into line from day to day. The precession of the Equinoxes produces an ever-varying relationship between the Constellations and the Fixed Zodiac, so that these influences will gradually pass on through the Zodiac and eventually become obsolete, or at least subject to revision. Not so the natures which are attributed to specific degrees of the Fixed Zodiac such as we have in the present work and others already mentioned. And yet the question which lies at the root of these diverse systems of Zodiacal influences is really founded upon this distinction of Star-points versus Degrees, or the Constellations as distinguished from the Signs of the Zodiac.

If the influence is that which naturally proceeds from the action of the stars (considered as Suns) upon the centre of our Solar system, then certainly it would be reasonable to suppose that there is some special virtue in these Star-points, irrespective of the exact degrees of the Fixed Zodiac to which they are temporarily related. But if, on the other hand, the nature of the fixed degrees proceeds from some correspondence of the Zodiacal parts with the human system, such as we find to be at the root of most astrological principles, then there is sufficient reason for giving these symbolic interpretations of the Fixed Zodiac a foremost place in our study.

At all events there can be no harm in adding this new series to the literature of the subject, and in the belief that it may be of some service in the cause of truth, I commend it to the notice of my fellow-students.

Sepharial.

ARIES

♈ 1° *A strong man standing, dressed in skins, or heavy, loose, and coarse material—the shoulders almost bare. In his hand he bears a club. The figure suggests a Hercules.* It denotes a man capable of sustaining much labour, and one likely to perform great acts in which force of character and endurance sustain him rather than goodness of principle or purity of motive. The native is aggressive, passionate and quarrelsome, and well equipped for the struggle of life in its practical aspects. STRENGTH AND PASSION seem to mark this degree of the ecliptic.

♈ 2° *A man standing, armed with sword and spear; richly dressed in scarlet and purple, with jewelled clasps, and helmet of fine brass or gold—apparently prepared for battle and confident of victory.* It denotes a proud, warlike nature, with much self-reliance and confidence in his own powers. One who will have few friends and be very independent in his way of living; at all times willing to assert his opinions and to evidence his powers. A nature somewhat fond of DISPLAY.

♈ 3° *A woman sitting in a chair as if conversing with someone. Her hands are folded lightly upon her lap, her face has a pleasant, smiling expression. She is loosely habited in a Grecian robe, her neck and arms are bare.* It denotes a person of easy manner, kind and accessible to all; one fond of cheerful company and pleasant life. The native would never be cruel or harsh, but impulsive in passion and yet gentle in manner. The native would go to some length in order to avoid a quarrel, and is pre-eminently a lover of peace and harmony and will have many friends on that account who will be of use to him. It is a degree of ease and LUXURY.

♈ 4° *A wood, in which which wild undergrowth abounds, and many plants of different kinds and colours.* It denotes a rustic nature, fond of the beauties of the country life; displaying not the least indication of learning, yet having much natural wisdom. A nature somewhat brusque and uncultivated, but rich of heart; abundant but untrained—one who will be very prodigal of his energies and wealth. It is a degree of crudity and RUGGEDNESS.

♈ 5° *A person climbing a rock in the midst of a fierce storm. Flashes of lightning reveal the figure in dark outline. It appears strong and climbs well.* It denotes a person who will give evidence of much force of character. One who will make his way against almost insuperable difficulties, but whose efforts will be finally crowned with a position of security and comfort. The native will pass through many perilous adventures and will make many conquests, but they will all be due rather to his own perseverance and force of character than to favouring circumstances. This degree seems to be one of UNCERTAINTY, PERIL, and FINAL SUCCESS.

♈ 6° *A man riding upon a horse near to the edge of a cliff, and looking down into a valley where people are at work.* It denotes a nature well qualified to undertake the government of others; it seems to indicate that the force of circumstances will frequently place such a person in a position over others which is not without its dangers, and many catastrophes are to be feared. The degree indicates SUPERIORITY, attainment and honour; but is fraught with many dangers.

♈ 7° *A fox running along a path beneath the shadow of a wall.*

It denotes a wily, prudent and cunning person: one endowed with much circumspection and diplomatic power. Such persons are inclined, most of all, to self-defence without violence, and they gain their ends more by avoidance of dangers than by strength or aggressive means. In extremities of peril, a clever ruse or extraordinary presence of mind will often be the means of liberation. The quality of this degree is CAUTION.

♈ 8°   *A man surrounded by others seeking a quarrel.* It denotes one who is quick to anger, stirring up strife around him; eager to combat the opinions and to disturb the peace of others. Persons under this degree have a tendency to run into dangers, and not unfrequently fall victims to their own imprudence. It is essentially a RASH and IMPETUOUS degree.

♈ 9°   *A man standing upon a lofty place with his arms folded and his head erect.* It denotes a person of great courage and self-confidence. One who makes an able friend or formidable enemy. In dangers he is cool and collected, at all times endowed with courage, and not infrequently a victim to pride and self-love. Iu most affairs of life he gains his ends on account of his temerity and positive disposition. In the service of others he is frequently presumptuous, restless under restraint, loving freedom, and despising assistance. Occasionally he is too lofty to command attention from any but himself. This degree is one of PRIDE.

♈ 10° *A man on horseback standing alone in the middle of a battlefield where around him lie the dead and dying.* It denotes a person who will occupy some singular position in life; one whose career will be remarkable, if not unique, and noted

86

for its daring and hazardous exploits. It gives success in undertakings and much prestige. It is a degree of VICTORY.

♈ 11°   A woman of beautiful and kind countenance, standing alone, and but half covered with a robe which falls from the left shoulder. It indicates a soft, gentle and amiable disposition; addicted to acts of kindness and charity; but of weak will, such as to be led astray through a desire to please others; forgetful of self and liable to acts of indiscretion. This is a degree of BEAUTY and GENTLENESS.

♈ 12°   *A man leading two children by the hands.* It denotes a sociable and bountiful nature, with strong instincts of a domestic nature. One who delights in his family relations and feels pride in the quality of householder and husband. The degree confers much dignity and honour upon the native in his social and civil life, but elsewhere he does not meet so much success. It is a degree of CONSERVATISM.

♈ 13°   *A man at the summit of a mauntain, illumined by the setting sun; holding a staff in his right hand, in his left a crown.* It denotes one who through suffering, pain and hard work, will at the close of life rise to much dignity and receive many honours. This degree is capable of lifting the native from obscurity to prominence as the reward of enduring effort. It is a degree of REWARD.

♈ 14°   *A man out in mid-ocean on a raft, famished and in pitiable distress.* It denotes loneliness and indigence in life; one who will lead a strange and outcast life, with few friends, and those either unwilling or unable to help him. It seems to contain the idea of much travelling, perhaps exile, and finally a lonely grave. It is a degree of ISOLATION.

♈ 15°   *A man struggling in the water with a broken footbridge above his head.* It denotes a nature prone to mistakes of judgment; liable to be too trustful of others and to misplace his confidences, so that he is often deceived, not only in his own powers, but in his estimate of the character of others. In a speculative life, the native of this degree would in the end be hopelessly unsuccessful, and he ought to cultivate self-knowledge and self-reliance and to exercise extreme caution in all his dealings and associations. This degree is one of TREACHERY.

♈ 16° *A youth, book in hand, wanders apparently through a glade overhung with the branches of surrounding trees. The sunlight is slanting through the trees, and falling upon the figure of the student.* It denotes one who is fond of nature, and studious of her laws; loving the peaceful contemplation of natural beauty; devoted to the higher interests of his soul; and of a reclusive disposition. Such would be successful in his pursuits of natural history, whether in one department or another, but would not apply his knowledge to the attainment of fame. This is a degree of PASSIVE BEAUTY.

♈ 17° *A woman holding scales, containing on the one side a cup of red wine, on the other a number of golden coins.* This is a degree indicating one of a speculative nature, selfish, and luxurious; one whose heart is divided between pleasure and wealth, but who knows not the true use of either. Such would gain wealth by speculation, but waste it in extravagance. "The fool and his money are soon parted." So here. It is a degree of EARTHINESS.

♈ 18° *A man and woman standing hand in hand, looking with affection towards one another.* This denotes a person of an amiable and pleasant disposition, friendly to all, and beloved of his kinsmen. One who desires peace and concord, and who will meet with success through the intervention of some female friend. It is a degree of AMITY.

♈ 19° *An old man, dressed in a simple and much worn gown, carrying two bags of gold clasped at his breast with nervous hands.* It denotes one who worships gold; a stingy and misanthropic nature. One who acquires to no purpose: self-centred and reclusive; whose constant fear is loss, a fear that is sure to be realised. It is a degree of ACQUISITIVENESS.

[NOTE.—Referring to our remarks on "Charubel's" delineation of ♓ 12°, it would seem from the significations here attached to ♈ 19° and 20° that Sig. Belloni's symbols were written at a time when the First Point of the *Zodiac of the Constellations* was situated between these two degrees. The old man would be the old year, and his two bag of gold the days of the year, seed time and harvest.—Ed.]

♈ 20° *A man equipped for a rough journey, belted and armed.* This degree signifies one of adventurous nature, fond of discovery and of travel. A pioneer in whatever field of labour he may undertake to work in; one who will open up new roads of knowledge and research; active, aggressive, bold and fearless; one who will travel into distant countries and gain applause for his discoveries. It is a degree of INQUISITIVENESS.

♈ 21° *A strong and prosperous-looking man stands with arms extended forward, holding in his hands a bowl full of wine.* It denotes a generous and hospitable nature; one that will succeed through good and worthy actions, yet has some sense of his own merits and powers, and is desirous of recognition. A steadfast and sincere man, who will make many friends and be held by them in respect. It is a degree of CONSCIOUS MERIT.

♈ 22° *A man of tottering and uncertain gait, carrying water which he spills on the ground.* It denotes a weak and disorderly nature which, by reason of its imperfection, will be prone to go astray. Such an one will lose credit and substance through his indecision and faulty judgment. One that will not attain to his end because of his wavering nature and his want of direction and stability. How shall he act who does not know what he desires? It is a degree of INSTABILITY.

♈ 23° *A man standing with a tankard in his hand ready to drink. Two others standing apart, talking together, with averted faces.* This denotes one who is likely to fall into evil habits by low associations, and who, through the envy and intrigues of his comrades, will suffer injury. Such an one has not the power of selection in his pursuits, and is likely to drift with the stream into all sorts of unpremeditated evil. It is a degree of WEAKNESS.

♈ 24° *A man playing with coloured balls, an immodest woman standing behind him.* This indicates one of a playful but careless nature, given over to pleasures and unprofitable pursuits. One who will be crossed in life by the opposite sex, and meet with troubles thereby. One with very little force of character or worthy ambition. It is a degree of FOOLISHNESS.

♈ 25° *A man of powerful form, riding upon a restive horse, whose mouth is curbed.* It denotes a man of strong character, capable of maintaining his dignity and position by means of his natural powers. One of strong and independent nature, who will so far have his own way as to be at times tyrannous and unjust. One who will brook no opposition, nor give quarter to an enemy. It is a degree of DOMINION.

♈ 26° *A kingly person, presenting a sceptre to one kneeling.* It denotes one who, whether by his merits, or by the influence of persons in power and authority, will rise above the level of his birth. The nature is one of merit allied to ambition, which will effect great things, not however without assistance. It is a degree of ATTAINMENT.

♈ 27° *A man, richly attired, having lost his foothold, is falling to the ground.* It denotes one whose nature will not sustain the reverses of fortune to which he will be subjected: Attaining to considerable dignity and influence, most likely as the accident of birth, he will not continue therein to the end of his days, but will fail for want of judgement and persistence. This degree signifies the breaking up of families and the loss of their traditions. It is a degree of DECADENCE.

♈ 28° *A fair woman, richly attired, stands alone.* It denotes one of a rich and beneficent nature, who will, by his goodness of heart, attract many friends and gain great attention. It indicates success through a woman. The nature is not free from love of luxury and approbation, but it is generous and gifted, and will, by friendly counsel, meet with opportunity for expression and due reward. It is a degree of FAVOUR.

♈ 29° *A man of humble appearance, but much strength, felling a tree with an axe.* It denotes a person of a practical nature; aggressive and sometimes destructive, One who finds success in simple and persistent effort, and who will meet with many obstacles in life, against which he will successfully contend. It denotes a simple, honest, and impulsive nature; one that will cut out his own part in life in spite of many difficulties. It is a degree of LABOUR.

♈ 30° *A horseman, armed as if for battle, is watching the waning moon.* It denotes a person of an independent and domineering nature; who will be forsaken by his friends and colleagues on that account, and whose fortunes will be severely hurt by a female. Serving himself alone, he will not receive assistance. "The dog and his bone are best left alone," It is a degree of ISOLATION.

TAURUS

♉ 1°   *A woman of pleasant face, neatly attired, stands holding a sword, whose point is earthward. Her head is kissed by the meridian Sun, her face is towards the north.* It denotes a person of a disputative mind, one who will have many enemies, and will need to exercise himself much in self-defence; one to whom life will open out into a great field of strife, but who, through his own native force and diplomacy, will eventually prevail. It is a degree of SELF-PRESERVATION.

♉ 2°   *A man lying upon the gronnd in the last moments of life. The Sun is setting amid clouds.* It denotes one for whom life will be a severe lesson; whose ambition is likely to outstrip his power; one who will attempt great things to his discomfiture; whose efforts will prove futile, and whose hopes will vanish as the clouds. It is a degree of SELF-UNDOING.

♉ 3°   *A woman is gathering grapes, with which she fills many baskets.* It denotes a person whose interests will be greatly enhanced in the autumn of life, who will reap benefits from old age and pleasures from maturity; whose chief characteristic is acquisitiveness, and whose designs will meet with much success. It is a degree of acquirement, of GATHERING TOGETHER.

♉ 4°   *A burning brand beneath the paw of a lion, whose rage is against it.* It denotes a person in whose life much sedition will prevail, whose affairs will be marred by his own violence, and whose house will be dismembered through strife, in whom wrath will effect great evils, and whose force will be turned against himself. It is a degree of DISINTEGRATION.

♉ 5° *A man of benevolent countenance stands near to a cottage chopping wood. Around him are orchards well filled with fruit. Near to him is a sheep grazing.* It denotes a person of a contented, happy disposition, a friend of Nature and well beloved of her. A man of natural goodwill, whose labour is its own reward, whose wealth is his own contentment, and whose ambitions are fulfilled with the day. It is a degree of HEART-WEALTH.

♉ 6° *A man in the prime of life stands upon a dais, holding in his right hand a scroll of papers; upon his head is a laurel wreath.* It denotes one who will attain the greatest victories in life by means of his intellect; who is possessed of great penetration and large understanding, through which he will acquire honours and dignity, and will be regarded with favour by the people. It is a degree of MIND-WEALTH.

♉ 7° *A well-favoured cow, grazing in a park, in the shade of two trees.* It denotes one whose wealth will lie in the direction of natural qualities, whose mind will be complacent, contented, incapable of great distress or very effective effort; one who will attract attention chiefly by his physical powers (or if a female, by her beauty) and his good fortune; not by the use of his mind. It denotes comfort and happiness dissociated from labour, and inclining to luxury; success and contentment in one's attachments. It is a degree of BODILY WEALTH.

♉ 8° *An old man, poorly clad, stands by the side of a river, from which he collects bits of wood and straw with a rake.* It denotes one of little wit, who will, through his own obtuseness, fall into errors which lead to his own despoiling. He will think to gain comforts by easy ways, and will scratch to himself heaps of sorrow and annoyance, and this chiefly from females. What substance he has he will hardly keep, and what he has not, that he will not readily gain. It is a degree of LASSITUDE.

♉ 9° *A portly man, walking among pigeons, which flock upon the ground at his feet.* It denotes a man whose chief interests will be in his home, and in the care of his children; one who is attractive to young persons, and whose mind is pacific and benevolent; one who has the ability to inspire confidence and faith in others; whose footsteps will be followed in security and whose life goes by easy ways to a peaceful end. It is a degree of MINISTRATION.

♉ 10° *An ox, lying upon the ground asleep, in the sunshine. Upon its back two birds are perched.* It denotes one of an idle and self-indulgent nature, whose pleasure is in his physical appetites and their satisfaction. One who will bring trouble upon himself and over whom the sirens will quarrel while they feed upon him. It is a degree of GROSSNESS.

♉ 11° *A man seated on a throne, holding a sceptre, crowned, and with signs of wealth around him.* It denotes one who, if born wealthy, will attain eminence by means of his care in the affairs of life; if born poor, he will acquire both wealth and fame. The position will be due to his shrewdness rather than his integrity, for the chief characteristic here is *watchfulness.* It is a degree of SELF-SERVICE.

♉ 12° *A flower of a bright orange tint, upon which two butterflies are resting and fanning their wings.* It denotes a sympathetic and graceful nature, ever ready to please others, and yet anxious of recognition and affection from those to whom it is devoted; one that desires peace and concord, and finds delight in associating with those of a similar character to itself; a hopeful and happy nature, upon which the heavens will smile. It is a degree of RECIPROCITY.

♉ 13°   *Two dogs running, one carrying a bone, the other in pursuit of it.* It denotes one who is prone to unlawful acquisition, to envy and strife; yet likely to cheat himself in the end by pursuing unprofitable things, without attainment of those which are nearer at hand. There is little satisfaction in this nature; and not much will come of its craving. It is a degree of SELFISHNESS.

♉ 14°   *A table upon which a right angle and a plane are lying.* It denotes a humble and industrious nature, that finds pleasure in good works. A man of justice, rectitude and strength, whose life will be full of peace in the service of others, and whose ends will be graced by the fruits of well-doing. The chief characteristic is the sense of justice and fraternity. It is a degree of LIBERALITY.

♉ 15°   *A venerable man seated in an uncertain light; before him are several books, and various scientific instruments surround him.* It denotes a studious and intuitive nature, whose mental vision will see where others are in the darkness; one devoted to the inner meaning of Nature's workings, and acting from obscure motives; one of much self-reliance, inclined to solitariness, and yet always surrounded by friends; one who will be sought after while himself seeking none. It is a degree of MYSTERY.

♉ 16°   *Two white cows are standing together in a jungle; behind them is a tiger ready to spring.* It denotes that one born under this sign will have many advantages in early life, will make a prosperous marriage, but through a false sense of security will afterwards come to ruin and sorrow. It is a degree of RELAXATION.

♉ 17° *A man swimming in the river against the current and making no progress.* This symbolises a life of toil without much fruits; the misdirection of effort through ignorance of natural laws; a straining after that which Nature has not designed, and consequent failure in life. The native will be unpopular, moving against the stream, and by much exertion, hurting himself alone. It is a degree of FUTILITY.

♉ 18° *Two bulls are seen fighting together.* This denotes a petulant and warlike character, who is ever ready to take up arms with the slightest cause. Danger by one's own hand as much as by that of opponents is threatened. The native will make many enemies. He who takes to the sword perishes by it. It is a degree of STRIFE.

♉ 19° *A woman, lightly clad, is lying in a field, surrounded by violet-coloured flowers.* It denotes a gentle, inoffensive but weak nature, inclined to indolence or hopelessness; and thus while Nature is luxurious and fertile, and all around speaks of wealth gained by industry, the native remains in a poor condition for want of determination. It is a degree of INCOMPETENCE.

♉ 20° *A crow, or raven, stands upon a water-pot.* This indicates a designing and crafty nature, planning mischief even in regard to harmless things, but one who will find himself reflected in his own designs, and will eventually injure himself thereby. It is a degree of ENVY.

♉ 21° *An owl, perched on a tree, in the branches of which a snake is coiled.* It indicates a silent, watchful disposition, inclined to caution, method, and thrift, but liable to assaults from unexpected sources, which will overthrow many carefully designed plans. It is a degree of ANTICIPATION.

♉ 22° *A field of rich grass in which stands a tree. A swarm of bees encircle the tree.* It indicates one whose efforts will be successful and whose diligence will lead to the acquisition of money and friends. Industry and thrift will be the characteristics of the native, and success will come by those qualities rather than by unexpected favours of Fortune. It is a degree of UTILITY.

♉ 23° *A king sits upon a throne; behind him stands a figure veiled in black.* It signifies one who will suffer misfortune in the height of his career and whose fall will be dangerous in proportion to the heigh he has attained. The native will be too apt to depend on his own powers and will essay feats which will be beyond his natural powers. Ambition will lead him into dangerous positions, and at a weak moment he will fall. Let this be taken as equally affecting his physical, moral, and social welfare. It is a degree of COLLAPSE.

♉ 24° *A bed of a dried-up river, wherein crows (black birds) are feeding.* It signifies one who will take his course through useless tracks, and by too much trust in others will suffer depletion. Yea, though all his life long he may minister to the wants of others, yet, in his advancing years, he will be abandoned to the mercy of wayfaring and deceitful men. This illustrates virtue misapplied. It is a degree of DECLINE.

♉ 25° *A lion rampant, standing upon an elevated ground.* It indicates a powerful and haughty nature; one who is disposed to justify himself by force of arms rather than by intrinsic merit. Such a person will make many his servants but few his friends and in the end his state will be as pitiable as that of a dying lion. It is a degree of PRIDE.

♉ 26° *A fair woman, leading a child by the hand, and gathering flowers by the way.* It denotes a person of a loving and agreeable nature, disposed to find happiness in the execution of common duties; a lover of domestic peace, and of tolerance in all things. It is a degree of CONCORD.

♉ 27° *An alchemist at work in his laboratory; upon his table is much gold.* It indicates a patient, thrifty nature. One who by industry and inventive faculty will acquire wealth, but yet will live simply. It denotes an eccentric vocation and success therein. Such a person is likely to have more means at his command than his nature requires to use. It is a degree of SUCCESS.

♉ 28° *A man is seen climbing a pole which is set upon an elevation.* It signifies one who will aspire after vain things and exert himself to no purpose; whose ambitions are in the clouds and who knows not how to reach them. It is a degree of VAGARY.

♉ 29° *A powerful man, holding a scourge in his right hand, and driving two slaves in manacles.* It signifies a tyrant, who takes delight in power apart from its uses, and whose opinions are bigoted and selfish. To rule, without regard to qualifications, is the passing ambition of one born under this degree. Death, which frees the slave, will bind the hands of a tyrant in irons forged from his own heart. It is a degree of DESPOTISM.

♉ 30° *A dark man, richly apparelled, and surrounded by servants and courtiers, reclines on a couch.* It indicates one whose tastes are luxurious but artistic, one who will have much wealth and influence, but whose love of ease will be his great fault and the cause of his worst misfortunes. He who would provide for a long journey must not carry water in his hands. It is a degree of LUXURY.

GEMINI

♊ 1° *Two yellow flowers growing beneath the shade of a luxuri-
ant tree.* It indicates a life of security, peace and prosperity.
The native will make friendships that will prove sincere and
advantageous; and by means of his friends he will meet with
success in life. He will be protected by someone greater than
himself, whose influence will be widespread and beneficent.
This native will have a kind nature, trustful disposition, and
his domestic life will be happy and prosperous. It is a degree
of SECURITY.

♊ 2° *A man scaling a wall by means of a rope ladder. In his teeth
he holds a sword, and in his right hand a firearm.* It signifies
one of a daring and courageous nature, who will, by his own
merit, rise to positions of honour, and overcome all obsta-
cles. He will be eloquent, carrying defence in his mouth,
and prominent in his avocation. He will, however, die on the
attainment of his greatest ambition. A degree of PROWESS.

♊ 3° *A troubadour stands with one foot upon the ledge of a rock,
his instrument slung at his side; he is listening to the music
of a cascade which falls at his feet.* This denotes a person
of Bohemian habits, refined tastes, a love for things beau-
tiful, music, poetry, art, etc. The native will lead a roaming
life, will have much happiness, but not great fame. He will
be talented, but may be too contented in the possession of
his powers and thinking too little of his wider uses. He will
have a strong imagination, love of the marvellous, and will
be very sensitive to the opinions and influence of others. It
is a degree of HARMONY.

♊ 4° A man dressed like a Minister of State, of venerable and kindly aspect. This degree will produce a person of kind and noble disposition; one who will occupy positions of trust, and, by his own merits, rise to eminence in his own sphere of work. It is a degree of DIGNITY.

♊ 5° *Two men standing in a wood in the act of fighting a duel. Between them lies a rich purple and gold vesture and a casket of jewels.* This indicates that the native will be of a jealous and warlike nature, winning a competence for himself by great hazards. He will make efforts at gaining wealth and position, but will meet with opposition, and will either succeed or perish in the attempt. This is a degree of CHANCE.

♊ 6° *A woman stands holding a book in one hand and a pair of scales in the other.* It indicates a person of learning, sound reason, dispassionate judgment, elegant manners, but cold and impassive nature. The native will succeed in his duties and profession, and will become famous, but not popular. He will be rich and will live to a good age. This is a degree of JUDGMENT.

♊ 7° *A peaceful valley; a lake on which a swan is floating. At the back rises a high mountain.* This indicates one of a generous, kind nature, full of contentment and quiet happiness. One who will suffer but few sorrows, and will have peace in all his relations. The mind will be passive, calm, and thoughtful; the manners courteous and graceful, and the body elegant. The native will have strong memory and small imaginative power. This is a degree of PEACE.

♊ 8° *A house on fire at night-time.* It indicates that the native will be rash and warlike, inclined to destruction, and successful therein beyond his desires. He will be apt to stir up disputes among others and to bring desolation upon himself through a false sense of security. His domestic life will be full of turmoil. It is a degree of STRIFE.

♊ 9° *The figure of a woman holding a globe in one hand and a sceptre in the other.* It indicates wide knowledge and power; a position of importance; a mind fit for governing, and a position of security after middle life. There are indications of pride and self-love in this symbol, but dignity, conscientiousness, and self-reliance are prominent features in the character. It is a degree of DOMINION.

♊ 10° *A woman of pleasing appearance stands offering a glass of some fluid to a child.* It indicates that the person born under this degree will have a kind, sympathetic nature, able and willing to help the sick and needy; one whose knowledge of human nature, of arts and sciences, will be thorough and well used. The nature is gentle and benevolently hopeful and inspiring, and disposed to self-sacrifice. This is a degree of HEALING.

♊ 11° *A group of vagrants or gipsies, seated round a cauldron, in which food is preparing.* This denotes a person of alien nature, whose fortunes will be fickle, and whose happiness will be centred in his family. Withal, there is a tinge of sensuousness in the nature, disposing to excess in the satisfaction of the appetites. This person will leave his native land and wander over the world, never satisfied with things as they are; but, ever seeking, he will leave many golden opportunities behind. It is a degree of EXCESS.

♊ 12° *A young laurel free, broken by the wind and withered.* The native will be of a hopeful and honourable character, full of projects for the future, but will lose many opportunities through misfortunes unforseen. His affections will be sincere, but fate will be against him in this respect, and few things in his life will come to maturity. Expected honours will be snatched from him, and the flowers of life will wither in his hand. Let him practice self-restraint and encourage contentment. This is a degree of (sfiorezza) SPOLIATION.

Ⅱ 13° *Two wolves are devouring a carcase in the moonlight.* It indicates one of a crafty, subtle nature, avaricious, given to treaties and associations of a dangerous character; secretive, revengeful, and of a quick temper. The native will lead a roaming and unsettled life. This degree is fatal to one born while the Sun is above the earth. It is a degree of VORACITY and SELF-SEEKING.

Ⅱ 14° *A man in a mask stands beneath the shadow of a tree at night. At his feet there is a dead cow.* It denotes a person of a wily nature, acquisitive, and disposed to use doubtful means in the pursuit of wealth. The native will show an excess of caution and self-regard, but he is liable to be deceived in his own powers. This is a degree of PLUNDER.

Ⅱ 15° *A woman holding a bundle of faggots, her hair loose and disordered, by the wind. She wanders in search of something.* It indicates a person of versatile character and eccentric nature. One who is disposed to undertake more things than he is able to complete, and who will either be brilliant on account of wide learning, or impotent through over much vexation and trouble. It is a degree of CONFUSION.

Ⅱ 16° *A man sitting upon his heels and breaking stones with a hammer.* It indicates a person of very few resources and of small intellectual powers; who, from lack of ability or through misfortune, will be able to bring but little to fruition.

One who may labour much to little profit. It is a degree of UNFRUITFULNESS.

♊ 17° *A broken pitcher lying upon the ground with spilled fruit around it.* It denotes one who will come to some untimely end through the hands of another. It shows the nature to be unpractical and the pursuits of the native to be mostly vain and of no lasting benefit, It shows loss of powers during lifetime, and perhaps loss of faculties. It is a degree of IMPOTENCE.

♊ 18° *A flying arrow.* It indicates a person of lofty aspirations, keen mental powers, penetration and executive ability. One who will cut out his own line in life and excite attention, but who may, by his destiny, fail in achieving the result aimed at. It is a degree of EXECUTION.

♊ 19° *A woman stands in an attitude of dejection and covers her otherwise naked breast with the hair of her head.* It indicates one who will have great sorrow in life, and will be deserted by friends and left to his own resources. To a woman it speaks of the worst of ills. Blighted hopes, betrayed confidence, sudden bereavement and void ambitions are the dire fruits of this black line in the scroll of life. This degree is PERILOUS.

♊ 20° *Two men, well clad, are standing together, the one holding a white horse by the bridle.* It points out a person who has much aptitude in spiritual things, a tendency to believe much in dreams and visions, and to pursue strange studies. It gives the friendship of notable persons and a taste for science among other things; but at the same time it may lead the native into dangerous paths. If influence falls to the hand of this man it may work him harm. It is a degree of DISPROPORTION.

♊ 21° *A youth is seen throwing coins into a cup as if in play.* It denotes a person of eccentric and, to a certain extent, unsociable habits, who will probably lose great opportunities by his carelessness and peculiar tastes while amusing himself after his own manner; he will be reckless of how others may be working, and will probably lead a dependent life. It is a degree of INDIFFERENCE.

♊ 22° *A young woman lying beneath a tree, throwing food to the birds which gather around her.* It indicates a person of gentle, winning disposition, kind heart, and generous, ardent nature. One who will be happy and make others so. Domestic peace and prosperity. Rustic habits, a lover of the artistic and beautiful in nature, fond of poetry, music and singing. Some disposition to follow the fine arts. A lover of peace and concord. It is a degree of GENIALITY or FELLOW-FEELING.

♊ 23° *An old oak, without leaf or bark, splintered by the storms through which it has passed, stands alone upon desolate moorland.* It denotes one who through his own actions, or the force of circumstances, will be deserted by kith and kin, and will pass through many trials. The storms of life will sear his heart and blight his nature ere the young world of his dreams can grow op around him to shelter and protect his years of falling leaf. It is a degree of ABANDONMENT.

♊ 24° *Several sparrows are collected together, chattering and pluming themselves in the dust.* It indicates a person of social and jovial nature, somewhat given to luxury and convivial pursuits, but very unselfish, happy in the company of others, attractive, forming many friendships. Ever ready to express his honest nature by word of mouth or in spontaneous action. Gifted in the art of persuasion, sympathetic. It is a degree of FRIENDSHIP.

♊ 25° *An old book lying open upon a table, and beside it a burning lamp.* It signifies a person of some exceptional mental powers, whose mind will be well stored with ancient learning. One of a studious and retiring nature, whose greatest happiness and whole wealth will be in the conquests of the mind. He will achieve something of importance to the world by dint of close and patient study. It is a degree of CULTIVATION.

♊ 26° *A market place, in which several young men are in dispute, and asserting their respective opinions by the free use of cudgels.* It signifies a person of a stubborn, wilful nature, easily persuaded of the merits or rights of others, litigious and quarrelsome, of few sympathies, jealous and revengeful. It denotes a life of many dangers and perhaps death by the hands of a man. It is a degree of CONTEST.

♊ 27° *A young man of dishevelled appearance sitting upon a barren rock by the sea, weeping.* It denotes a person of melancholy disposition, over whom the circumstances of life will have much influence, even to the extent of depriving him of all happiness. To a certain extent the nature is dependent and confiding, at all times sympathetic, but ill-fitted to the battle of life. It denotes also some great heart trouble, bereavement or disappointment in love, death of husband or wife as the case may be. It is a degree of MELANCHOLY.

♊ 28° *A large and well cultivated tract of land.* It signifies a person of broad, open and genial temperament of mind, a healthy body, keen appreciation of nature's beauties; love of rustic pursuits; successful life, large family and many friends. This individual will live more in the physical and emotional aspects of his nature than in the mental or spiritual; yet the reflection of these in the life of the native will be apparent and will work for good in him. It is a degree of FRUITFULNESS.

♊ 29° *A gloomy sky filled with scudding clouds. A flight of black-birds are struggling against the wind.* It denotes a person of pessimistic nature; one who will abandon his many projects for want of hope and perseverance. The mind is filled with an endless succession of thoughts and schemes, but always in the black mantle of doubt and misgiving. The nature is weak and easily thrown off the track; prolix, versatile, but lacking, as such natures mostly are, in continuity. This individual will have many dreams and yet none will be fulfilled. Hence he will have no confidence, either in himself or his designs. It is a degree of DOUBT and CHANGE.

♊ 30° *A wolf following a sheep along a secluded pathway.* It signifies a crafty nature, capable of intrigue and deception; one who will form associations with a design of ultimate conquest. A seductive nature, living at the risk or others' happiness. A man of considerable powers of persuasion, but not to be trusted. It is a degree of DECEPTION.

CANCER

♋ 1° *A well-fruited vine hanging upon an old wall beneath the sunshine of a summer day.* It signifies a person of tender sympathies and strong attachments, capable of extreme self-devotion to one who is beloved; fruitful in good acts, happy and contented in disposition. One who will have enough of the good things of life and will use them wisely. The native will marry well, and frequently it will be found that the native of this degree abides long in one place, and is held by strong associations to country and to kin. It is a degree of SYMPATHY.

♋ 2° *A dog standing over a bare bone; in front of it are two others half starved.* It denotes a person of a very selfish and jealous nature, unproductive of any good to himself and of no use to his fellows; a mere hanger-on. The disposition is indolent, but what it lacks in energy is supplied by suavity, *finesse* and subtlety, so that the native is never at a loss for the means to live; but buys comfort at the cheapest price, and is often a respectable beggar. It is a degree of INDOLENCE.

♋ 3° *A woman seated in an attitude of grief, her clothes disordered and her hair unkemt, holding some faded flowers in her hands; among the flowers are lilies and roses.* It indicates a person of fateful inclinations and strong passions, whose life will be subject to the influence of the opposite sex, and who, if not extremely cautious in those relations, will suffer injury and perhaps disgrace. It points to one of weak will, but strong feelings which are apt to over-rule reason and experience. It is a degree of SPOLIATION.

♋ 4° *A well-appointed table, with the remnants of a feast lying upon it.* It indicates a person of worldly tendencies, with an appetite for the good things of life, which will not be denied. The nature is extravagant and reckless, prone to all kinds of excess and passionate impulses, whereby the fortunes will be most seriously damaged. These things arise from a certain richness of heart and *camaraderie*, but goodwill in this individual finds expression mostly through the sensuous nature. It is a degree of SENSUALITY.

♋ 5° *A young tree or sapling, bent about the middle, and thence growing awry.* It indicates a person of warm affections, but incautious nature; who confides, without sufficient grounds, in those around him; and is apt to misplace his trust. To those of the female sex it is a bandul degree. In general, it shows a loving and trustful nature without much knowledge of human weaknesses. It is apt to be bent, and perhaps broken, by the storms of passion, and to lean where there is no real support. It is a degree of BETRAYAL.

♋ 6° A woman clothed in gaudy apparel, plays with some jewels in her lap. It indicates a nature of wasteful and unpractical habits, yet gifted with some degree of *savoir faire* and knowledge of human nature. The native will be inclined to habits of excess, will be fond of dress and ornamentation; fortunate in the acquisition of wealth, but wholly unacquainted with its right use; good-hearted but foolish and extravagant, and yet frequently unjust therein. A nature too prone to externals and outward show. It is a degree of SEMBLANCES.

♋ 7° *An iron gauntlet, a sword, and a scourge lying together upon the stump of a tree.* It indicates a person of strong personality, but of a tyrannous nature, who, by force of arms and aggression generally, will press forward regardless of the merits of others and insensible of their feelings. His band, though strong, is frequently unjust and cruel in its action, impelled by the motive that "might is right"; and, when opposed, is capable of extreme cruelty and selfishness. In certain natures the influence of this degree generates the common-place "bully." It is a degree of SELF-ASSERTION.

♋ 8° *A dove lies upon the ground, while over it a snake is poised in an attitude of attack.* It indicates on the one hand a nature capable of extreme self-indulgence and licence; and, on the other, one who is apt to succumb to worldly seductions. The influence of this degree acts most powerfully to destroy domestic happiness and to fracture marital relations; and the fate of the native will hang upon the nature and influence of a subtle fascination or a secret attachment. It is a degree of SELF-ABANDON.

♋ 9° A little village lying in a fertile valley. It indicates one whose heart is full of native goodness, whose hand is set to great work in modest ways, and whose patience, thrift, and true humility will bring his work to perfection. There is very little aggression and no self-assertion in this nature; but, like the valley, it is fruitful in good things because of its lowliness, while surrounding high peaks of the mountains are barren. The native, though never famous, will be always successful, even beyond his ambitions, which are modest but steadfast. It is a degree of CONTENTMENT.

♋ 10° *A wide-spreading oak tree, around the roots of which are many young shoots, while the birds of the season sing among its branches.* It indicates a steady, strong and reliable nature, which by much industry comes at length to the fruits of its labour, and in the autumn of life will be surrounded by the most grateful evidences of its own energy and perseverance. While sustaining itself it will afford shelter and comfort to others, both among its own kindred and among strangers, so that with integrity and competence there will go honour and esteem to enrich a good old age. It is a degree of FRUITFULNESS.

♋ 11° *A stranded vessel on a low, sandy beach.* It indicates a person whose affairs in life will come to an unfortunate end, or will be oftentimes totally arrested. The nature is one where ambition is not joined to sufficient experience or discretion; and, in avoiding obvious rocks, is liable to run upon unsuspected sand-banks. Yet through all risks the native will hold together without serious injury to himself, and will somehow always gain a new start in life after each failure. The nature is hopeful and even confident; but not qualified for independent work. If a sailor or traveller, the native will be in danger of shipwreck. This degree is fateful to those on the sea. It is a degree of OBSTRUCTION.

♋ 12° *A dagger lying beside a skull.* It denotes one of fatal tendencies, destructive to a degree; inclined to cruelty and oppression. This person will need to hold his passions in strong check or some fatality will surely come upon him. The nature is melancholy and taciturn; yet silently discerning, and capable of keen feelings. "It makes not, but it mars; and with the hollow eyes of death looks back with secret self-condemnation upon its unfruitful work." The end of life is tragic. It is a degree of UNDOING.

♋ 13° *A caduceus between two moons, one crescent and the other gibbous.* It denotes a person of extreme capacity in the pursuit of knowledge, a penetrating mind, and retentive memory; the native will accomplish wonders in the pursuit of the subtile sciences. The temper is changeful like the moon, and subject to fits of hope and despondency of more or less rapid alternation. The native is likely to travel much and to be subject to many changes of fortune. But the chief characteristic is versatility and aptitude in the gaining of knowledge. With the symbol of Hermes dominant the native will either be a linguist, doctor, or a distinguished scholar. It is a degree of KNOWLEDGE.

♋ 14° *A bunch of spring flowers, over which is set a bright star which flashes and sparkles in a deep blue atmosphere.* It indicates a person of poetical and gentle disposition, fond of sublime subjects and the study of nature in its gentler phases; may be a botanist or astronomer, or one with a strong taste for such associations. In early life this individual will rise to a good position, and if not born into an illustrious family will marry a person of high rank or fame. In all cases the native attains a good position and generally marries early into a family devoted to the fine arts. It is a degree of SUCCESS.

♋ 15° *A dais on which is set a throne, on the cushion of which a dog is lying asleep.* It indicates a person of idle habits, to whom hard work and care are foreign and distasteful; but who will, whether by watchfulness, force or strategy; attain to a good position and hold offices for which he is not by nature qualified. It frequently produces a mere charlatan; or one who hides under a passive and indifferent exterior a vicious and spiteful nature. It is a degree of USURPATION.

♋ 16° *A man like a Hercules or Samson standing over a slain lion.*

It indicates a person of much tenacity and strength of purpose; who by dint of extreme power, whether physical or mental, will overcome his greatest and most terrible enemies. The native will have much to contend with in life, and will encounter many dangers; but, as indicated; will finally overcome them. Together with this native strength, there may be blended a softness and gentleness of manner, which may induce others to attempt an advantage over him; but those Philistines who may have this Samson out (shorn and eyeless though he be) to make sport with him will rue the day. It is a degree of CONQUEST.

♋ 17°   *A lightning flash.* It indicates a person of extreme nervous energy and force of character, who, by reason of his executive ability and great fund of energy, will take a leading part in the affairs of his community. The native of this sign will, among other things, be a great reformer. He will clear doubts as lightning rends the clouds, and will, while overturning much of existing belief, become a source of illumination to many. It is a degree of PIONEERING.

♋ 18°   *A cluster of faded exotics, very sweet and sickly to the smell.* It indicates a person of extreme frailty of character, unable to hold his own in the broad fields of life, and very timorous of exposure to the keen winds of criticism. One who will live in luxury even when of small means; a person with very little mettle, fond of pleasures and of fictitious stimulants. The native will eventually fall on evil days. It is a degree of SATIETY.

♋ 19°   *An escutcheon containing a harp and a gauntlet.* It denotes a person of noble aspirations and refined tastes. One whose family is connected with the musical or military worlds, and who will have tastes in one or the other direction. In either he will show much aptitude, but in music the executive powers will transcend the ability to compose. As an interpreter of others' works he would shine. In the character there is a peculiar admixture of gentleness and irritability, of playfulness and gravity, which will render the native difficult to deal with. It is a degree of EXECUTION.

♋ 20° *A man dressed as a groom, riding upon a spirited horse.* It indicates a person of general aptitude, quick perception, steady mind and able body, who, in some secondary place, will serve the cause of truth: may be as a teacher, or as a priest, or one connected with the Church. Success in life is shown, but not pre-eminence. The life, while useful, will be obscure. It is a degree of SERVICE.

♋ 21° *A waning moon, amid a bank of clouds, dimly reveals a ship at sea, but all disabled.* It indicates a person of roving, unsettled habits, whose ill-fortune will lead him to many pursuits in quest of wealth, but who eventually will be badly placed, and with little hope of improvement. It indicates that the native will have much aptitude and versatility, but not much perseverance or hopefulness, and this continually, passing from one bad thing to something worse, instead of improving that which he holds. It is a degree of INSTABILITY.

♋ 22° *A man asleep in the heat of the day; some implements beside him.* It denotes an unsuccessful person, whose indolence, lack of interest and energy, will prove the source of much misfortune. Yet the middle of his life will be bright and happy; only, dreaming when he should be working, he will go to a sorry home in the evening of his life. It is a degree of INDOLENCE.

♋ 23° *A man standing upon a mountain with a staff in his hand. The setting sun shows his figure in relief.* It indicates a person of aspiring tendencies, fond of adventure and doing hardy things. In some respects a unique character and, may be, a striking personality. One who, by some effort of his own, will attract attention in the latter years of his life, not by any learning or invention, but by prowess or the use of his natural powers. The native may show a strong tendency to mountaineering or to geographical discovery, and will be a great pedestrian. He will be in great danger during the middle of his career, and will eventually triumph over obstacles, and avoiding dangers will terminate his life extremely well. It is a degree of ELEVATION.

♋ 24° *A strong castle on a high rock, and upon the battlements of the castle a flag with a crown upon it is seen extended in the wind.* It denotes a strong, masterly character, of great endurance, stability and daring; ambitious of honour and capable of withstanding his enemies while achieving greatness and fame for himself. It is a degree of MASTERY.

♋ 25° *A horseman armed, moving across a desert towards some woody hills.* It indicates a person of much independence of spirit, self-willed and daring. Such is capable of carrying out designs conceived by himself without the aid or companionship of others. He may be a pioneer; it is certain he is venturesome and self-reliant; and where such qualities may have influence, he will succeed and be singular in honour as in action. The native will be somewhat estranged from his kindred; taciturn and self-contained; but will make his mark in some field of work requiring independence of spirit, courage and perseverance. It is a degree of SELF-RELIANCE.

♋ 26° *A meteor, or falling star.* It denotes a person of somewhat poetical or æsthetic nature, but wholly unsuited to the routine of daily life in its sterner and more prosaic aspects. Like the meteor, he has an eccentric path, and his appearances are spasmodic and evanescent, although bright. His position in life will be always subject to reversals and changes and his success will not be lasting. If he should attain to eminence he will be in danger of a fall. It is a degree of UNCERTAINTY.

♋ 27° *A well-conditioned heifer standing to the plough.* It indicates a person who will owe his success in life to uses imposed upon him by others of greater will and intelligence. It shows a docile and tractable spirit, capable of patient service under the direction or initiative of others; much silent force and endurance, but little self-assertion, originality, or ambition. As a servitor this native will succeed, but would not need to be urged, for both nature and inclination are adapted to patient work. It is a degree of DOCILITY.

♋ 28° *A beautiful scene of the country, wherein all the elements conspire to enchant the eye and hold the spirit in a mood of silent adoration.* It indicates a nature of extreme susceptibility to the influence of the natural forces; a kind, harmonious and devotional nature; extremely attractive, gentle and thoughtful. It shows one capable of sustained sympathies, of patient and peaceful mood, pure instincts and elevated mind. The native will be fond of the open country and the beauties of Nature in every one of its many and changeful aspects. It may induce a taste for horticulture or farming. It is a degree of HARMONY.

♋ 29° *A tethered horse, upon which a tiger is covertly approaching.* It indicates a person of docile and tractable nature, combined with a certain subtlety of mind and high order of intelligence. One who will be held in restraint by others, or whose freedom will be taken by the hand of Fate and the force of circumstances. Although thus held in check, the native will be subject to dangers of an unknown character from secret enemies and jealous foes, and will be in peril of an untimely end. It is a degree of forced RESTRAINT.

♋ 30° *A young horse running across a field with a leading cord in trail; it lifts its head against the breeze and sniffs the air.* It denotes a person of much intelligence, ardent spirits, somewhat wilful and daring nature; having a great love of freedom, contempt for public opinion, and much selfreliance. The mind is quick and alert, but somewhat untameable and wilful, and the emotions are apt to run away with the reason. There is, however, a good deal of intuitive judgment in the native, and this degree gives a keen sense of justice, a warm passional nature, strong will, little self-restraint and much insight into human character. It is a degree of FREEDOM.

LEO

♌ 1° *There stands a lion upon an elevation looking towards a rising sun.* It denotes a person of extreme dignity of character, with much self-reliance, fearlessness, nobility and freedom of nature; an ambitious person and somewhat jealous of honours, being much subject to praise and flattery. The native will be apt in the government of others, and equally so in self-control; but unless the heart be kind, the native will be a mere pompous tyrant. It is a degree of DIGNITY.

♌ 2° *A pennant or streamer, such as is used by mariners to indicate the course of the wind.* It denotes a person of an extremely vacillating and uncertain disposition; weak minded, and subject to be driven about from one opinion to another; generally moved by consent to prevailing sentiment, and incapable of any firm and independent position. The native will be liable to experience strange caprices of fortune; and will wander, with many a change of object, from one place to another, but little permanence for good will be assured to him. At times exceedingly hopeful, and anon depressed and nervous, the native will make little headway or progress. It is a degree of WEAKNESS.

♌ 3° *A wave-line of nebulous light, obscured by a cloud in the midst.* It denotes a person of elastic and undeveloped mind, uncertain principles, liable to lead to licence and moral turpitude. The native will lead a somewhat irregular life, and will be generally inconsequent and unreliable in his actions. Much of the obscurity into which this person will be thrust from time to time will be due to the unfledged condition of the mind, and the misdirection, through ignorance, of the moral faculty. It is a degree of WANDERING.

♌ 4° *A cat upon the watch for prey.* It denotes a person of the most prudent, circumspect, and patient mind; capable of sustaining great fatigue in the accomplishment ol his desires; a mind gifted with much diplomacy, suavity, self-restraint, and watchfulness; keen in observing but slow to draw conclusions; capable when aroused, of much malice, but not of open anger. Firm in his attachments, a fast friend and unrelenting enemy. The native will succeed in life by dint of caution and perseverance. It is a degree of CIRCUMSPECTION.

♌ 5° *A snake coiled around a tree, its head raised ready to strike.* It denotes a person of scientific powers and learning in the subtle arts; one who is capable of carrying out the most elaborate researches with patience and intelligence of the highest order. Withal there is within the mind of the native a certain degree of cupidity and cunning, which, wisely directed, will be of great service in daily life. There is also a keen sense of rivalry and competition, a love of personal advantage, which the native will use in a very subtle manner. Generally speaking, the native is acute, cunning, cautious, and very intelligent; but jealous and envious, and to be warily dealt with on that account. There is moderate success in life shown. It is a degree of SUBTLETY.

♌ 6° *Two crossed swords above a gauntlet, forming an escutcheon.* It denotes a person of a proud, martial nature, with considerable tastes for athletics, deeds of daring and prowess, contests, feats of arms, and the like. Somewhat given to argument and contention, ever ready to rush into disputes regardless of danger. The native will succeed as a soldier, or in active service requiring courage and strength; but will be liable to some reverses of fortune following upon undue self-assertion. It is a degree of PROWESS.

♌ 7°   A sceptre, on the crest of which shines a diamond like a magnificent star. The native is born to power, eminence, fame. He will, by the use of his many talents, supplemented by a powerful will, rise to a foremost position in his sphere of life. There is in the character a large amount of courage, nobility, energy and endurance, and the free use of such qualities will, under a benign fate, bring the native into a field of life where he will be a central figure. It is a degree of SUPERIORITY.

♌ 8°   *An aureole of clouds, in the midst of which appears a triangle of flame, and an eye within the triangle.* It denotes a person of exalted nature, gifted with spiritual faculties, by means of which he will attain to some degree of eminence in things devoted to the fiery art, and likewise will be distinguished in matters of a spiritual nature. The mind is just, aspiring and noble; hopeful, full of the divine fire of a worthy ambition; intuitive, but not logical, yet ever intense and sincere. It is a degree of ARDOUR.

♌ 9°   *A fine chateau, with gardens and terraces. In the foreground a peacock in full feather struts leisurely.* It denotes a person of tasteful, but luxurious habits; one who will spend much upon mere show, and will depend much upon appearances to the neglect of more desirable uses. Together with these characteristics, there is a great deal of pride, which in the uneducated may run to ostentation and snobbishness. Yet, in any sphere of life the native will be fortunate among his compeers. It is a degree of DISPLAY.

♌ 10°   *An oak tree broken by the wind, and beneath is the skeleton of some dead creature.* It denotes one whose chief ambitions will not come to completion; but, either through disaster or untimely death, will be prematurely brought to nought. To whomsoever this degree may appertain, the warning goes forth: build not for the future, but for eternity, for it is very nigh; and if thou sowest aught, make no count of the harvest, for the seasons are not to thy hand; yet both sow and build for the greater good, and work in hope! In character the native will be versatile, somewhat morose and despondent, but strong in trial; and giving shelter even to the worthless out of pure goodwill. It is a degree of PERIL.

♌ 11°   *A man and woman are seated at a table, whereon viands and wine are lavishly abundant.* It indicates a person of a very sensuous nature, addicted to extravagant habits, and apt to be easily led into dissolute ways by illchosen companions. There is very little firmness or strength in the native, though the disposition is genial, kind and sociable. The instinctual sense, however, is stronger than the moral sense, and therein lies danger of self-debasement and loss of virtue. It is a degree of SELF-INDULGENCE.

♌ 12°   *A fine bull, of a white colour, grazing in the shade of a large tree which stands in a park.* The person denoted by this degree will lead a quiet and successful life, and will either be born into large estates, or will join such by marriage. In character, the native will be steadfast, firm, independent, very reserved, benevolent, yet outwardly forbidding, patient and cautious. This degree is one of ADVANTAGE.

♌ 13°   *A jutting rock, upon which some tufts of grass hold a thin, but certain existence.* It indicates a person of firm and steadfast character; one who will resolutely hold to his own beliefs and principles, though it be to his disadvantage. In some ways the mind will be precocious and there will be some degree of self-assertion shown; but, whatever the native may determine upon as the right thing to do will assuredly be done if within the compass of resolute striving. It is a degree of CONSTANCY.

♌ 14°   *A broken wheel lies upon the ground, while a horse grazes near by.* It indicates one of small resources, little power of invention, and not much executive ability. The native is very laissez faire, and drifts too easily through life; and this want of direction will be apt to lead him into evil conditions. The native may be fortunate, but it is certain that he will not retain his wealth owing to his own fault. It is a degree of AIMLESSNESS.

♌ 15°   *A figure like the angel of the Sun (Michael), standing erect, and striking the earth with the point of a dazzling sword.* It indicates a person of very superior ability in some special direction; one in whom the power of government will re-side; a mind somewhat ambitious, but conscious of its own powers—which are of no common order—so that no unjust advantage is taken. In some sphere of life the native will be an imposing figure, or may do something which may call for wide recognition. Fame and power attend this degree. It is one of SUPERIORITY.

♌ 16°   *A ram standing upon a barren rock, pawing the ground.* It indicates a person of a headstrong and rash disposition, extremely given to impulse; difficult to restrain; a formidable opponent and a warm-hearted, generous friend. The native is effusive, enthusiastic and restless, but capable of subsisting upon small fare and in all probability he will be poor though in some sense eminent. It is a degree of IMPULSE.

♌ 17° *A man riding a camel with attendants following.* It denotes one who will be noted for his wide and prolonged travels. One whose life will be beset with dangers of a physical nature; one who will leave a humble home and become a prominent figure in a foreign country. The character is stubborn, persevering, very vindictive and revengeful; not ungrateful but never forgetting injuries. The native will be somewhat fond of parade and self-advertisement, and in the end will be highly successful in life. It is a degree of JOURNEYING.

♌ 18° *A bright mirror in which the Sun's rays are reflected.* It denotes a person of extremely brilliant and powerful intellect, who will make his mark in the world by means of his learning and assimilating the ideas of others, but on the other hand he will be equally apt in original inventions and brilliant schemes, The nature is sympathetic, kind and generous, and will be admired for his good deeds. It is a degree of SHINING.

♌ 19° *A man running in the face of a strong wind, but making little headway. His garments fly in tatters behind him.* It indicates one of small wit and lacking in executive power and originality of thought. One who will nevertheless set himself against public opinion and incur severe criticism and loss thereby. There is in the nature a certain foolish pride and obstinacy which is wholly unallied to anything of originality or distinctive merit. It is a degree of FOOLISHNESS.

♌ 20° *A crescent moon joined to a shining star.* It denotes that the native will have many changes in life and will eventually become eminent through his association with some person of high rank and merit. The native will be gifted with a powerful imagination, much versatility and keen intuition. He will travel to distant countries, and will become eminent for his own mental brilliancy, apart from his associations, which however will be the means of his success. It is a degree of DISTICTION.

♌ 21° *A human face surmounted by a coiled serpent; a raised hand also appears.* It indicates not only a powerful and commanding nature, but a keen understanding of the laws of life; much introspection and knowledge of human nature; strong sympathies; much discretion; careful balance of power and effort; intuition and foresight, as well as diplomacy of no mean order. The native will have strong powers of concentration, good memory, and will be successful in commanding others, through his insight into character. It is a degree of PENETRATION.

♌ 22° *A nest of young birds, over which a hawk is seen hovering.* It denotes that the native is his own enemy, and that he will suffer through want of care in his actions. Apart from this, which arises from a certain native innocency, he will be in danger of injuries in his own house and through his own kindred. The life is fraught with dangers of an incendiary character, and he should avoid risks of personal injury as much as possible. In business or profession he will be supplanted. It is a degree of INJURY.

♌ 23° *A bright, pale blue star, shining over a clear lake.* It indicates one of a quick, refined, and well-trained intelligence, who will gain distinction by menial powers. The nature will be peaceful, harmonious, and beneficent. The mind is highly intuitive, and capable of lofty and sustained flights. Withal there is a good knowledge of character and a quiet but potent reserve of diplomatic power. The native will shine like a star in his sphere at life, and will have many followers. It is a degree of INTELLIGENCE.

♌ 24° *A man felling a tree.* It indicates a person capable of enduring long and hard work. A humble and unambitious mind, of large sympathies, and warm feelings; much attached to rustic things and to the wild habits of the woodland life. One who sees good and finds contentment in the rudest work, so long as it be manly and productive of current necessaries. It denotes a person of an ingenuous and rugged mind, harsh manners, but soft heart. A good friend. It is a degree of SIMPLICITY.

♌ 25° *A reversed triangle upon a red ground.* It denotes a person of a very passionate and emotional nature, who will suffer through the allurements of the other sex, and at some time in his life will be liable to suffocation or drowning. The native will certainly be in danger through the watery element. The fortunes will be in danger of reversal, and that through the passional nature of the native. The nature is incapable of any steady effort, and is, in short, as soft and unstable as water. It is a degree of INSTABILITY.

♌ 26° *A thick wood at the back of a field, in which is a man ploughing with an ox.* It indicates a person of laborious habits, very much attached to the country life, and a close student of nature. The mind is retiring and modest, very intelligent, and gifted with patience and firmness, capable of sustaining close researches or yet heavy labours of a purely physical kind. The native will be fortunate, but never very rich or very prominent. It is a degree of STEADFASTNESS.

♌ 27° *A dagger.* This is an ominous sign! It may mean danger to the native at the bands of an enemy, or, yet more unhappily, it may mean the reverse of this. The native will certainly be of a quarrelsome, argumentative nature; given over to impulsive actions. A restless and destructive mind, always on the alert to attack, to oppose, to argue. Very executive, but by no means constructive in disposition, and hence liable to go through life like a tornado, remarked but not esteemed. It is a degree of DESTROYING.

♌ 28° *Two hands linked in a close grip of friendship.* It denotes a person of a very amiable and social nature, filled with concord and goodwill towards his fellows. A rich, unselfish nature, capable of those little greatnesses in daily life which make a man beloved, if not remarkable. It is probable that the native will be instrumental in forming some large associations for social co-operation, or intellectual improvement. The native is essentially constructive, harmonising and humane. It is a degree of SUSTAINING.

♌ 29° *Two golden circles joined by a blue ribbon tied in a double bow.* It denotes one of a kind, benevolent nature, who will be fortunate in marriage, and may marry twice. The native is a lover of peace and concord; an idealist; embodying two lives in one; a reseacher in celestial things. He will make many and sincere friends. His life will be useful, lovable and sincere. He will attain his ambitions, and will end his days in peace. It is a degree of UNION.

♌ 30° *A dog in poor condition stands whining and cringing.* It indicates a person of a narrow, servile disposition, given to complaining and lamenting, instead of acting and achieving. A nature self-centred and morose, of no great comfort to its owner or of use to others. It is a degree of INDIGENCE.

VIRGO

♍ 1° *A festival or occasion for the assembling together of villagers in gala costume.* It denotes a person of a sociable, friendly and flexible nature; capable of adapting itself to its environment; having a strong taste for pleasures of various kinds, luxuries, festivities, etc. It promises friendships and good fortune to the native, who will be much esteemed for his convivial spirit. It is a degree of FEASTING.

♍ 2° *A solitary rock jutting up from a waste of sand.* It indicates one of much fixity, steadiness and gravity of character; inclined to agnosticism or atheism. Cold, mathematical, hard, and very just in his methods of thought, but lacking those emotional qualities which make of life something more vital than a problematical theory. The native is somewhat indolent and wanting in direction and purpose; but there is a great power of resistance and endurance. The fortunes of the native will be poor, partly due to lack of executive ability on the side of the native, and partly to the conditions of birth and environment. A degree of POVERTY.

♍ 3° *A man in a skull-cap, busy at work with some scientific instruments.* It denotes a person of industrious habits; quick insight into natural laws; an investigator in the chemical or other scientific world; fond of experiment, eager in his undertakings, very hopeful, though during life will be hardly used at the hands of fortune. The native will, however, eventually succeed in his endeavours, and will assuredly reap the fruit of long and earnest labours. It is a degree of RESEARCH.

♍ 4°   *A field of corn standing high and ripe.* It denotes a person of simple and rural habits, who will succeed in the cultivation of natural products, and in husbandry or farming. The mind, although simple, is full of the essential elements of the right thinking, and the nature is ripe with well-directed aspirations and endeavours. Such an one will live a useful and successful life, and will come to the length of his days in competence and peace. It is a degree of PRODUCE.

♍ 5°   *A soldier prepared for battle.* It defines a man of ready spirit, quick to respond to the calls of duty and honour; a man of noble instincts and well-disciplined habits. Such will prove a ready and willing friend and a redoubtable opponent. He will succeed in life through his own executive powers, and the credit which falls to him will be well earned. It is a degree of EFFICIENCY.

♍ 6°   *A man and a woman playing together, with fruits, flowers, and wine upon a table beside them.* It indicates a person of a joyous, youthful nature, full of animal spirits and mirthfulness; fond of all kinds of pleasures; seldom seriously disposed; endowed with some personal beauty and the qualities which make a cheerful companion and a successful lover. There is, however, very little stability in the nature, and no power to sustain courage under trial. Money will come readily to the hand, but it will go as quickly, leaving its scars behind. It is a degree of PLEASURE.

♍ 7°   *A man and woman standing with their backs to one another.* It denotes a person of reserved and bashful disposition; not unsociable, but awkward in the presence of others, particularly so with the opposite sex. The native will be indifferent to marriage, or will have troubles therein. The affections are very sincere, the mind pure and chaste, and the disposition kind and generous. The manner, however, is retired, cautious, sensitive and delicate. It is a degree of MODESTY.

♍ 8° *A woodland scene, at the back of which there stands a tower upon a hill.* It indicates a person of free, open and generous spirit; frank and natural mind ; with a strong taste for natural beauties; exalted ideals; contemplative nature. The native will have some inclination to mountain climbing or to the ascent of high places. It denotes success in life of a quiet order, and a retired old age. It is a degree of CONTEMPLATION.

♍ 9° *A stagnant pool filled with weeds and rank verdure.* It denotes a person of an indolent and wasteful character, prone to let duties slide and to procrastinate with fortune. It further indicates that the native will form an alliance with a female which will be to his detriment. In general, the native will be unfortunate, his marriage especially so. It is a degree of STAGNATION.

♍ 10° *A bag of money upon a table, near to which stands a dark woman masked.* It denotes a person of a fortunate nature, who will attract both friends and money. The latter will come to his hands as birds to the net of the snarer. But, see! he will not know how to use it, and it will become a source of danger to him through the machinations of a woman. In character, the native will be sociable and generous: weak-willed, but highly industrious and fortunate. Apt in business, but with small knowledge of the deeper levels of human cupidity and passion, hence liable to be victimised. It is a degree of SEDUCTIVE FORTUNE.

♍ 11° *A man's hand, with the index finger pointing upward as if in command.* It denotes a nature of the most high utility.

A flexible nature, capable of fulfilling many and various positions in life; a generous and kind disposition; a high order of intelligence; always seeking after the *uses* of things; ingenious, inventive; one who will succeed in life, and will have many tributes to his intelligence and usefulness. It is a degree of UTILITY.

♍ 12° *A woman blindfold, and a man leading her.* It denotes a person of a weak yet seductive nature, one who will have much influence upon the other sex, and who may be led into dangerous relations with them, so that the life may be compared only to a tangled skein in which the complications are more various than the nrnterials which enter into them. It is a degree of ENTANGLEMENT.

♍ 13° *A broad tract of open fields under the moon's rays; a river winds its way through them.* It denotes that the life of the native will be calm, joyous, tranquil aud useful. In character the native will be gentle, peaceful, obliging, calm, not forceful, but exerting an influence of a very effective kind which persuades through harmony. The native will be very romantic and imaginative, and will favour the fine arts, music, poetry, painting, etc. The life will be fortunate. It is a degree of HARMONY.

♍ 14° *A man mining in the rock with a pickaxe.* It denotes a person of practical and unimaginative nature; a negationist or agnostic; a man of the people; laborious, honest and just. The life of the native will be of a sedentary nature, occupied in hard work to little personal profit. There will be exposure to accidents and danger to life and limb thereby. The native will not care for supremacy or advancement, and will follow along the track made by others, devoid of worldly ambition. It is a degree of SERVICE.

♍ 15°   *A beautiful woman nesting two doves upon her breast, one in each hand.* It indicates a person of the most tender and humane instincts, imbued with gentleness, love and devotion; capable of service in the meanest capacity, providing it to be an office of usefulness to others. The native will be remarkable for his womanly tenderness and gentleness. His life will be successful, but on account of his timidity, he will be in danger of being pushed into the background at critical junctures, and will thus lose credit where it will often be due to him. It is a degree of DEVOTION.

♍ 16°   *Several men in festive attire assembled together are talking.* It indicates a person of sociable and versatile character, having strong humane feelings and sympathetic mind; one who will make many friends and will have some considerable benefits from associations formed casually. Without attempting the native will be most successful in the bringing together of persons mutually advantageous one to another. It is a degree of ASSOCIATION.

♍ 17°   *An old man cutting grapes in a vineyard.* It denotes a person of an industrious, watchful and prudent nature, who will work with an eye to the future, and will exercise providence over his means. In old age he will reap the reward of a steadfast industry, and gather in the fruits of foresight and care. It is a degree of PRUDENCE.

♍ 18°   *An old white-headed man surrounded by happy children.* It denotes to the native a long and happy life; an old age invested with the comforts of homely affection. It endows the native with a kind, benevolent and fatherly interest in his fellows, especially those of tender years. He will be much beloved, and will end his days in prosperity and peace. It is a degree of GUARDIANSHIP.

♍ 19° *A husbandman or cattle-dealer holding a stock-whip in his hand.* It indicates a rough and rustic nature, with a taste for excitement of the chase, or for the breeding of cattle. The nature is rugged, but genuine; lacking in suavity; critical, but invested with unequivocal sincerity, which will cause him to be respected. The native will prefer country life and its freedom to the more varied but less thorough liberties of the town. It is a degree of ROBUSTNESS.

♍ 20° *Two men fencing with swords. A man in black stands aside watching them.* The native is born with a predisposition to disputes and quarrels, and he will be involved in some *fracas* in a foreign country or with a foreigner. He will be further liable to hurts from secret enemies, and his life will be overshadowed by a melancholy fate. It is a degree of FIGHTING.

♍ 21° *A man carrying a money-bag in each hand.* The native will be of a penurious, acquisitive, and mercenary nature; always counting the cost of all he does, and looking well to it that whatever he performs shall first be remunerative; then, if possible (though this is not important), just. He will acquire wealth by easy means, and will indulge in some very notable speculations. It is a degree of COVETOUSNESS.

♍ 22° *A well-favoured woman, bitt of evil aspect, stands before a mirror.* It denotes a person of a sensuous and worldly nature, very susceptible to flattery; vain, easily led away, and in great danger of a downfall. Unless the native urges a strong moral resistance to his instincts he will incur shame and dishonour through his alliances with the opposite sex. The same applies *mutatis mutandis* to a female. It is a degree of SENSUOUSNESS.

♍ 23° *A ship in full sail.* It indicates a person of a roving and fanciful nature, always on the alert for some new experience, a new sensation, and some *soupçon* of romance and danger therein. The native will travel to foreign countries and will either become a sailor or will gain his reputation and means of subsistence by work connected with the sea. It is a degree of ROVING.

♍ 24° *A man sitting naked upon a sea-girt rock, covering his eyes with his hands.* It denotes a person of misanthropic spirit and unsociable disposition, who will be estranged from his kindred and may be exiled or outcast from his country. In addition, the native will be short-sighted or have some moral obliquity, so that he will incur severe troubles through this defect in various ways. It is a degree of LONELINESS.

♍ 25° *Crossed swords, over which is seen a crown.* It indicates a person of a military, aggressive character, and who will take things by force and cut his way through life by dint of energy and executive ability. He will have many and powerful enemies, but will overcome them. Yet peace will not abide with the man of war, and the native, while gaining fame, will lose his happiness in life. It is a degree of AGGRESSION.

♍ 26° *Two women walking together with linked arms talking confidentially.* It denotes a person of a sociable, kind, sympathetic and cordial nature, who will attract many sincere friends of both sexes, and by means of them will prosper. In mature years the native is destined to preside over a united and happy home. It is a degree of CONCORD.

♍ 27° *A broken hammer or mallet, lying upon a carpenter's bench.* It denotes a person of a peculiarly incapable nature, unhappy disposition, and a certain awkwardness in his bearing. He will suffer ills through want of practicalness and executive power, and by reason of his backwardness will be liable to be victimised and deceived by the more active and wary. It is a degree of BLUNTNESS.

♍ 28° *A wide-branching tree laden with fruit.* It denotes a person of a full, rich and generous disposition, superior intelligence, industrious and husbandly habits, predestined to success in life by reason of inherent merits. He will gain many friends and have a large family. Whatever else is needful to success and peace of mind will fall to him. It is a degree of FRUITFULNESS.

♍ 29° *A man attired as a cardinal of the church.* It denotes one of a quick and energetic nature, short temper, reclusive habits; highly imaginative and capable of much creative work; inclined to religion of a ceremonial nature; subject to spells of sensuousness, but of strong self-commanding faculty. It is a degree of ECCLESIASTICISM.

♍ 30° *A man standing, either headless, or with the head shrouded in black cloth.* It denotes a person of a very melancholy disposition and eccentric mind, a searcher of secret things, and fond of midnight studies; a recluse. It threatens the native with some mental affection, or danger of wounds in the head. The native will have to exercise great care in his mental efforts or he will end his days in chaos and confusion of mind. It is a degree of OBSCURATION.

LIBRA

♎ 1° *A man with a drawn sword in an aggressive attitude.* It denotes a person of martial and quarrelsome character, ever ready to pick a quarrel and to rush into danger. Such an one will fight his way through life with little regard to the feelings and prejudices of others, and though he may become notorious for his executive readiness, he will meet with disgrace and trouble through his impetuosity. There is danger of a fatality at the hands of the native. He will do well to keep his action under control. It is a degree of WOUNDING.

♎ 2° *A man in the garb of a doctor of the monastic order (misericordia).* It denotes a person of kindly and humane disposition, but very melancholic and predisposed to religious mania. The native will possess a high order of intellect capable of investigating the laws of the most recondite sciences; inclined to spiritual pursuits and to the monastic life. It is a degree of SEARCHING.

♎ 3° *A man in chains.* It denotes a person of reticent and self-centred character, disposed to take life according to his own views and beliefs. He will suffer much in consequence, and will be estranged from his people; will be often in distress for the means of a livelihood and will at some time in his life be deprived of his freedom. It is a degree of BINDING.

♎ 4° *A man with a broken plough standing in an open field.* It indicates a person of fair abilities, but one who will suffer from lack of opportunity in life. He will be debarred from reaping the fruits due to him by reason of misfortune and hindrance in the early stages of his worldly career. He will more than once lose his office, and will be reduced to the necessity of menial work. His life will be difficult and troublesome. He will have a taste for farming or for cultivation in some form. It is a degree of PRIVATION.

♎ 5° *A red triangle.* It indicates a person of high intelligence and lofty aspirations, but very prone to the use of force instead of persuasion. A man who is always getting in front of himself, so to speak, losing his temper against his desire, and letting his energies run away with his reason. He will be in danger of hurt by the sword or by fire. He must be careful of the martial element. It is a degree of IMPULSE.

♎ 6° *A heifer drawing a plough, and urged by the goad.* It denotes one very unfortunate, who will be constrained to severe and hard work for a certain period of his life. The native is patient, enduring, and capable of much self-government. In the end he will assuredly reap the reward of his labours. It is a degree of LABOUR.

♎ 7° *A naked man in the act off falling from a rock into a lake.* It indicates a person of susceptible and weak nature, easily led away, and liable to be drawn to his destruction by the agency of the opposite sex. The native may attain to a high position in life, but whatever his position, he is in danger of an untimely fall. Let him take heed against the allurements of the world. It is a degree of FALLING.

♎ 8° *A young maiden weeping over a grave.* It denotes one of a melancholy and retiring nature, very sensitive, and of keen sympathies. The native will be in danger of early bereavement, and will at an early age be left devoid of family ties and friends. It is a degree of EFFACEMENT.

♎ 9° *A gladiator, armed with dagger and shield, ready for the fray.*

It indicates a person of quick, impetuous, quarrelsome, and aggressive nature, who will cause many disputes in life on account of his irascible disposition, and will make many enemies. The native will be in danger of losing his life while engaged in some affray or quarrel, and should know how to forefend himself by self-command, which is the greatest of all conquests. It is a degree of FIGHTING.

♎ 10° *A prison door, fitted with iron spikes, and framed with iron girders.* It indicates a person of vicious tendencies, which will lead him into dangers of the gravest kind. He will suffer restraint or imprisonment, or will lead a life of forced seclusion. He will not escape open criticism, and misfortune will press heavily upon him: yet even the caged bird will sing, and to every prison house there is a way out. It is a degree of SECLUSION.

♎ 11° *A centaur—half man, half horse—armed with bow and arrow.* It denotes a person of a subtle and changeful nature, capable of simulating the virtues and vices of others from motives of diplomacy. The native will be alternately impelled to paths of high endeavour and to those of debasing instinct. The father of the native will die early or will be unknown to him. It is a degree of ALTERNATION.

♎ 12° *A fair woman looking at her face in a handglass.* It denotes a person of a frivolous and lighthearted disposition, improvident and foolish, neither regarding the future nor profiting by the past: laughing in the face of fate, and closing the eyes to experience: self-centred and worldly. The native will come by much misfortune, but will flaunt his colours to the end of a foolish career. It is a degree of FOOLISHNESS.

♎ 13° *A pillar of black marble standing upon a rock, roughly hewn.*

It denotes a person ot peculiar and sometimes melancholy and misanthropic nature: apt to contract false or unprofitable relations with his fellows and with the opposite sex. The native will make a bad match, and will be untortunate in wedlock, with probable separation. The native, in centring his affections upon one object, will be liable to disappointment in life. It is a degree of SOLITARINESS.

♎ 14° *A mummer's mask.* It denotes a person of a subtle nature, capable of simulating the character of others, and given to mimicry and imitation: not always sincere, and apt even to deceive himself in matters relating to the emotions and feelings. The native has natural aptitude for theatricals, especially comedy, and is capable of much foolishness and flattery. If a female, a coquette. It is a degree of IMITATION.

♎ 15° *A man walking with two women, their arms linked in his.* It denotes a person of untrustworthy nature: frivolous, insincere, capable of duplicity: of a light, joyous spirit sometimes running away with the reason. The native will be given to self-indulgence, and to the flattery of women. There will be trouble in love affairs and in marriage. It is a degree of VACILLATION.

♎ 16° *An iceberg, at the back of which is seen a display of the aurora borealis.* It denotes a person of immense reserve forces, of much activity, energy and brilliance: a quick, alert and original mind, which will win for the native some distinctive honours. The native will be disposed to travel to distant northern countries, and may explore arctic regions or pursue electrical science. It is a degree of FORCE.

♎ 17° *An old door in which a dagger is stuck.* It denotes a person who has a critical and quarrelsome nature, apt to find fault with the opinions of others for the sake of controversy: striking at existing systems and laws even when unable to improve upon them. A mocking, taunting spirit, which will bring upon the native a series of troubles in life. Eventually he will be convinced of his foolishness by the strong band of retribution. It is a degree of FOLLY.

♎ 18° *A well-lighted house with open door.* It denotes a person of hospitable and homely nature, ever ready with the best of fare to entertain friends and acquaintances. The native will grow to be much beloved for his open-handedness and sincerity of feeling. He will be both prosperous and happy, and will rejoice in the company of his friends. It is a degree of HOSPITALITY.

♎ 19° *A square block of marble, upon which is the regalia of sceptre and crown.* It denotes a person of proud, ambitions nature: desiring to be held in esteem, and possessed of such force and firmness of character that he will triumph over his rivals and opponents. In whatever station of life he may be, the native will evince the characteristics of rulership and government, and will sway the destinies of others. It is a degree of RULERSHIP.

♎ 20° *A man in the robe of a priest standing in the cloister beneath the light of a window.* It denotes a person of sincere, religious tendencies: a taste for ecclesiastical work, in which he will probably indulge. The life will be quiet, peaceful and free from much of event, perhaps secluded. The native will have protection and favour from persons of high position and intellectual dignity. It is a degree of RELIGION.

♎ 21 *A bridge in a broken and dilapidated condition spanning over the dry bed of a river.* It denotes a person of an unpractical nature, serving in positions for which he is, not qualified, and making little or no progress in life. His resources will run dry at short notice: he will be deserted by friends: will serve in a lowly position: will form projects only to see them fall through one after another, and generally will work along a false trail. It is a degree of COLLAPSE.

♎ 22° *A man asleep by the side of some money-bags.* It denotes a person of little vigilance: much given to selfindulgence: wanting either in sense of duty, or in energy to fulfil it. The native will lose heavily on account of his carelessness, false sense of safety and want of caution. He will live much in the memory of the past and in dreams of the future, being the while oblivious to the demands of present duties. It is a degree of CARELESSNESS.

♎ 23° *An old man in a gown and skull cap like a doctor surrounded by chemical and other instruments.* It denotes a person of careful, systematic, and patient observation: much inclined to the study of science, especially chemistry, medicine, or alchemy. A researcher in the secrets of Nature, given to the careful and accurate tabulation of results which will prove of use to science, and by this means the native will gain for himself certain distinction and honour. It is a degree of RESEARCH.

♎ 24° *A solitary tree upon a rocky height, behind which is a dark and threatening cloud.* It denotes a person of much independence of spirit, self-confidence, pride, and no little love of distinction. The native will suffer on account of his isolated feelings, and will be in danger of betrayal by the machinations of perfidious enemies. At a time when he has reached a height of isolated distinction, he will fall under the jealous hand of his enemies. It is a degree of PRIDE.

♎ 25° *An elevated promontory, illumined by the noonday sun and crowned with many and variously coloured flowers.* It indicates a nature that is prone to self-conceit, amenable to flattery, proud in heart but light-headed and trifling in many relationships of life. It may confer considerable personal charm and attractiveness, and will render its subject the recipient of many of fortune's favours. It is a degree of ELEVATION.

♎ 26° *A strong man mailed and plumed, with couched lance, ready for attack: a knight of the field.* It denotes one who will be steadfast in defence of his rights and those of his country, ever ready for the fray of daily life, and possessed of a courage and determination which, together with his alertness and caution, will give him the victory over all his enemies. It is a degree of VICTORY.

♎ 27° *A rustic cottage, overarched by a spreading cedar tree.* It indicates a nature that is attuned to works of benevolence and homely simplicity, careful in the affairs of daily life, solicitous of peace and comfort, and ever ready to shelter, befriend and succour the wayside traveller without neglect of those within his doors. It is a degree of BENEVOLENCE.

♎ 28° *An ass tethered to the shaft of a grinding mill.* It indicates a nature that is inured to arduous and homely work; one who will pursue the beaten track of an unambitious life with but slight regard to his own limitations and still less to the wider projects and life of others. It is a degree of SERVITUDE.

♎ 29° *A dark pool of water in the shadow of dense foliage.* It indicates a disposition towards a quiet and ineffectual life; a nature that is ambitionless and effortless, disposed to a gloomy fatalism which renders the life insipid and melancholy. Yielding without reason and showing adaptability without purpose, the nature will be devoid of any degree of brilliance and the life will be rendered obscure. It is a degree of GLOOM.

♎ 30° *A man sleeping upon a bundle of clothes. Over him hovers a vulture, while upon one side of him is a serpent ready to strike and on the other a leopard in the act of springing.* It indicates a nature that is careless and imprudent; one who is foolishly oblivious to his environment, believing himself secure while yet he is surrounded by dangers, and given over to self-indulgence and untimely pleasures which will render him subject to misfortune and violence. It is a degree of INDIFFERENCE.

SCORPIO

♏ 1° *A nomadic warrior, equipped with javelin and firearms.* It denotes a character that is ever ready for the fray, liable to become involved in many strifes and quarrels, and to resort to force rather than reason for his victories over others. Such an one is liable to become subject to the accusation of violence towards others, and will hardly pass through life without wounding some one or more of his fellow-creatures. In body robust and in mind offensive to the peace of others he will not fail to make numerous enemies. It is a degree of OFFENCE.

♏ 2° *A great headland over which the Sun is rising. It overhangs the sea.* It indicates one who is great and magnificent, imbued with feelings of magnanimity and reposeful strength. His opinions are lofty and elevated, his views wide as the seas, and his stability of purpose in all respects equal to his strength of mind. He looks forward to the future with confidence, and his hopes will not be frustrated. It is a degree of MAGNITUDE.

♏ 3° *An old man seated beneath a shady tree, his head bowed in thought. A pilgrim.* This symbol is the index of one given to solitude and deep philosophic thought, a lover of the mysterious and abstruse. Impressed with the unreality of things around him and the changefulness of human relations, he is disposed to the study of eternal verities and feels in no need of companionship. He is not a misanthrope nor a pessimist, but he has a true perspective of life and regards things and persons according to their true value. It is a degree of DISILLUSION.

♏ 4°   *A lyre, upon the arm of which there hangs a wreath of laurels.* This is indicative of a nature almost wholly given to the pursuit and cultivation of the fine arts. The mind is harmonious, generous and peaceable. The life will be free from disquieting and distressful elements, and the inherent harmony and refinement of this character will be reflected in all his works. He will strive by the use of the gentle arts as well as by the more liberal, to illustrate and interpret the finer emotions of the soul. In art or the drama he will meet with great distinction. It is a degree of SOUND.

♏ 5°   *A storm-swept prairie.* Free as the wind that blows will be the mind of him who shall answer to this degree of the circle. Violent withal and rash, he shall put forth much strength to no purpose, and the path of him will be marked by waste and extravagance. Fallen idols and desolated temples will be the outcome of his genius, and to destroy where he cannot build will appear his aimless pursuit in life. Nevertheless in the end he will become himself the desecrated tomb of many forlorn and blighted hopes. It is a degree of WANTONNESS.

♏ 6°   *A great mound of earth and stones, on the summit of which there is a single flowering shrub.* It is the index of a mind that is given to carefulness in small things and attention to detail; whose heart is in his task; and whose soul is content with the simple fruits thereof. Such an one will build up a name and position for himself by dint of patient and laborious toil, whether in natural science or in the ordinary avocation of a commercial life, and in the end he will be sure of his due reward. It is a degree of CONTINUITY.

♏ 7°   *A man standing with his left foot upon the shoulder of a spade. A pick-axe lies upon the ground, and in his hand he holds a jewel which reflects the Sun's rays.* This symbol denotes one who shall gain his position in the world by fortuitions means, and acquire considerable wealth by exploration and discovery. He may become a great trader in precious stones, a discoverer of rare minerals, or the pioneer of some undeveloped country. Such as may be his calling, he will have unusual success therein, and by means of his good fortune will be raised to a position which he had neverlooked to enjoy. It is a degree of FORTUNE .

♏ 8° *An archer shooting his arrows towards a flight of birds.* It indicates one who is restless, flighty, and indeterminate; effecting operations without design, using his forces at hazard, and frequently engaging in strife upon small occasion. In social life he will be disposed to be dissolute and disrespectful of convention, and will become involved in more love affairs. than he will be able to manage successfully. Intensity, enthusiasm and nonchalance are the chief features of his character. It is a degree of INCONSEQUENCE.

♏ 9° *A nest of young and unfledged birds lying upon the ground.* This symbol is indicative of a childhood spent in adverse circumstances; and of a nature that may be in danger of degeneration through neglect in the earlier stages of its growth. Bereft of parents and guardians at an early age, the nature is doomed to self-assertion and effort, or else to desolation and despair. Obscure in origin, and reared among strangers, the nature is yet capable of attaining to considerable distinction, It is a degree of ORPHANAGE.

♏ 10° *A man wearing a mask as in a play.* It denotes one whose character is never wholly expressed, but who is capable of simulating qualities and characteristics which are not proper to himself. The nature is taciturn, sarcastic, and critical; sometimes deceptive; and always capable of playing a part, whether it be for good or evil. Difficult to understand and to penetrate, the thought is yet more playful than malicious, and is capable of attracting friends and admirers without committing itself to any obligation. It is a degree of SIMULATION.

♏ 11°   *A hare seated upon a knoll above its burrow, behind it is the rising Moon.* It is the indication of a timorous and watchful nature, apprehensive of dangers that are not apparent and unmindful of those which are inevitable as the nightfall. Such an one is liable to be taken unawares and deceived in the chief affairs of life; and while showing astuteness in all that he has regard to, he will yet prove himself to be more watchful and cautious than wise and far-sighted. It is a degree of INSECURITY.

♏ 12°   *A small cottage surrounded by a thicket.* It is the index of a mind that is prudent and resourceful, provident and reserved. But it also shows one who is surrounded by enemies and liable to ambushes and deceit. This circumstance will unfortunately call forth all the lower and ruseful faculties of the nature, and while rendering the person free from harm by such enemies will at the same time tend to degenerate the mind. It is a degree of SELF-DEFENCE.

♏ 13°   *A great and lonely tower rising from an eminence of rock.* It shows one of a powerful and independent nature, relying on his own counsel and capable of standing alone. A degree of taciturnity and reserve will add to the general inscrutability of the mind of this person, and dispose him to command the respect and regard of others. His position will be elevated, his success in life will be assured by his own innate strength, and his fortunes will remain untouched by the hand of change. It is a degree of STABILITY.

♏ 14° *Two men seated at a table with beakers of wine before them.* It is an indication of a jovial and sympathetic nature, disposed to some qegree of self-indulgence, and liable to indiscretions which will prove harmful to the fortunes. It augurs much liberality and frankness of mind, a kindly but weak nature, and a very intimate knowledge of human character. It is a degree of COMRADESHIP.

♏ 15° *A bear sleeping beneath a tree around which is a swarm of bees.* This symbol indicates a mind that is slothful and inactive, relying on a false idea of the invariable necessity of things rather than upon his own efforts, and disposed to take a fatalistic view of life. But both Heaven and Earth conspire against him, and while he remains heedless of the busy workers all around him, the sweets of life also remain unknown to him; eventually he will be spurred into a blind and fruitless activity, and will suddenly be bereft of his natural powers. It is a degree of INDOLENCE.

♏ 16° *A cup or goblet from which rays of ruddy light are emitted.* It is the index of a kind and benevolent nature; a generous and humane disposition; ever cager to befriend and comfort those who may be in distress of body or mind. The grandeur and spiritual loftiness of this soul will attract many friends, and the work of charity and benevolence will increase continually, gathering volume as it goes, till it reaches the ocean of human life, and enfolds all mankind. It is a degree of HUMANENESS.

♏ 17° *A battered hulk lying upon the seashore.* It is the symbol of a life that is wrecked and battered about by the winds of adversity, a condition of misery and abandonment the most profound. The life will be a wandering and rudderless drifting upon troubled waters; and whether through his own fault or folly, or the yet more relentless hand of a most inimical fate, the fortunes will eventually be in danger of wreck and ruin, and the native will become a derelict from the great sea of life. It is a degree of ABANDONMENT.

♏ 18° *A woman charming snakes, one of which is twined about her neck.* It is the index of a watchful, brave, but suspicious and jealous nature. Such an one will brave many dangers for the sake of mastery over the passions of others, and will be active in the attainment of the arts of conquest. Nevertheless it is probable that eventually the life will be endangered thereby, and, beyond the loss of power where it is most to be desired, the danger of a poisoned love, or a yet more sinister folly, will threaten to crush and obliterate this person. It is a degree of JEALOUSY.

♏ 19° *A stiletto and tavola.* It is the index of a mind that is given to disputes and assaults, eager in contention and yet cautious in self-defence. Such an one will prove a formidable and untiring adversary, yet at the same time a convivial companion. With a somewhat abnormal taste for the good things of life, a good trencherman, and a man of sharp wit, he will make friends easily; but his enemies will be equally numerous. Headstrong and quick-tempered, he will yet bear himself bravely and honourably in strife, and his enemies will have much respect for him, while his friends will hold him up as a champion. It is a degree of AVIDITY.

♏ 20° *A Sun that is rising upon the ocean waters.* This symbol is indicative of a mind that is given to restlessness and travel for the sake of discovery. The rising of the Sun is a symbol of elevation and coming honours, while the ceaseless motion of the waters denotes many changes and long voyages, especially in the direction of the Orient. There both fortune and distinction will await him, and in some field of exploration and discovery he will become celebrated, It is a degree of ILLUMINATION.

♏ 21° *A buffalo standing on an eminence pawing the ground and snorting.* It is the symbol of a bold, independent and forceful nature, that knows neither restraint nor law, and that will suffer great privations in order to maintain the semblance of freedom. It is a degree of INDEPENDENCE.

♏ 22° *A cataract falling from one rocky ledge to another.* It is the index of a nature that is impelled by force of circumstances to precipitate and hazardous projects. A restless and impulsive mind, defective in foresight and never aware of danger till it is encountered. The life will be narrowed and confined, and so largely determined by the force of circumstances that it will be in danger of falling from one level to another until it is lost in obscurity and swallowed up in the sands of time. It is a degree of COMPULSION.

♏ 23° *A man sowing in the wind.* It is the index of a character that has little regard to the fitness of things, and is for that reason apt to waste his substance and dissipate his energies, continually occupying himself with vain and illusive projects; sowing where he has no advantage and constantly going counter to the opinions and advice of others. Such an one may lay hold of a fortune and it will be scattered, or being endowed with superior faculties he will use them to small advantage. It is a degree of DISSIPATION.

♏ 24° *A man habited in rough clothes hewing timber close to a log hut.* It is the indication of a mind that is contented and laborious, peacefully employed in useful arts, and naturally adaptable to circumstances. He will fashion and shape a world of his own from materials which nature will supply in response to industry, and out of such rude elements he will eventually acquire a habitation and a name that will be handed down to future generations. Industry and stability will mark his character, while virtue and humility will adorn his soul. It is a degree of UTILITY.

♏ 25° *A wolf standing upon the carcase of a horse.* It is the inclication of a predatory and adventurous spirit, a mind that is avaricious and cunning, quick to perceive and enforce its own advantage, but slow to cultivate the more useful and social habits of life. Such will lead a distressful and contentious life, and will not long enjoy the benefit of his conquests. He will snatch an advantage and will be forced to surrender it to others; and because of his selfishness his own friends will berail him. It is a degree of SEIZURE.

♏ 26° *A man swimming in an angry sea.* It denotes a person of resolute and brave nature, reckless of danger and disposed to take great risks upon himself for the benefit of others. He will have a troublesome life, with many changes of fortune, and more than the usual amount of buffeting by the waves of adversity. Yet he will endure, and in spite of his disposition to help others at his own disadvantage he will meet with recognition, and even honour, as the leader of a forlorn hope. It is a degree of SACRIFICE.

♏ 27° *A warrior plumed, haranguing a multitude of armed soldiers.* It denotes one who has a forceful and yet pliant mind, a persuasive tongue and a brave spirit. Such an one will lead others by the power of authority which is vested in reason and sustained by the ability of expression. From such a man an appeal is equivalent to a command, and an exhortation equal to a rebuke. He will undertake high duties and grave responsibilities in life and will largely be moved by a power that is within him, unrecognised but potent. It is a degree of PERSUASION.

♏ 28° *A rocky eminence out of which is carved a cross in stone. It stands against the rising sun as if haloed in divine light.* It is the index of a nature that will give evidence of a superior faculty, and a disposition for spiritual and religious studies. The mind is firm and dependable, the tastes are monastic and austere, and the whole character luminous yet ponderable, faithful and reclusive. It is a degree of SECURITY.

♏ 29° *A man seated at a table holding a pen. Before him are some pebbles on a sheet of paper.* This denotes a mind that is studious and of serious bent, delighting in the higher problems of the intellect, and disposed to the more serious studies, such as literature, science and especially mathematics. He may become the originator of some new methods of computation, or the demonstrator of a new science. He will lead a sedentary life and fortune will at length wait upon him. It is a degree of FACULTY.

♏ 30° *A woman in trailing robes waving a wand around which is coiled a serpent.* It is the index of a nature that is both clever and cunning; capable of asserting its power over others by persuasion or fascination. To such will be given some lofty command or position of trust, and success will be achieved by personal charm and magnetic power. It is a degree of ATTRACTION.

SAGITTARIUS

♐ 1° *A man lying upon a heap of stones by the roadside.* It is the index of a mind given to projects that are unprofitable and to dreams that lead to no practical result. The native's associations will be controlled rather by caprice than prudence, and in the end his bed will be a hard one to lie upon. Nevertheless, his freedom of spirit and love of natural simplicity will reconcile him to much of hardship and privation. At heart he is content. It is a degree of PRIVATION.

♐ 2° *A man standing with drawn sword.* This indicates a character that is given to strife and aggression, whether in assaults-at-arms or in polemics. He will lead a life of continual warfare, and litigation, and will be in danger of wounding and of being wounded. Wherever he goes he will make enemies and will be in peril of his life thereby. Armed, he is yet unshielded, and this is a challenge which even gods will not ignore. It is a degree of WOUNDING.

♐ 3° *The Goddess of Mercy enthroned.* It is the index of a nature that is humane, fruitful and full of good works. Beloved for works, as for inherent virtue, he will make many friends, and what of hardship he may endure, will be voluntarily undertaken for the sake of others. He will be attached to his home and family, but his sympathy will not be limited to its circle, but will extend beneficially in many directions. It is a degree of SYMPATHY.

♐ 4° *A soldier, holding a crossbow, stands behind an embrasure.* It is a symbol of prudence and carefulness, allied to a certain degree of daring and love of combat. It is a nature that

152

takes no risks, but while armed for the battle of life, makes full provision against its hazards, and is continually on the defensive. Reserved and cautious, the nature must be drawn out by circumstances, before it is fully appreciated; it is then found to be well equipped. It is a degree of PRUDENCE.

♐ 5°   *A man of middle age watching over a cradle.* It is the index of a nature that is given to repining and solitude yet bound by ties of kinship or love to those who are either enfeebled or bereft of health and fortune. In this character there is a melancholy resignation to the decrees of destiny, and an un-complaining submission to the wrongs of this world. Himself a sufferer in silence, he will be little able to help in removing the load of care from the brows of others, yet his fidelity and natural sympathy will prevent him from deserting them altogether. Such a person will suffer severe bereavements and sorrows. It is a degree of REPINING.

♐ 6°   *A mill-wheel driven by the wind.* This denotes one of an ingenious, inventive mind, and given to the study and prac-tice of useful arts; but of such a yielding nature that he is always liable to imposition and injustice from others. His life will be spent in bringing new inventions to the service of the world, without great advantage to himself; he will be utilised without gaining much credit or respect. It is a degree of SERVITUDE.

♐ 7°   *A group of cattle browsing in the sunshine.* It denotes a nature that is patient, contented, happy and self-possessed, capable of following sedentary and homely occupations un-complainingly, and much attracted to the calm joys of do-mestic and rustic life. He will lead an uneventfol and peaceful existence, happily suited in his domestic ties, and patiently

devoted to the work of an unambitious calling. It is a degree
of PLACIDITY.

♐ 8°   *Two men playing cards together.* This denotes one given to
the hazards of speculation, hopeful, jovial, and venturesome.
He will follow a life of change and chance, counting on noth-
ing beyond the day, and content with his lot, so long as he
comes by it without effort. In the midst of want and privation
he will keep a hopeful countenance and good heart. It cannot
be said that he will do much good to others, yet he will do no
intentional harm, and his good spirits will cheer others, who
else might despond too easily. It is a degree of HAZARD.

♐ 9°   *A house on fire.* This symbol is indicative of an enthusiastic
and inspirational nature, highly impulsive and headstrong, but
having a definite purpose in life to which all else is subservient.
He may be a visionary, or a man consumed by fire of a subtle
genius, but his unpractical nature will subject him to severe
penalties, and after a short and fevered existence, the cruse
of his vital powers will be exhausted. It is a degree of ZEAL.

♐ 10°   *A full moon shining in a clear sky.* It is the sign of a sympa-
thetic and adaptable nature, of superior abilities and consid-
erable powers of imitation and assimilation. He will shine by
reflected light, but will display his faculties with such ease
and grace, in places where they are appreciated, that he will
pass for one of inherent genius, will acquire fame and wealth,
and finally will outshine all others in his particular sphere of
life. It is a symbol of CAPACITY.

♐ 11°   *A tiger crouching as in the act of assault.* It denotes a char-
acter that is treacherous and aggressive, disposed to seek
his ends with subtlety and to secure them by force. There
is here a combination that is both diplomatic and assertive,

and therefore to be treated with reserve and firmness. The native will attain many of his ambitions and will make many enemies in the course of his career. His projects will lead him into many dangers and may even bring about his premature end. It is a degree of STRATEGY.

♐ 12°   *A fair woman sporting herself on a couch.* It is the index of a mind that is given to the delights of the senses, voluptuous and sybaritic, self-indulgent and indolent, yet ambitious of honours and wealth. The pleasures of the senses will prove to the native a delusion and a snare, leading him on from one indulgence to another until at length he will fall into a premature senility and ineptitude which he will not have strength enough to rouse himself from. Women under this degree should be carefully cherished and forefended. It is a degree of SENSUOUSNESS.

♐ 13°   *A large portcullis guarding the entrance to a prison.* It is the symbol of a nature doomed to seclusion and separateness of life, either on account of some incurable hurt to the flesh or by reason of a mind that is misanthropic and perverse. Such an one will move in narrow limits, and his walk in life will be circumscribed by a stern necessity. He will be in danger of restraint, captivity, or imprisonment, and his life will be full of dangers. It is a degree of RESTRAINT.

♐ 14°   *A quantity of books and papers in disorder.* It is the index of a mind given to the study of literature, history and other intellectual pursuits. The literary and scientific taste will be cultivated and trained to useful but somewhat unpopular or novel ends. The memory will be highly retentive, and the imagination lively but well under control. Such an one may become a prolific writer, combining science and invention with a facile power of romantic fancy. A strenuous worker and temperate liver, he will not fail to meet with due distinction. It is a degree of INTELLECT.

♐ 15°   *An arrow in mid-air.* This is the index of a mind that is penetrating, intent and ambitious. Such an one may gain distinction by fortuitous flights of fancy. He will meet with distinction, will obtain a position of some elevation, but being sustained solely by his own inertia, he will suffer a rapid decline, and in the end will meet with reversal. Enterprising and progressive in spirit, he will succeed during the first part of his life and later will have causa to regret his projects. It is a degree of DIRECTION.

♐ 16°   *A black hole or cavern in a rock.* This is an indication of a mind given to futile or vacuous projects, inconstant and fruitless work, so that his fortunes will be meagre and his position of no account. Always open to receive benefits from others, but yielding nothing of his own, he will fail of friends and fortune and in the end will afford but a black and barren prospect. It is a degree of VACUITY.

♐ 17°   *A man afloat upon a raft.* This symbol denotes one of isolated and lonely mind, given to projects of alien kind, daring enterprises and unique adventures. Such an one will be estranged from his relations and kindred, and will lead a life of great vicissitudes and hardships, failing in the latter part of life in some bold adventure whereby he will become involved in many troubles. His position in life will be unstable and as it were founded upon the waters. He may be a sailor and become shipwrecked, or in other capacity will meet with wreck of fortunes and be deserted by his own. It is a degree of ABANDONMENT.

♐ 18°   *A man's face painted with grotesque scrolls, and surrounded by a mass of tangled hair.* It is the index of a mind that is without proper balance, given over to vain and wild projects, neither useful nor fortunate. Such an one is in danger of losing his reason by disappointment of foolish and inconsequent efforts. His mode of life will be eccentric, and the expression of his thought touched with a singular grotesqueness and peculiarity. There may be genius; but, if so, of an unpractical and fruitless type: more probably there will be lack of reason. It is a degree of DISORDER.

♐ 19°   *A serpent surrounded by a circle of fire.* This symbol denotes one whose mind is subtle and tortuous, resentful and passionate. He will be continually involved in difficulties, and surrounded by dangers. At some time in life he may find himself in a beleaguered city, or in a cruel distraint, from which he will escape only with some hurt to his person or fortunes. In one form or another he will be called upon to pass through a fiery ordeal, and throughout life his mind will be chafed and tortured by stress and limitations. It is a degree of CAPTIVITY.

♐ 20°   *A garden of many-hued flowers.* It is the index of a mind that is genial, kindly and sociable. Such an one will find many friends and admirers. His life will be filled with happy and fortunate associations, and his mind will be devoted to the artistic, ornamental and æsthetic. The beautiful in nature will attract him, and his life will be surrounded with elements of concord and amity. It is a degree of CONCORD.

♐ 21°   *Two triangles interlaced, with a third superposed.* It is the index of a mind of more than average ability, to which the conquest of things mental and spiritual will be the chief object in life. Such an one will combine in himself the balance of physical and mental forces in an equal degree, and will hold the power to utilise them to considerable extent. It gives an aptitude for the study of the social sciences, and confers ability for self-government and rulership. It is a degree of MASTERY.

♐ 22° *Two arrows crossed.* This is the symbol of an aggressive spirit, a mind given over to contention and strife, and a soul that is set against the current of public feeling and opinion. Such an one will run counter to the established laws of social life, and be continually engaged in the pursuit of his own eccentricities. There is danger of litigation and a menace of a violent end. It is a degree of STRIFE.

♐ 23° *A human heart encircled with a band of iron and pierced by a dagger with jewelled hilt.* Insecure affections, misplaced confidence, bitter resentment and jealousy are the unhappy results of love divorced from discretion and a good judgment. Such an one to whom this symbol applies will go through life attended by a host of forlorn hopes, loving without power to evoke response, acting by impulse unallied to reason, and in the end will become cramped and misanthropic, the iron of selfish disappointment eating into the soul. Danger of heart disease may be indicated, or what is worse, the canker of jealousy may prove fatal. It is a degree of RESTRICTION.

♐ 24° *A broken tree struck by a lightning flash.* This is the index of a mind occupied with abortive projects, vain ambitions, and un-fortunate relationships. His life is likely to be short and his end sudden. All his ambitions will fall short of accomplishment, and dire catastrophe will cut off his hopes ere he can reap the harvest of his endeavours. It is a degree of ABSCISSION.

♐ 25° *Three cups of wine standing upon a table in the form of a triangle.* It is the index of a mind that is given to excessive indulgence and undue enthusiasm in matters of a spiritual and mental nature; one who will follow out his projects regardless of consequence, impelled as it were by a species of mental intoxication. The substance and form of this symbol is allied to the higher nature, but should the carnal appetites gain an ascendency over him, he will in all probability degenerate into a debauchee. Moderation should be his watchword even in spiritual things. It is a degree of EXCESS.

♐ 26° *A mask representing the face of a hound.* This is the sign of one to whom appearances are apt to count for much, but who will nevertheless be possessed of a really deep and sympathetic nature. Fidelity and friendship will be prominent characteristics of his nature. He will be dexterous in the use of arms, apt in the imitation of mannerisms, and would make a capable actor, being gifted with powers of dramatic representation. Of a kind and sympathetic nature, he will readily attract friends, and yet few will know him for what he really is. It is a degree of IMITATION.

♐ 27° *A man beneath the paw of a lion rampant.* This is the index of a nature lacking direction of force and initiative. Such an one will find many enemies, both powerful and aggressive, to bar the way to success in life. He may rise to a good position, but will be in danger of falling under the reproach of his king or ruler. His path will be beset with difficulties and dangers, and such will chiefly be due to his lack of stability and want of purpose. It is a degree of IMPOTENCE.

♐ 28° *A tortoise.* This is the symbol of a patient and steady nature, one to whom all tasks are trivial, to whom hardships come as a matter of course, and who is not dismayed by the prospect of unending toil. Steadfastness, patience and endurance will characterise his life and work in the world, and in spite of all obstacles he will attain to the position he has set out to gain for himself It is a degree of PATIENCE.

♐ 29°   *A hare.* This is the symbol of a mind that is both cultured and timid, yet possessed of considerable moral force and remarkable physical energy and agility. Such an one may easily lose his way and come to an unfortunate end, because of his strong sense of the direct and honest course in life and his extreme diffidence in asserting that sense or conviction. He will be in danger of some brain affection, which may lay him low and render him incapable of action for many years together. There is a twist of some sort in the nature. He may be driven to extremities by the force of circumstances. It is a degree of INEFFICACY.

♐ 30°   A spade protruding from the soil. It is the symbol of a mind that is capable of sustaining great and arduous work, one to whom some of the dark secrets of Nature will be revealed. He may show some taste for agriculture or may follow the fortunes of some great mining industry or archreological research, and in such he will be a discoverer. Whatever his walk in life, his work will be difficult and protracted, but success will ultimately crown his labours. Endowed with a sharp, incisive mind and strong purpose, he will ignore the advice of friends and rely wholly on his own efforts. It is a degree of DISCOVERY.

CAPRICORN

♑ 1°   *A boy and girl standing with arms entwined.* It is the index of a mind that is given to duplicity, or at least to dissimulation and diplomacy. There is considerable *finesse*, and also an extraordinary degree of adaptability in the nature, which will enable it to gain some distinction and even a position of honour. The native may become an ambassador or consul, or otherwise serve as a connecting link between two peoples or nations. In a lower degree, the native will follow more than one occupation at the same time and will in general show considerable versatility. It is a degree of ALTERNATION.

♑ 2°   *A vane of which the arrow is pointing North.* This is an indication of a vacillating and uncertain disposition now turning this way and now that, and finally falling away into negation and ineptitude. Many enterprises will be undertaken and abandoned. Procrastination will be a besetting fault, and will lead to many difficulties. This is one whose efforts will be strenuous but fitful and lacking endurance, so that with more than usual effort he will achieve less than the ordinary. His end is obscure and darkly veiled. It is a degree of VACILLATION.

♑ 3°   *A serpent coiled around an uplifted beacon.* It is the index of a mind that is unusually wise, subtle and profound. Endowed with much prudence, foresight and circumspection, the native may apply himself profitably and creditably to almost any work in life and with every prospect of success. But that for which he is by nature especially fitted is without doubt diplomatic service, the law, or the administration of government. In some special form of literature or science he will show extraordinary ability, maybe in medicine, in chemistry, or other of the chymic arts. He will shine and his light will be seen from afar, while those who are near will manifest much reliance on his knowledge, and will follow the light of his leading. It is a degree of ILLUMINATION.

♑ 4°   *A vestal lamp burning brightly.* This is an indication of an elevated and superior mind, given to the study of things that are essentially spiritual. There are aspiration and intuition in a superior degree, and such an one will probably seek and find in the silence of his own chamber the key to many of the higher mysteries of life and thought. In any capacity he will attain to a superior position and will be an acknowledged leader of men and moulder of human minds. From all that is essentially mundane and sordid his thoughts will be estranged. He will have an intuitive perception of eternal verities. It is a degree of INITIATION.

♑ 5°   *A small cottage with wide-open door.* This is the sign of an hospitable and generous nature, a kindly and warm hearted disposition. Austere and rigid in his own methods of life he will nevertheless show much sympathy for others, and compassion for their weaknesses and foibles. Withal he will evince a singular lack of prudence, and though denying himself and sustaining others he will be liable to imposition and theft. Such an one should safeguard the doors of his speech and be select in the choice of his friends and confidants. It is a degree of HOSPITALITY.

♑ 6°   *A heart surmounted by an aureole.* This is the symbol of an affectionate and devoted nature, one who will centre his affections upon a single object and continue steadfast all his life. In such an one there is little of guile, little of fear, and perfect confidence in those to whom he gives his heart. Such devotion as he is capable of manifesting is worthy of a higher tribute than the average life or mind can render, and it is all but impossible that he can escape disappointment, sorrow and dismay. In whatever path of life his work may lie he will succeed where others have failed, merely because of his whole-heartedness and concentration. It is a degree of DEVOTION.

♑ 7° *A heart pierced by a nail.* This is the index of a nature that is capable of strong attachment, both to things and persons, and yet with something of selfish design in all that he es-pouses. Consequently he cannot fail to meet with trouble, and his chagrin will arouse bitter feelings of resentment against others who may have thwarted his designs. Hence spring various rivalries and feuds, and these operate in his life to produce ruin and desolation, so that in the end he has nothing left but himself to care for and all the world besides to hate and rail against. It is a degree of JEALOUSY.

♑ 8° *An eagle carrying its prey in mid-air.* This is the index of a mind that is given to extraordinary flights of fancy, making of purely mundane things the substance of many and pro-longed cogitations and solitary musings. The nature is rather isolated and misanthropic, while the mind is endowed with faculties of no mean order, so that the world will afford few attractions, and ordinary subjects will form only the pabulum of a more ethereal and spiritual food. There will be wasting of flesh in nightly vigils, and much strengthening of the spirit in lonely meditations. Contented, supremely indifferent to the things of this world, his taste of happiness in this life will be evanescent and brief. It is a degree of LOFTINESS.

♑ 9°   *A cross and a broken key.* This is the index of a nature that is aspiring and eager to penetrate into the experiences of life, but doomed by an adverse fate to failure and disappointment. The broken key is the sign of those abortive enterprises in which he will engage to his undoing and loss of reputation. Where he should knock and wait in patience he will essay an entry by craft and worldly wisdom, and even as he turns the key in the lock it will break off short in his hand. If he should restrain his impetuosity and daring, and cultivate humility of spirit, haply his cross will not be found too heavy for him to bear. With that as key to the treasures of this world he may enter the Gates of the Temple of Wisdom. It is a degree of IMPOTENCE.

♑ 10°   *An owl sitting in the moonlight.* It is the index of a mind that is wise and patient, prudent and self possessed. Where others see nothing he will discern many indications of the trend of events. He may study astronomy and become a discoverer of things occult or distant. For the ordinary work-a-day world he has little interest, but to those who are disposed to deep philosophical speculations and abstruse studies he is likely to be a figure of some consequence and esteem. His life and work are centred in the things that are hidden from the common eye, and in the hours of the night will lie the greatest dangers of his life, as also in things remote from sense. It is a degree of OCCULTISM.

♑ 11°   *A roll of parchment, sealed and lying across a sceptre.* This is the index of a person who is born to occupy positions of trust and responsibility, most probably in connection with the Ministry, or in a minor degree occupying some office in Government service. The sealed parchments show diplomacy, a taciturn disposition and ability to keep secrets and confidences. The life-work will be carried on under conditions which require great secrecy and caution. The nature is reserved and self-reliant. He will rise to positions of authority, and will serve his country and king. It is a degree of AUTHORITY.

♑ 12° *A fox running apace in the moonlight.* It shows a person who is given to acts of subtlety and craftiness and disposed to lead a predatory life, relying on the fortunes of chance, aided by his skill and cunning, for a livelihood. He will show considerable zeal in the pursuit of his designs, and much secrecy will be required in the conduct of his affairs, for there will be incidents therein which cannot bear the light of day. The nature is cruel and rather crafty. He will depend on the activity and industry of others for his means of support, and eventually will be in danger of excommunication, exile or imprisonment, or may even have to fly the country. It is a degree of CRAFTINESS.

♑ 13° *A tripod with flames of fire issuing from a brazier.* This is the index of a nature that is aspiring and active, disposed to lead a life of adventure and hazard, but honourable in the pursuit of lofty ambitions. He may become attached to the military service, or in some other form will be a representative of the fiery and devouring element. He has a restless and aspiring nature, such as will impel to action upon a wide scale. He will travel and explore, lighting up dark places and devastating ancient sites in the quest of new food for the mind. Chastity and purity of life will mark him as of singular temperament, and his efforts will thereby become concentrated and highly successful. Alive to all the higher ambitions of this world, he will nevertheless be zealous in the conquest of worlds that are beyond normal ken. He may be an ambassador, consul, spiritual researcher, or explorer. It is a degree of ASPIRATION.

♑ 14° *A harrow standing on an open field.* This indicates one who will manifest an extremely critical, sarcastic and aggressive nature. It will be his business in life to dig into the common soil of the human mind, to lay bare and expose its true nature, and to create dissensions, divisions and strifes, stirring up and leavening the pabulum of popular beliefs, and bringing to light their fallacies, impedimenta, and imperfections. The mind will be pugnacious in the extreme, and although it may attract admirers it will have few sympathisers or adherents. In removing the weed-growth of the ages and in the ruthless examination of things as they are in the broad field of human life and thought, will consist the main work of this peculiarly angular and incisive nature. It is a degree of CRITICISM.

♑ 15° *A soft cloudy cumulus upon a bright horizon.* It signifies one who has a kind, pliant and sympathetic nature; adaptable to environment, hopeful and confident. He will receive many favours from Fortune, and will be the friend and associate of those who have influence and power in the land. His mind will be set upon the attainment of high truths, and his course in life will be marked by a singular degree of inoffensiveness, gentleness, forbearance and suavity. Thus his friends will rejoice in him, and his enemies will find his gentleness and softness a foil to their sharpest weapons. His fortunes will lie in smooth places, and with intelligence added to gentleness of nature, he will be regarded with favour by all who come into contact with him. It is a degree of MOLLIENCE.

♑ 16°　*A man riding at high speed upon a well-conditioned horse.*
This denotes one who has a taste for and ability in the man-
agement of horses, and to whom the delights of horseman-
ship will not be less than those of hazard and adventure.
He will lead a romantic life, will travel afar, and undertake
many hardy exploits. His occupation may bring him largely
into touch with foreign people and strange lands, and either
he will be an importer of foreign wares, an explorer, or an
archæologist. Should he incline to the law he will make great
progress therein, and honours will attend his efforts on all
occasions. In scholastic work also he finds his prevailing
passion fully satisfied, for in the taming and bridling of the
untrained mind and the right directing of its powers he will
prove himself not less successful than capable and zealous.
It is a degree of INSTRUCTION.

♑ 17°　*A lyre lying upon a wreath of flowers.* It denotes one who
will show some remarkable powers of expression, and by the
power of sound will persuade where others cannot compel
by force. He may become a poet or musician, and in the gen-
tler offices of life will show considerable talent. His nature
will be docile, tractable, harmless and inoffensive. He will be
constant in his attachments and will undergo some singular
persecutions and tests of his fidelity, emerging there-from
victorious and undismayed. Should he follow the highest
expressions of his faculty he will be capable of enunciating
in language that is harmonious, persuasive and subtly com-
pelling, a new body of doctrine or a new phase of philosophic
truth. It is a degree of PERSUASION.

♑ 18°　*Two men in fierce strife.* This symbol denotes one whose
aggressive and quarrelsome nature will lead him into all sorts

of difficulties and dangers, from which it is to be feared he will not escape unhurt. Contentious, reviling and unorthodox, his mind will be at war with prevailing opinions and popular beliefs. He will create discord wherever he goes, and be a sorry test to men of humane and benevolent dispositions. His nature is devoid of frankness and he does not admit the truth even to himself, but opposes all and everyone on whatever ground is open to debate. In a word, he is an Ishmaelite, and will finally be deserted and abandoned to the mercies of his mother Nature. It is a degree of STRIFE.

♑ 19° *A rocky eminence in the midst of a turbulent sea.* This symbol denotes a character of great self-reliance; firmness, stability and originality, one who is capable of standing alone and combating with the steady resistance of enduring strength all the assaults of adverse fortune or popular displeasure. Alone, undaunted and impassive, he will stand amid the angry tumult of contending forces. He will show real strength and the firmness that is born of conviction and direct perception of the truth. He cannot hope to be popular, but he cannot fail to be great and singular. The waves sweep on and dash themselves in futile wrath upon his moveless body. They are driven back, and expend themselves in seething comment and hissing impotence: he remains. It is a degree of STOLIDITY.

♑ 20° *An ape seated before a mirror.* It is the index of a mind given to vanity and capable only of the intelligence which characterises the superficial worldling. He sees himself as the one object. He is an egotist. Nevertheless he will aspire to some distinction as a leader of fashions or as a comedian or mimic. His powers of adaptation are considerable, and his physical activity very great. He would succeed best as an actor, but that only in the lighter vein. His person is more considerable than his mind, and his reputation will be dependent on his powers of adaptation and expression. It is a degree of IMITATION.

♑ 21° *An ancient hieroglyphic manuscript with a retort and crucible upon it.* This symbol is the index of one who will essay the Magnum Opus or great work of alchemical science. It may be that he will attempt the solution of some scientific problems, and in such would be successful beyond his belief. On the other hand its scope may be restricted to the world of commerce, or even extended to the spiritual world, so that the transmutation of the gross and external body of the soul may be effected. In any case the native will be a deep researcher and will study ancient methods and principles with benefit to himself and advantage to the world. He will begin a new school of thought and his mind will be set upon reforms in the scientific and philosophic worlds. It is a degree of RENOVATION.

♑ 22° *A plough.* This symbol belongs to one that is capable of arduous and protracted labours. His inherent force of character will carry him through all difficulties and beyond all obstacles. He is endowed with much definition of purpose, determination and incisiveness, so that he will make headway against all obstructions and cut out a line in life for himself. He will in all probability find the recompense of his labour in association with agricultural projects, and in the utilisation of old and waste materials. It is a degree of DETERMINATION.

♑ 23° *A wineglass overturned.* This is the index of one who will be unable to contain his feelings and passions, and will in consequence run to excesses, extravagance and waste of substance. He will be endowed with a fine intelligence, a genial and pleasant nature, and a generous and convivial disposition. But his inability to control his passions will lead to his reversal and undoing, so that he will—unless he be under the guidance of a strong and steady hand—eventually be left to his fate, denuded of all that makes him a desirable companion or useful agent in life. It is a degree of INCONTINENCE.

♑ 24° *A tankard set upon a table.* This denotes a steadfast and capable person, whose life will be orderly and useful, whose mind will be open to the reception of truth and knowledge and whose passions will be well regulated. He will display a frank and even blunt nature, being free from all craftiness and subtlety; and his mind will have a sincere regard for all that is simple and natural in human nature, and a rooted distrust of the non-transparent. It is likely that he will be disposed to seek his livelihood in the vineyard or hostel, but in the highest capacity he can he will aspire to become a teacher and purveyor of spiritual truths. In any case he is a man of the common walk and his sympathies are with the people. It is a degree of SINCERITY.

♑ 25° *A series of bubbles floating in the air.* This denotes one in whose nature the light, fantastic and ephemeral is predominant. A certain elasticity and expansiveness of soul will render him reflective of the world around him in all its more sparkling and bright aspects, but he will lack solidity of character, will be given over to vanities and in the end these will be the source of his sudden and untimely collapse. He is liable to be a mere dabbler, but his sympathies will be in the direction of occult verities, and a certain superficial reflection of these things may render him a fashionable mountebank. It is a degree of SUPERFICIALITY.

♑ 26° *A wide, open seascape on which are distant sailing boats.* This symbol denotes a person of calm and thoughtful temperament, a kind, genial and sunny nature, smooth and tranquil manners, and peaceful disposition. When roused to anger, however, he is capable of excessive strength and display of power, and the forces in reserve within him are only to be known under stress and excitation. He is yielding, but cannot be reduced. He is gentle but irresistible. His sympathies are wide and his taste for travel will be marked. It will lead him to distant countries and maybe to the pursuit of nautical life. That he will have interests in distant lands is certain. It is a degree of COMPLACENCE.

♑ 27° *A stretch of broken country with a fringe of woodland.* This symbol denotes a nature that is rugged and natural in its expression and wholly devoid of the superficialities and polish of conventional life. Left to himself he will prefer a life of quiet retirement and rustic work, but in the busier haunts of men he will pass for one who is ungracious and uncouth, though none will question his sincerity and genuineness. He may be disposed to seek his living in the cultivation of the soil, or the sale of its produce. His temper will be uneven, and at times morose and lowering, but a certain off-hand gruffness of expression will only veil a kind and ingenuous nature. It is a degree of RUSTICITY.

♑ 28° *A sextant and compass.* This symbol is related to one whose tastes are of a very catholic nature. His learning and rectitude will make him a reliable and useful guide to others, and in some special capacity of learning he will gain distinction and honour. In a sense he is a cardinal man and cannot fail to become famous. His inclinations will be expressed in the study of navigation, astronomy, exploration and the mathematics. In a narrower sense he will become a director of some successful trading company and his path in life will be marked by a series of successful ventures. He will never lose his way, nor fail to attain his end, for all his undertakings will be regulated by rigid and exact principles, and carried out with precision and certainty of success. It is a degree of DEFINITION.

♑ 29° *A dark and lonely pool overhung by wooded banks.* This is the index of a nature that will be given to contemplation and philosophical musings. In the silence and solitude of his own soul he will enter into an intimate communion with Nature and will be blessed with an understanding of her more obscure laws and his mind will be pervaded by a peace which none will be able to disturb. His affections will be deeply rooted in all that appertains to the simpler and more natural life, and his poetical and visionary nature will lay hold upon eternal verities. As for himself, he will walk by the side of his mother Nature, and his soul will be lifted to a place of rest. Unpractical though he may be in many things, yet his message will be one of authority as appertaining to a favoured child. It is a degree of CONTEMPLATION.

♑ 30° *An arrow in flight.* This symbol denotes an aspiring and ambitious nature, impelled by the strength of a force behind him to the attainment of a certain high or distant project. Gifted with extreme directness and celerity of action, and endowed with remarkable powers of concentration, he will be in a fair way to attain his intentions and accomplish his ambitions. But everything will depend upon his start in life as to whether he will reach his goal. Heredity and training will count for more than usual in his case, for he is one of those who will follow his inherent impulses and has little or no individual power of direction and scarcely any adaptation. The breath of public opinion may carry him wide of his mark, and with the decline of his natural forces there will be a falling off of ambition and purpose. It is a degree of DECLINE.

AQUARIUS

♒ 1°   *A man lying upon a sheaf of corn, asleep, with viands at his side.* This is a symbol of one whose life will be wasted in dreams and visions and vain projects to which he cannot lend the power of action. He will be dreaming where others are working and in consequence will lose the virtue of utility and the right to sustenance. Moreover, because of his unpractical and indifferent nature, he will be at the mercy of others, and will suffer depredation and fraud at times, and at others will be pushed aside to make room for the more intelligent and responsive workers in the world's great field of action. He will dream of wealth while others are making it, and all the while he will neglect the opportunities which lie as simple everyday occurrences close to his hand. It is a degree of LASSITUDE.

♒ 2°   *A book on which stand a compass and an hourglass.* This is the index of one who has a scientific and highly versatile mind. He will be disposed to the study of the laws of nature, will gain an intimacy with the principles of scientific and philosophic investigation and may be the inventor of some instrument, or the discoverer of some force in Nature, by which the elements of space (the compass) and time (the hour-glass) are annihilated to a great degree. Undoubtedly he will be a man of considerable depth of thought, and will make some useful discoveries. It is a degree of EXTENSION.

♒ 3°   *A man walking with bended head, leaning upon a staff.* This symbol is related to one whose life is liable to many and severe shocks of misfortune, the severing of ties and the disappointment of hopes. Nevertheless, he will show a spirit of steadfast resignation to the will of Heaven and therein will find consolation for his griefs and sorrows. The task which he will have to perform in life will be honourable but unprofitable, and many will be the difficulties which encumber his upward path. He is nevertheless equipped for a long and arduous journey, and being endowed with a patient and firm will, he must eventually attain his goal. Only in the interval he will have to surrender all that he holds most dear in life. It is a degree of PERSEVERANCE.

♒ 4° *An officer arrayed much like a Chineze mandarin in an official robe of purple and gold and blue.* This is indicative of one who will show considerable meritin diplomatic or governmental work and who may become a minister of state or high official. To him will be entrusted the care of high secrets and charges, and he will be associated with persons of high estate and power in whatever land he may be called upon to serve. It is probable that he himself will be able to boast an ancient lineage and there is, apart from his destiny, an inherent dignity and repose which will enable him passively to withstand the assaults of his enemies and by patience finally to overcome all and succeed to the highest positions of trust and confidence. It is a degree of AUTHORITY.

♒ 5° *A woman nude, looking at her reflection in a pool of water.* It is not necessary to say, perhaps, that this is a symbol indicative of extreme danger to the moral nature of the person born under this degree. There is an element of dalliance and self-love in the nature which will be liable to lead to serious complications and entanglements. It may be that this egotism will only veil a weakness which cannot withstand the temptations of the carnal nature. The nature will be sympathetic and to a large degree reflective of the immediate environment, in which, however, there will be too strong an accent of self. It is probable that the native may show artistic tastes and a marked ability for portrait painting or sculpture. It is a degree of EGOTISM.

♒ 6°   *An archer drawing a long bow.* This symbol is related to one who has considerable faculty for teaching (prophecy), and skill in manual crafts. As a director of thought, an exponent of religious teachings, as traveller, lecturer, even handicraftsman, he will show himself capable and will meet with distinction. He will be ambitious and will have a mind set upon things that are remote from his environment. Careful in his methods, and ambitious in his designs, he will have to travel far, nevertheless, for the results of his actions, and of him it may be said that what is remote from the sense is ever more attractive than things corporeal, and that which is afar than that which is near. It is a degree of APPERCEPTION.

♒ 7°   *A target pierced by a rapier.* This symbol denotes one who has extreme powers of penetration and yet will be incapable of adequate self-defence in the ordinary affairs of life and will fall a victim to his own want of discretion. In him the knowledge of the truth does not entail the following of it, and this denial of his own convictions will lead him to sore troubles and possibly to disgrace. He will show an impulsive and headstrong nature, such as may lead him into serious conflict with others, thereby laying him open to the danger of assault and hurt in the passage of arms. Let him beware of the direct thrust and practice the use of the two-edged sword. It is a degree of VULNERABILITY.

176

♒ 8°   *A lion standing in the open arena.* This symbol is indicative of a nature that is strong, forceful and independent, loving freedom above all things and desiring death by hunger rather than servitude or restraint. Such an one will prove himself to be of greater service to the race when left to his own resources and given full freedom of action than when bound to a narrow or restricted walk in life. Nevertheless, he is liable to captivity or imprisonment, whether it be as a prisoner of State or as the victim of a hard and unrelenting Fate, and this will be entailed by his inordinate love of freedom. He will suffer and will serve, and thus gain both wisdom and freedom for all time. It is a degree of ESCAPEMENT.

♒ 9°   *A huge rock rent by a flash of lightning.* This symbol denotes one who has a powerful, aggressive, forceful and executive nature, capable of driving his way through all obstacles, however hard and enduring they may be. Quick, energetic and alert, he will make considerable progress in his particular walk in life, and may be the means of convincing the most sceptical concerning certain matters of a celestial and ethereal nature. His spirit is too intense and forceful, too incisive and critical not to be the occasion of much reviling and bitterness of spirit in others. He will do his work in the world with celerity of action and directness of execution, and he will let light into dark places. His departure will be sudden, but will not transpire till he has done some work of magnitude. It is a degree of CONVERSION.

♒ 10°   *A head and a hand separated from a body.* This is the sign of one who lacks coordination of thought and action, and who may eventually be liable to paralysis or similar affections of the body by woundings and the severance of nerves. Possibly he will be separated from his kindred and will be bereft of guidance and sustenance at an early-age. He will only learn by severe affliction and many sufferings how to coordinate his thought and action, and useless projects, irresponsible and foolish actions, and a badly regulated life will thus be turned to the service of the body corporate of humanity. It is a degree of DISJECTION.

♒ 11°   *Two bulls fighting on the edge of a precipice.* This symbol is related to one in whose nature there is more force and energy than power of direction and self-restraint, and who in consequence will be continually running into dangers which to him will be wholly unforeseen though obvious enough to others. He will rely upon his strength and push fulness to overcome his enemies, but it will be shown to him that there is nothing so insignificant as the strength of a man. Since he cannot overcome Nature let him learn to use her forces with discretion and moderation or he will be wounded in the conflict of life, and unseen dangers will lurk within the hour of exultation as snakes beneath the flower. It is a degree of FORCEFULNESS.

♒ 12°   *A lion raging against the bars of its cage.* This symbol imports a nature of considerable. native strength and dignity, yet unfortunate and in danger of being earned away by his passions and love of freedom. Hard though it may be to force his spirit into submission it will be well with him should he early learn that his compeers and superiors are equally jealous as himself of their rights and privileges. At some time in his life he will be the victim of a nature superior to his own and will suffer restraint and curtailment of liberty thereby. Let him adapt himself to his environment. His will else be the hard fate of those who are born of free spirit into the bonds of necessity. It is a degree of RESTRAINT.

♒ 13° A cavalier fully armed. This is the index of a militant and naturally aggressive nature, the sign of one who, while outwardly cautious and suave in manner, is ever alive to his own interests and on the defensive. At times he will be led into dangers by the aggressive attitude he will display in regard to his fellows, and although well equipped by Nature for all emergencies, he will never be so safe and free from harm as when observing regard for others. He will show a vigilant and alert nature, much power of self-defence; and will be remarkable for his capacity either in the military world or that of polemics. It is a degree of ASSERTION.

♒ 14° *A broken bridge spanning a rapid stream.* This is the symbol of one whose life will be beset with unforeseen dangers, and who should therefore go warily and with much circumspection into the narrow walks of competitive life. About the middle of his life there will be a great catastrophe, by which he will either lose the use of a limb, or will suffer a total collapse of his affairs. He will then be in danger of liquidation and may become involved in serious trouble. Almost from his boyhood he will have to be selfsupporting, and while he is sure to be of considerable service to others, and may even be author of much wise counsel, he will himself stand in need of help and sustenance ere his days are half completed. His future thereafter is in the keeping of Heaven. It is a degree of COLLAPSE.

♒ 15° *A ship in full sail upon a sunlit sea.* This is the symbol of one who will possess an enterprising and somewhat adventurous spirit, such as will lead him into associations with others remote from him in nature or in clime. He will show a catholic and cosmopolitan spirit, a versatile and ambitious mind, and a benevolent and sympathetic nature. If he should be induced to leave his country it will be to form alliances that are productive of the greatest good to himself and to others. If he should follow the mercantile life, he will be fortunate therein. But whatever may be his calling, he will prosper and gain for himself a position of affluence and distinction. It is a degree of AFFLUENCE.

♒ 16° *A smith's forge and bellows.* This symbol is related to the one who will show considerable aspiration in things of a spiritual nature and will be instrumental in awakening in the breast of man a belief in things supernormal, by fanning the spark of intelligent faith into a flame of conviction and consuming desire. His profession will be allied to the useful arts and his walk in life, although simple and devoid of ostentation, will nevertheless be of singular service to humanity. Great in soul and of immense aspiration, he will prove a veritable Vulcan. It is a degree of INSPIRATION.

♒ 17° *A man lying prone upon a bed of sickness.* This is the index of a mind that is inept, a nature indolent or perverted, and a fortune that is wholly dependent on the goodwill of others. It denotes one who will evince but little interest in the wider and more virile achievements of his fellows, whose mind will be cramped and warped by egotism and selfish indulgence, and whose body will grow sleek and nerveless in default of proper use and adequate exercise. In a more fortunate circumstance, it may depict only a physical malady requiring constant rest. In the worst case it denotes imbecility. It is a degree of APATHY.

♒ 18° *An old woman seated on a stool with a hooded cloak wrapped closely round her.* This is the index of one whose nature will be warped by feelings of selfishness and jealousy. He will exhibit little, if any, interest in the common lot of humanity, and will assume an attitude of melancholy, silent and envious misanthropy. Such an one cannot fail to become a source of hatred and malice to his own hurt and that of others. Wrapped around with the cloak of selfishness, he will fail to attain happiness in his own life and will be jealous of it in that of others. Hence bitterness and secret enmity will poison his soul, and in the end he will be in danger of an isolation not less painful because merited, and will be cut off from kith and kin and left to his own imperfect and cramped resources. Let him study to preserve interest and sympathy in all that is human and so escape being abandoned of Heaven and Earth. It is a degree of ISOLATION.

♒ 19° *A boat upon the sea to which a submerged man is clinging for support.* This symbol is related to one in whose life some great catastrophe will occur at a time when providentially there will be a friend at hand to rescue him from his danger. It indicates that a deficiency of tact and skill is liable to render him subject to adversity of fortune, and he will suffer financial disaster and even peril of death. But there will be raised up to him a friend capable of sustaining him in his extremity, and he will not therefore sink into the depths. This will be in response to his great faith. The nature, although daring, is lacking in tact and strength. All his troubles will arise from failing to admit his own incompetence. He will travel afar. It is a degree of INSECURITY.

♒ 20° *A great tortoise.* This denotes one of patient and plodding disposition, disposed to rusticity of habit, endowed with great powers of endurance, an even disposition and contented mind. His position in life will always be secure, owing to his great prescience and providence, and he will create about him by slow and patient toil the means of his own security and well-being. His life is likely to extend to phenomenal years, and his position in old age will be one of independence and security from all harm. Of rather solitary and retired nature, deeply philosophical, patient, and contented with simple ways of living, he will yet evince a kindly disposition and will live long to enjoy the fruits of his labours and the esteem of his fellows. It is a degree of PROVIDENCE.

♒ 21° *A man lying wounded or sick upon the ground.* It is the symbol of one whose nature is void of virility and ambition, and who, consequently, will fail to assert himself in the fight for life. Where others are in intense activity, he lies nerveless and powerless amid surroundings which, although natural, are devoid of comfort and unreflective of the arts and sciences of human evolution. Such an one will show moral apathy, mental ineptitude, and physical weakness, all of which will conspire to render him an object of pity to the passer by, and a burden to his kindred and friends. In some cases it may indicate incapacity merely. In others it will predict a moral paralysis. It is a degree of WEAKNESS.

♒ 22° *A raging bull stamping upon the body of dog.* This symbol denotes one whose passions are liable to run to excess and whose anger may lead him into the commission of acts of violence. It shows one of a strong and forceful nature, capable of forcing his way in the world by push and energy, yet not so strong as to be capable of controlling his own feelings. At such times as his passions are aroused he is capable of acts of brutal ferocity, and though he may gain the victory over all his outward enemies, there will yet be one within remaining unsubdued. It is essential that an otherwise fortunate nature should not ruin a great career by actions of impulsive ardour and indiscretion. It is a degree of VIOLENCE.

♒ 23° *A beaver at work upon a tree overhanging a gorge.* This is the index of one to whom work will be a matter of daily and continual pleasure, and whose efforts will be sustained with diligence and fidelity. He will show much executive ability, exceptional constructive faculty, and extreme powers of endurance, so that his pathway to success is sure. There is, however, the danger that, at the supreme moment when the fruit of his labour falls due, it may be swallowed up and lost to him forever. Except for this his position is beyond all power of assault or harm, for habits of industry and strenuous energy are sure of recognition. He may become a well-known worker or dealer in timber and the building trade. It is a degree of INDUSTRY.

♒ 24° *A bent stalk bearing a full ear of corn.* This symbol is related to one of undoubted faculty and mental ability, but with too little courage and power of attack to make his merit felt in the world. Such an one will be bent and broken by the winds of adversity, and having but small physical stamina he will find it difficult to sustain the highest expressions of his mental growth in the face of much want and physical distress. Yet he will not be bent or broken by adversity till he has given expression to an extraordinary amount of learning and will be popularly appreciated. It is a degree of BENDING.

♒ 25° *A dark face wearing an expression of fierce anger, and across the forehead a red band of blood.* This symbol indicates one whose nature is vindictive and passionate almost beyond power of control. There will be some danger of frenzy or even acute mania, such as will warrant his enforced detention. His thoughts are those of the Ishmaelite and avenger of hereditary wrongs, and he is as one who sees blood in the air and runs amok. It shows a dangerous predisposition and unless controlled by the power of moral persuasion, intellectual training and social culture, will assuredly lead to trouble and disgrace. It is a degree of MALICE.

♒ 26° *A man walking blindfold towards the opening of a deep pit.* This indicates one whose thoughts and projects are liable to become chaotic and confused, so that he may be said to be walking in the dark, and to that extent may be led into grave dangers. It may be from ignorance or from want of alertness and responsiveness to his surroundings that he will come by hurt to himself, but save by the helping and directing hand of some wise friend, or the overarching love of Heaven, he cannot escape downfall and ruin. The higher the position he may occupy, the greater the danger of falling. Let him therefore study to walk warily and in humility in the simple ways of life and not aspire to tread paths which are unfamiliar and full of pitfalls for the unwary. It is a degree of BLINDING.

♒ 27° *A stately mansion surrounded by trees in an expanse of pastureland.* This symbol denotes one who will be "house-proud," fond of his home and desirous of acquiring estate, so that he may have the uninterrupted joys of continuous home life. He will prove himself to be a capable and polished member of society, a good patriot, and an earnest upholder of the traditions of his people and country. Of a pleasant and frank nature, and humane disposition, he will readily attract friends around him, and will be never so happy as when entertaining them in a homely but unostentatious manner. He will prosper in the world and will be beloved for his breadth of mind and wide sympathies. It is a degree of POSSESSION.

♒ 28° *A cup, a pack of playing cards, and dice.* This symbol denotes a person of dissipated and irregular life, whose weakness for wine and gambling is likely to lead him into sore difficulties and many excesses. His mind will be addicted to the pursuit of fortune by adventitious means, so that while he may succeed in attaching himself to others of like propensity and habits, he will lack even their confidence, and failing, will lose their adherence also. Thus, unless he shall elect to follow the paths of simple industry and patient toil in the ordinary walks of life, he will come to ruin and will be forced to pick up a precarious livelihood in the byways of social activity. It is a degree of SPOLIATION.

♒ 29° *Two crossed swords surrounded by a wreath of laurels.* Whoever has this astral signature will be remarkable for his powers of attack and defence. He may be a clever barrister, a successful diplomat, or a man of the sword. In the passage of arms which will constantly fall to his lot, he will prove himself capable and skilful to a degree. He will show considerable powers of execution, a pointedness and directness of speech, an incisive manner, and sharp, acute, penetrating mind. He will gain honours in his special walk in life, and should he take to the sword either in the defence of his own country or the conquest of another, he will meet with distinction and honours. Yet he will bold but little of this world's goods and must rely continually on his power of cutting his way through life by his own continuous exertions. It is a degree of EXECUTION.

♒ 30° *A sceptre surrounded by a crown.* This symbol denotes one who will rise to distinction and offices of great power and influence. He will display capacity for government and rulership, and, however humble his origin, will speedily attain to a foremost position in his own sphere and may successfully attempt even greater heights than many of his predecessors and contemporaries. In mind he will show himself to be rigid, strict, upright, and unbending in his integrity. His affections, although by no means warm, ary yet sincere and constant, and his ambitions are compassed by the one word AUTHORITY.

PISCES

H 1°   *A man and woman standing face to face, their hands clasped.* This symbol denotes a nature of genial, friendly and sociable qualities to which the ties of domestic and social life will constitute the sum of possible happiness. Such will live in harmony with his fellows, preserving his relations in the most perfect accord, and on all occasions giving evidence of fidelity, devotion and self-control. He will rule others by the power of persuasion, and will attain his ambitions by the exercise of unusual powers of adaptability. As a man of business he will be chiefly successful in bringing together elements of contrary natures, forming combinations of utility, and uniting forces which singly would prove incomplete and ineffectual. It is a degree of UNION.

H 2°   *A chest floating on an open sea.* This is an index of a nature that is placid and calm and disposed rather to carelessness and lassitude. He will be willing to sacrifice much for his own comfort and peace of mind, and will rarely distress himself on account of others. Nevertheless there is a strong undercurrent of feeling and passion, which, when aroused, will prove formidable. Left to himself he will prove inoffensive and dilatory, careless and haphazard. But when opposed he will show himself capable of fierce resentment and irresistible force. There is little doubt that he will lose much of his property by allowing things to drift and take their own course, where he should be taking the direction and management of them in hand. Although by no means a weak character, he will pass for such on account of his indifference to his own affairs and those of others. It is a degree of INDIFFERENCE.

♓ 3°   *A boar's head upon a dish.* This is indicative of a headstrong and rather petulant nature, to whom the good things of this life will count for much. He will have a taste for high living and may show exceptional faculty in the culinary arts. His disposition will be generous and hospitable and the best of his nature will be evident when he is entertaining his friends in convivial feasts. Possessed of a fiery and petulant nature, he will make many enemies, but will always succeed in bringing them to accord with him by some subsequent act of generosity and goodwill. At heart he is bountiful and humane, but he will be adjudged coarse and self-indulgent and a slave to the appetites. It is a degree of CONVIVIALITY.

♓ 4°   *A trilithon consisting of two strong pillars of stone with a horizontal thwart of the same material. Within the trilithon is a strong iron gate.* This is the index of one whose nature is set about with the security which arises from a prudent and cautious nature, a high order of intelligence and a strong stability of character. He will prove to be a haven of refuge for the weak and helpless and a protection to all who stand in need of a friend. Within his gate there is peace and security, rest and satisfaction. He will successfully withstand the assaults of his enemies, and although it will be at all times difficult to get at the inward nature and motive of his life, yet to those who are admitted to his confidence he will justify his reticence, his retirement and his independence of action. Justice and self-restraint will be the keynotes of his nature. It is a degree of DEFENCE.

♓ 5°   *Three men advancing arm in arm.* This indicates one given to friendship and the delights of social intercourse, and whose nature will find chief expression in the fostering of amicable relations between others. Prolixity and diffusion of effort may render his best intentions void of good results, but that they are animated by the best feelings none of his friends will ever doubt. He will have many supporters and his confidences will be esteemed by them. He may profitably be engaged in the instruction and leading of others, whether as a teacher, director, overseer or officer, and he will be one of those to whose instruction and advice men will naturally incline. His fondness for pleasure, however, may ruin his prospects. It is a degree of ACCORD.

♓ 6°   *A wreck floating on a peaceful sea.* This indicates one to whom the Fates are likely to prove unkind, either in the fact of giving him birth in the family of one who has suffered complete wreck of fortunes, or by leading him to hazards of a speculative and adventurous nature which will lead to his certain ruin. Let him therefore be ever on guard against the seductions of becoming rich in a hurry, and let his efforts be those of one who, having a long distance to travel, and a great height to attain, measures his strength with care and goes at a moderate pace. Should he attempt the seas of fortune he will be driven back and his chances of success will be for ever ruined. If he should wisely keep to the broad highways of life, and pursue the common path, he may retrieve the family fortunes and acquit himself with honour. It is a degree of SALVAGE.

♓ 7°   *A niche in which are set a lamp and a book or missal.* This indicates one to whom the secrets of nature are likely to be revealed as the result of long and patient study of her laws.

He will be endowed with considerable devotion, enabling him to sustain long and patient vigils, and pursue his studies where others would have abandoned him. His intelligence will be of a high order, and will induce him to the pursuit of religion, philosophy and the fine arts, in all of which he will show more than ordinary ability. He may show a taste for the conventicle. It is a degree of ILLUMINATION.

♓ 8° *A man with upraised arms submerged in the water, over which a heavy rain is falling.* This is the index of one who is liable to suffer many affronts of fortune, due chiefly to his own incompetence and the attempting of things and enterprises that are beyond his powers. Let him study humility and service of others, and cultivate a proper understanding of his own aptitudes and powers. Thus he may escape a sudden and unlooked-for ruin which otherwise must attend him in the boldest venture of his life. He may go into liquidation and become submerged, and crying for rescue from his helpless state, there may be found none to weep for him save Heaven, which yet is kind in that it permits this warning. Independence is not for those who have no knowledge of their own weakness. The strong swimmer alone can attempt the deep waters. It is a degree of INCOMPETENCE.

♓ 9° *An old man with a pack upon his back and a long staff in his hand walking down a hill.* This indicates one whose fortunes are likely to prove very remarkable. Estranged at an early age from his kindred he will follow an adventurous fortune and his livelihood will be to that extent precarious and uncertain. He will roam into distant countries and experience many privations, always sustaining his lot with quiet resignation and singular indifference of spirit. He will attain to some distinction, but will suffer reversal and in the end will carry his load of cares downhill to the grave. In some special manner he will prove himself to be a man of singular character and remarkable powers. It is a degree of PILGRIMAGE.

♓ 10° *On a table of plain surface lie a number of chemical instruments, a retort, a pestle and mortar, a bent tube and a crucible being the chief.* This indicates one with some special aptitude for the study of chemistry in one or another of its many phases. His mind will be analytical and acute, capable of resolving things into their principles and perceiving causes where others only take note of effects. His mind is of that nature which while avowing no religion has no thought which is not essentially religious, and which, in its quest after the secrets of nature is moved primarily by a sincere devotion to the Spirit of Nature. In daily life he will evince much reticence, caution and wariness, being very distrustful of things and persons not known to him, but will show considerable animation when discussing the particular studies and subjects with which his mind is occupied. It is a degree of TESTING.

♓ 11° *A wild horse leaping a barrier.* This denotes a man of considerable freedom and energy of nature, one who will be restless under restraint, free and open in expression of his thoughts and feelings and very emphatic in his dealings with others. He will show aspiration and may incline to forensic study. His nature will be adventurous and his actions will be characterised by a supreme contempt for danger and peril. If he should incline to law, literature or ecclesiastical work, he will have distinction. It is a degree of LIBERTY.

♓ 12° *A truncated cone.* This indicates one who has undoubted aspirations and will rise to a good position, although when that position is assured there will be danger of a sudden cessation of fortune, and his life may thereafter continue to be filled with troubles and vexations. On the other hand, there will be some born under this degree who will give promise of high attainments, and who will be cut off in the midst of their career. In either case the pinnacle and end of their ambitions will never be reached. Therefore let such aim higher than they mean to hit, or yet remain contended. It is a degree of CURTAILMENT.

♓ 13° *A circle within a circle, both concentric.* This indicates a life that is bounded by another, a happiness that can never be shared alone. To such an one as is born under this degree the circle of existence will embrace the close relationships of domestic life in perfect accord. The nature will be symmetrical and of abundant endowments, and the life will be rounded by a full experience of all those sweet influences which are engendered by a life in accord with environment, a mind at rest within itself, and a nature disposed to harmony. To him will be given the guarding and cherishing of those of smaller attainments, and less mature life. It is a degree of GUARDING.

♓ 4° *A man stripped to the waist hewing timber.* This is the index of one whose life will abound with difficult and laborious work. Endowed with a good will and an earnest soul, he will make good use of his powers, and however humble his station he will magnify it, however slender his means he will so work as to deserve more. For the rest, he may be disposed to a life of rustic simplicity as an agriculturist or worker in the orchards and woods, or he may even be the builder of a house, of a city, and at best the founder of a colony. He will be remarkable for the simplicity and naturalness of his mind, and for the strenuous character of his work in the world. It is a degree of LABOUR.

♓ 15° *An arrow in flight passing through a cloud of smoke.* This symbol denotes one whose mind will be penetrating and ambitious, keen and incisive and endowed with considerable power of determination and direction of force. What he sees he will pursue without vacillation. He feels himself to have a path in life already marked out for him and he will be swift to follow it. His nature will be somewhat aggressive and headstrong, and there will be times when he will incur enmity in consequence and be in danger of secret hurt. He will make long journeys and will reach to inaccessible or remote parts of the world. It is a degree of DIRECTNESS.

♓ 16° *A tiger standing guard over its young litter.* It is the index of a nature capable of strong attachment and devotion and able by watchfulness and caution to command success. He will show great attachment to his kindred, and his family circle will be secure in the vigilance of his devotion. Very cautious, circumspect and patient, he will seldom fail in his enterprises; what he cannot attain by his energy he will secure by his patience. In the defence of those related to him he will show exceptional strength and even ferocity of temper, while to them he will display only the gentlest and most tender nature. It is a degree of WATCHING.

♓ 17° *A man falling with upraised arms between the parting timbers of a broken bridge.* This symbol has reference to a life that is liable to be cut off in mid-years, and probably by means of an accident connected with the water. Such an one should exercise great care in his going, especially about the middle of life, and should avoid hazards both commercial and physical. It may be that he will be in danger of ruin and liquidation at some middle period of life, determined by the sum of his years; but certain it is that all that he depends upon for a safe passage through this world will be liable to a sudden and unforeseen collapse. Let him keep to the broad highway of life and not take an isolated path. There is safety in companionship: misanthropy has many expressions and counts many its victims. He who aspires to rulership is a misanthrope, the humble man has safety with the people. It is a degree of COLLAPSE.

♓ 18°   *A horse and its rider falling at a fence.* This symbol denotes one whose career will be broken either in some foreign land or in the pursuit of an enterprise that is strange and foreign to his nature and capacity. He will be adventuresome and headstrong, and will pursue his course regardless of con-sequences. His taste for outdoor sports will be prominent and will lead him into dangers, especially if he should follow equestrian pleasures. To some who are born under this de-gree calamity will accrue from transgression of the law. Let all such keep their passions in subjection by the power of the will and bridle their desires. It is a degree of CATASTROPHE.

♓ 19°   *Two daggers crossed.* This indicates a nature given to con-tention and litigation and there will be a corresponding el-ement of danger in the life and fortunes of such. Incisive, aggressive, and endowed with keen and penetrating intel-lect, there is here a nature capable of gaining considerable distinction in the use of arms or in the pursuit of the le-gal profession. But it is to be feared that the nature is too contentious to excite any but the worst passions in others, whilst a paucity of friends and a precarious fortune may be assigned to this radical want of harmony in the nature. It is a degree of WOUNDING.

♓ 20° *A helical scroll.* This degree denotes a nature which is un-decided, changeful, fickle and of no stability. Such an one will lose himself in the multitude of his projects and imag-inings. His path in life will be circuitous and will lead back to himself. His imagination will run riot with his reason, and his efforts will lack that definition of purpose which makes for success in life. His mind will be tortuous and chaotic, filled with dreams and fancies to the exclusion of useful and practical measures. He may suffer brain diaorder, or some continuous affection of the nervous system, which will ren-der even his bodily actions limp and uncertain. To such an one healthful and virile companionship in youth will prove a lasting blessing. It is a degree of WANDERING.

♓ 21° *A lunar crescent emerging from a cloud from which also proceeds a flash of lightning.* This denotes a person of strong and forceful nature, proud and conflicting spirit, great des-patch and celerity of action, penetrating and swift thought, and tremendous executive faculty. Here there is determinism and direction of force in the highest degree, effective in all the affairs of life, but not for that matter always productive of success or happiness. Hopeful though the nature is, its schemes and projects will not always bear the light of day, and as in a dark imagination the highest hopes and fancies of the nature will be elaborated, so in the night time also will judgment strike home to the sundering of root and branch. Let him beware of the dark hours. It is a degree of CLEAVAGE.

♓ 22° *A woman of dark countenance standing over a prostrate man.* This is warning of a nature that is disposed to be brought under the malignant influence of womankind, to his hurt and ruin. Or let it be said that a woman's influence is here predominant for ill, and a sinister fame attaches to all of the female sex who are generated under this degree. It is a man's undoing through weakness, a woman's victory through dishonour: to either sex it is full of warning and threat. Let such as vitate under this radius look to their charge and the account they shall make of it. It is a degree of PROSTRATING.

♓ 23° *A warrior in helmet drawing a long bow to which the fletch is duly set.* This symbol is capable of two renderings, the first of which points to a strong character, a set purpose, a lofty aim and in some particular sense the gift of prophecy and knowledge of future events. On the other hand, there is the weakness which depends on the hazard of life, the care-lessness or indifference which arises from lack of interest and finds expression in vanity and self-inflation. At its best it signifies the higher indifference which affects the mind secure of its achievements, in the worst case it denotes. improvidence and carelessness, a life set upon a hazard. It is a degree of SPECULATION.

♓ 24° *A woman reclining upon a couch, scantily attired.* It is the index of a mind given to the ease and luxury of life, the soft effeminate pleasures of the senses. Such an one will eat the lotus and make chains of flowers more difficult to break than the strongest bonds of steel. Such an one will dream while others work, and drift upon the river of life while others ply their oars and brace themselves to nervous effort. The opiate fails, the soul is sick with its satiety, and the sleeper awakes from nerveless indolence to a life of dull ineptitude, futile regret and selfcondemnation. It is a degree of SENSUALITY.

♓ 25° *A crown through which is set an upright sword.* It is the index of a mind set upon high resolves and capable of sustaining the assaults of its enemies in such a degree as to achieve its purposes without loss of fortune, prestige or honour. Such an one may prove to be a great warrior, a man of the sword, to whom honours will be given without stint. A king, he will sustain his throne by the use of aggressive measures and by victories gained over all his enemies; while one of lowly birth will gain his crown in the service of his king. His mind will be upright, astute, aspiring and sustained by an unswerving faith. It is a degree of VICTORY.

♓ 26° *A man in armour, fully equipped and bearing a shield.* This indicates one who will walk through life warily, but with that assurance which is the result of being forearmed against danger. While cautious and circumspect, he will evince a brave and dauntless spirit, and with the double equipment of caution in defence and courage in attack, he will surmount the machinations of his enemies and break down all opposition. Such an one will be faithful in his dealings and just to his fellows, so that he will abide in safety, defended at all points by the goodwill of his friends and the faith of his associates. It is a degree of SECURITY.

♓ 27° *An earthquake.* This is a sinister indication and refers to one who will be overcome by sudden and unexpected calamities, which will undermine his labours and,reduce his hopes to ruin. Let him be careful where he builds, and test with discernment and understanding the grounds of his faith and hope in others. Let him labour diligently and sow in the broad valleys of the world the seeds of his yet uncertain harvest. For the rest let him trust in Heaven and invoke its aid in all humility. But if he should aspire to build his castles of many stages, or spread his vineyards up the mountain side, then he shall have the greater need of care and stronger faith in God, himself and man. It is a degree of REVERSAL.

♓ 28° *A serpent standing erect within a circle of fire.* This is the index of a mind of more than usual powers of intellect and a soul disposed to the searching out of the deeper secrets of nature. Such an one will manifest much wisdom and will attain to high distinction in the pursuit of scientific study, but more particularly such as is related to the art of healing, as chemistry, medicine and anatomical science. From him, as through a lens, the rays of a higher truth and deeper understanding will converge and he dispersed again for the better instruction of the world and its manifest and manifold advantage. He will take life at the crisis and turn it back from the Gates of Death. It is a degree of KNOWLEDGE.

♓ 29° *A man upon a raft floating in open sea.* This is the index of a mind that is in danger of misanthropic isolation and abandonment of self to the winds of adverse fortune. Such an one will show a lack of initiative, small power of direction, a wandering and uncertain mind, and a helpless nature. He will be in danger of meeting adversity while yet young, and of being discouraged thereby and frightened into a nerveless apathy. In some instances there will be danger of actual shipwreck or accidental submersion. Let him take in hand the rudder of intelligence whereby to guide his course, and spread his sails in hope. Let him follow his chart with care and trust in Heaven for a favouring wind which shall carry him safely into port. It is a degree of ISOLATION.

♓ 30° *A straight column with square capital and base.* This indicates one of considerable personal influence, one in whom egoity is strongly developed and plainly asserted. The mind is elevated, aspiring and precise, the nature plain and unaffected, but strongly didactic and self-assertive. The spirit of rectitude is dominated by the spirit of egotism. The attainments of the mind are marred in their expression by the evident lack of flexibility and deference. Without a high order of intelligence nothing but vanity and self-centred egotism is here discernible. Intelligence will render him dictatorial, but uncouth. At all times rigid and unbending, intelligence will give him mastery, and ignorance will render him a Goth. The character is capable of singular distinction. It is a degree of EGOITY.

"The Unreal hath no being; the Real never ceases to be."
Bhagavad Gîta

Isidore Kozminsky

ARIES

♈ 1°   *A ball of fire bursting across a rainbow.* Denotes one of strength, force, and daring. By nature he is aggressive and martial, desiring to conquer at all costs. He is restless and impelling, taking many risks and enduring many hardships. The degree is a dangerous one, threatening mind and body. The symbol is a symbol of ACTION.

♈ 2°   *A man with a sword in his hand falling through a skylight of coloured glass.* Denotes one of a rash and impetuous nature. He is strong and brave, but is wanting in restraint, and is apt to involve himself in unpopular or regrettable actions. Such a one will, all through life, have to exercise a strong hand over himself and his actions. It is a symbol of RASHNESS.

♈ 3°   *A prince saving a child from a burning castle.* Denotes one of brave and noble qualities whose sense of duty holds danger in contempt when the call is for the help of the weak. As a leader such a one can be relied on in any emergency which may arise. He aims high materially and spiritually. It is a symbol of NOBILITY.

♈ 4°   *A mailed hand holding a dagger with a bent point.* Denotes one protected against external hurt, yet who, with a powerful desire for martial action in all affairs of life, may be tempted to use protective armor for offensive purposes, forgetting that the point of the dagger of aggression is blunted. Such a one needs to restrain impulse and to bestow thought and study on any contemplated action, then let him be sure that his dagger be true before he strikes. It is a symbol of MISCONCEPTION.

♈ 5°   *A feudal knight in full armor standing on the walls of his castle defying a multitude of armed people. A mysterious figure at the back of the crowd strikes a note on a curious six-stringed harp, the massive walls crumble and fall, and the defier is at the mercy of the defied.* Denotes one who is apt to place infinite reliance on materialistic things and to exult in the strength which their possession gives him over the masses of men. In the midst of his power a spiritual force, acting on invisible agencies and sending forth a note softer than the trumpet sounds of Jericho, may rudely disturb him. Then, if his soul truly awakes, the native becomes a valiant knight in the cause of enlightenment, but if the soul slumbers back again into the sludge of materialism, then will the native again place all his hopes on things that seem, and the defier will be truly at the mercy of the defied. It is a symbol of FALSE SECURITY.

♈ 6°   *A metalsmith in his workshop fixing a silver caduceus of Mercury in a base of copper. Around are scattered various metals and instruments.* Denotes one of inward understanding. The smith by his craft glorifies the power of love and intelligence which he cements together. The base of copper indicates that no form of learning matter unless it is engendered by love and held by its soft and holy influence. One with this degree rising has a noble destiny. He is the metal smith, and this is the mark of his mission. It is a symbol of MENTAL PERCEPTION.

♈ 7°   *A man saving himself from falling into a deep cavern by clutching a wild rose-tree. The thorns cut into his flesh but the plant supports him.* Denotes one lacking self-confidence, relying too much on the weaker things which wound him whilst they hold him. To this native, luxury is hurtful, for the senses are active and the feelings quickly respond to environment. To rise superior to external conditions and the tyranny of sense is the task of the native of this degree. The symbol is a symbol of WEAKNESS.

♈ 8°   *A silver axe shattering a shield of iron.* Denotes one possessing understanding and a penetrative intellect who will be compelled many times in life to exert his abilities for the removal of obstacles and formidable enemies. He is gifted with much moral bravery and a high sense of duty. Here we have a hero whose weapon of defence and offence is the mind. It is a symbol of PENETRATION.

♈ 9°   *A Roman general gaudily appareled receiving a wreath of flowers from an empress.* Denotes one of proud bearing who delights in fine clothes and display. He will always attract admirer., and gain honor and advancement. In some way he will bear rule. If fate leads him into the theatrical profession, he will lead. If into business, he will be strong, courted, and successful in finance. If into the army or navy he will be a powerful officer. It is a symbol of GAINING.

♈ 10°   *A ship illumined with the rosy rays of morning sailing towards the rising sun.* Denotes spiritual and material advancement. The native will in some way be a pioneer whose labors will be hailed and recognized. He will be favored by the people, and will easily attract influence. To obtain the best promises of this degree he may have to move about as indicated in his horoscope. It is a symbol of INFLUENCE.

♈ 11°   *A little child tying a ribbon round a lamb's neck, the flock playfully frolicking around.* Denotes one of simple manners and lovable personality who has the power to change sadness into joy and wipe away tears from the faces of the afflicted. One to whom trust is given and who will not abuse it. It is a symbol of IDEALITY.

♈ 12° *A druid cutting the acorn from the sacred oak with a sickle of silver.* Denotes change and romance. The native will suffer fluctuations in thoughts, feelings, and conditions. As the body ages, the higher side of the native asserts itself and the allurements of youth fail to hold power over him. Much wandering and many strange adventures make up his experiences in the worlds spiritual and material. It is a symbol of ROAMING.

♈ 13° *A bright steel cross-sword with a handle of gleaming copper, above it a heart of gold from which stream shafts of golden light.* Denotes bravery, love, and sincerity. Honor will come to this native, his thoughts and ambitions lead him upwards. By Love's guidance he passes over obstacles and pursues an honorable course. His nature is somewhat proud, but he is generous and noble-minded. Influence and favor come to him. It is a symbol of LIGHT.

♈ 14° *A man standing on a mountain gazing sadly on the valley below, where some men are fighting for a bag of gold whilst a monkey is eating their food. On his right is the spirit of Truth; on his left the spirit of Love; behind him, holding on to his garment, is the spirit of Hate.* Denotes one who reaches a position of responsibility, power, and influence, and seeks to find in man the spark which being agitated blazes forth in glory, guiding by its perfect light. Here we have the teacher who strives to lead men from the valley of darkness into the light of understanding, but who himself is threatened by Error and Hate, which if he permits to influence him will drag him from his throne. But if he join his own great soul to Truth and Love, what wonders may he not perform! It is a symbol of INTERCESSION.

♈ 15° *A Crusading knight with red cross on white corselet sinking in the quicksands, an Arab mocking at him from the safe ground he has left.* Denotes an adventurer or one who follows risk and courts trouble, for he carries the cross of suffering on a field of light. He may be gifted with some noble sentiments, feelings, and impressions, but his very rashness and impetuosity force him to miscalculate, threatening to make him the sport of his enemies. It is a symbol of DEVIATION.

♈ 16° *Wild flowers growing amidst the corn in a sunlit field.* Denotes a person of charm, a lover of freedom- mental and physical-of nature, and of simple loveliness whose works in life will be blessed with success, and whose individuality will make itself felt amongst men. It is a symbol of ABUNDANCE.

♈ 17° *A beautiful woman, richly dressed, reclining on a couch, with fruits and golden vessels around her. At her hand, on an ornate table of white marble, lies an opened book.* Denotes a lotus-eater, a lover of pleasure, who delights in ease and the sweets of life. The fortunes are favored, but the native makes no personal effort to increase them. The mind is romantic and art-loving, and the form graceful. It ii a symbol of LUXURY.

♈ 18° *The goddess Venus holding out her hands to a wounded soldier, who is painfully trying to reach her.* Denotes sympathy. Many times will the native stumble and fall by the way, but ever will there be a bright light before him to dispel the darkness of the night and to dissipate his fears. The mind is aspiring, but to reach its ideal, pain and struggle are involved. The native must not falter, for very nigh unto him is his hope-a little sacrifice and endeavor will unite him to it. It is a symbol of UPRAISING.

♈ 19° *A harp resting against an altar, from which a volume of smoke arises.* Denotes one whose soul is full of poetry, harmony, and true religion, whose endeavors may be thwarted, but not suppressed. One to whom peace and goodwill are more precious than mere words, and whose prayers are unselfish, thoughtful, and sincere. It is a symbol of CONSECRATION.

♈ 20° *A blacksmith hammering a piece of red-hot iron on an anvil.* Denotes a determined worker, vigorous in the fight against opposition-a transmuter of himself and those who contend against him. Gifted with so strong a spirit, this native can never be mean. Baseness does not find a place in his nature. He loathes idleness, for energy, pain, and experience have taught him the power of industry. It is a symbol of RESOLUTION.

♈ 21° *A man struggling with a fierce serpent whilst others armed with large knives are hurrying to aid him.* Denotes one who will be assailed by secret and open enemies, who will be liable to troubles and false accusations. In his dealings he should always exercise great care, and should not rely on word-of-mouth agreements. He will not be without devoted friends, who will not neglect him in the hour of his greatest need. His intense feelings will cause him trouble, danger, illness, and regret, and he will have to strive with the dark serpent. Let him unite himself with noble and good-living people, and put away from himself votaries of evil. It is a symbol of CONTENTION.

♈ 22° *A pilgrim crossing himself in front of an ancient temple, an overdressed official and a soldier mocking him.* Denotes a devout person who will be subjected to many trials and taunts in life, but who will, by the strength of his faith, overcome them all. He comes from the masses rather than from the classes, and his sympathy will ever be with the struggling people of the nations. From officialdom and materialism he receives scant courtesy. It is a symbol of FAITH.

♈ 23° *A king absorbed in the flatteries of a courtier whose mistress is stealing important documents from a drawer.* Denotes one who is too ready to delude himself and to live in an insincere atmosphere of adulation and deception. Without accomplishing anything of particular merit, he accepts praises from flattering parasites. Thus is he lulled into a sense of false security, and loses those things which are truly of worth. It is a symbol of ENTRAPPING.

♈ 24° *A youth grasping a beautiful woman, who turns into a skeleton in his arms.* Denotes one who may lose his way following his desires. He is highly passionate, and allows himself to be shaken by his senses as the wind shakes the autumn leaves. He is then apt to grow selfish, and to disregard the feelings and rights of others, with consequences bringing to him death, defeat, and disaster. It is a symbol of ILLUSION.

♈ 25° *An old man with a scythe cutting down a field of nettles.* Denotes one who cuts his way through pricks, scratches, and wounds. The "coldly useful" may rise up against him to again be cut down to his advantage. The native is not tied to mere sentiment, and will be keen and enthusiastic in research, leading to discovery. It is a symbol of REVEALING.

♈ 26° *The governor of a city surrendering the keys to a dark frowning conqueror.* Denotes one who struggles bravely against great odds who is beset by enemies who harass and worry him. After a great fight he may have to hand over what he holds to one stronger than he is and be content with what consideration is given to him afterwards. It is a symbol of

DEPENDENCE.

♈ 27° *A huge hour-glass, the sands in which are running low.* Denotes one who is apt to delay the following up of matters of importance and to procrastinate until the hour grows too late to serve his purposes. His tendency is to move too slowly when the nature of an event demands hasty action. It is a symbol of DELAYING.

♈ 28° *A lapidary holding in his hand a magnificent amethyst, at which he gazes admiringly.* Denote one gifted with mental and moral strength, power, and forcefulness, who brings hope to many a sad or fearful heart. He is magnetic and iconoclastic, and by his faith and will he gains many adherents. it is a symbol of FASCINATION.

♈ 29° *An artist laying a mosaic pavement in a large public building. He works slowly and with great patience.* Denotes one of refined and patient nature who is content to work hard and slowly in the endeavor to accomplish worthy and enduring objects. He may be skilled in the arts that uplift, or an admirer of them. Still his destiny is bright, especially after his forty-fifth year, when his merit will receive recognition and favour. It is a symbol of DEVELOPMENT.

♈ 30° *A man endeavoring to subdue a raging forest fire with a pail of water.* Denotes one who will endure sorrow and who underestimates the strength of his adversaries. He is apt to enter into great schemes with very little backing, and to provoke argument without being prepared to meet it. Hence he is continually at the mercy of forces into whose grip he enters without regard to consequences. He is apt to fight a hard fight with insignificant weapons, and thus to court defeat. It is a symbol of UNREADINESS.

TAURUS

♉ 1° *A grey vapour surrounding a bush of red roses upon which is a brilliantly coloured butterfly.* Denotes one whose life is threatened in early infancy. The ideals are high, and he delights in all that is beautiful and sweet. The native is somewhat erratic and inconstant, loving "fresh fields and pastures new." He inclines to the poetic and artistic, and may excel in such paths. It is a symbol of CULTIVATION.

♉ 2° *A heart crowned on the summit of a barren rock jutting out of the ocean—a bevy of white sea-birds speeding towards it from the east in crescent form.* Denotes one capable of immense sacrifices who surrenders self, expecting no reward. The life will be often lonely, but ever threatened by storms. In the end wisdom and worth will triumph and the second half of life brings good promise. It is a symbol of DEVOTION.

♉ 3° *A man tossing handfuls of seed to the earth, which, as soon as they touch, fructify and incline towards him.* Denotes one favored by fortune. He will possess good judgment, and will do the right thing at the right time. His early life will be filled with struggle and with promise, expanding to favor as he advances in years. With a good insight into human nature the native can well choose others to assist in his work, and whilst holding work to be the true necessity of life, he knows the value of relaxation and pleasure to others as to himself. It is a symbol of FORTUNE.

♉ 4° *The arena of a circus during a night performance, the ringmaster in the centre urging forward the movements of a large white horse galloping round the ring, a lady gymnast standing on the animal's back holding a hoop of fire.* Denotes one whose destiny it is to come before the public in some professional capacity. The native will be impulsive, bold, and brave, and will be gifted with controlling and magnetic force. He will travel and move about a great deal, and will be exposed to danger with little or no hurt. It is a symbol of INTREPIDITY.

♉ 5°   *Two young men carrying huge bunches of large grapes on a pole between them, giving freely of the fruit to troops of children.* Denotes one who will gain greatly through his own efforts and perseverance, and who will be blessed. He will bring happiness to, and relieve the burden of, many, accounting it pleasure. Thus will he draw unto himself the good thoughts and prayers of others. It is a symbol of BENEFACTION.

♉ 6°   *A judge in his robes of office handing a book to a student, who is stretching out his hands to receive it.* Denotes one who will rise to a position of importance, and whose mission and ambition it will be in life to give instruction and to secure the advancement of worthy people of wit, talent, and inspiration. These acts will reflect his own glory as the Moon reflects the brightness of the Sun. It is a symbol of ILLUMINATION.

♉ 7°   *A beautiful white swan swimming on a smooth lake edged by lilies and grasses and pretty little wild flowers.* Denotes a tranquil and romantic life. The native is gifted poetically, and can express his feelings in the book of Nature with charming simplicity. He will not have much to trouble him in the world of men, and should keep away from crowds and mixed atmospheres, as he is singularly sensitive to external conditions. It is a symbol of TRANQUILITY.

♉ 8° *A leafless tree, on a plain, bending before a violent gale of wind, which whistles wildly through the branches.* Denotes one who meets with opposition, obstacles, and trouble who will be compelled to battle against adversity. Such a one should never take risks in anything, no matter how promising, but be content to work on in the very teeth of the enemy, remembering always that the strong are chosen to fight the battles of the weak. It is a symbol of IMPEDIMENT.

♉ 9° *A farmer driving a cart filled with fruit, at which birds are pecking.* Denotes one who acquires much by work and application, but who lacks the faculty of watchfulness in protecting his gains from the greed of others. He has an easygoing tendency, but gains come from labor, craft, and the management of his own affairs. He may be the victim of deceit or treachery, and should never put himself in the hands of others when his own well-being is concerned. He should avoid things and circumstances he does not understand. It is a symbol of MISLEADING.

♉ 10° *A daintily dressed woman sitting by a placid lake, gazing intently at a man's face reflected in the water.* Denotes a person of refined tastes and feelings, gifted with clairvoyant power and artistic skill. A union with one of psychic power-a soul-mate-brings harmony or complications (as indicated an the nativity) into a life which commands power and influence. It is a symbol of DESCRYING.

♉ 11° *A monk on a rocky road giving drink and food to a poor traveler who has fallen by the way. A rayed anchor above his head.* Denotes one of religious and charitable nature whose high understanding of the brotherhood of man and the absolute unity of human aims, when not diverted by the evil powers, makes him ever ready to divide his substance with those who, less fortunate in worldly matters, give a higher payment-human blessings and gratitude. His trust in humanity is never shaken. He is ever to others a harbinger of hope. It is a symbol of DELIVERANCE.

♉ 12° *Two diggers working on a mountain-slope unearth a large mass of glittering gold.* Denotes one of a searching nature who knows the true value of sincere work. He will never spare himself until his purpose is achieved. With him persistence wins by virtue of his fate. It is a symbol of ENDURANCE.

♉ 13° *A judge in a court of law frowning at a man holding up a document.* Denotes one who is energetic and active, but who is threatened with disfavor, prejudice, and adverse judgment. He has trials in life, and suffers much, and he is likely to oppose or be opposed by authority. If Mercury is weak or afflicted in the horoscope, the native suffers in business and from law; but if this planet is strong he is a mental pioneer fighting for liberty. It is a symbol of GRIPPING.

♉ 14° *A virgin clothed in white, with a bright star above her head, joining the hands of two men about to quarrel.* Denotes one whose love of harmony adds to the beauty of a spiritual nature. To him there is no virtue higher than peace, and nothing so unworthy of man's high mission as inharmony and hate. Gifted with a sweet and lovable personality and fine magnetic force, his power is felt and respected. It is a symbol of HARMONIOUS LOVE.

♉ 15° *A student with lamp in hand, standing at the entrance of a cavern from which issue clouds of soft, light, rosy vapour.* Denotes a person whose tastes and desires are directed to the understanding of the secrets which rest beneath the veil. He has brought to earth from other sources the knowledge which enables him to find the entrance to the cavern of hidden jewels, but it is doubtful if he can enter, for the gateway is guarded by sublime and intense colors caused by more excessive vibrations than can be endured by the human body. The light vapor approaching the "Ultra" stage is more powerful and effective than dragons of fire. It is a symbol of INITIATION.

♉ 16° *A white dove, adorned with a rose-coloured ribbon to which is attached a little bell, standing on the right shoulder of a man drinking wine.* Denotes one of a merry and convivial spirit who will be favored by women and Venus. There is a tendency to too much indulgence, but ever a restraining power which holds the native to a right and rosy course. It is a symbol of GOOD LIVING.

♉ 17° *A sea-gull flying over the waters of the ocean.* Denotes one free as air, brave, spiritual, restless, and unfitted for the regular routine of daily life. Care in infancy is essential. He is of a wandering disposition and frequent changes are for him. It is a symbol of WANDERING.

♉ 18° *A gaudily dressed herald blowing a trumpet, at the sound of which two knights, one on a white charger, the other on a black, rush towards each other with set spears.* Denotes one of a strongly martial disposition who delights in struggle and contention. He has a love of show and glitter, and desires to make himself heard. Within him is a continual war between good and evil, and victory depends on himself alone. It is a symbol of COMBATIVENESS.

♉ 19° *An archer, dressed in red, firing arrows at the Moon.* Denotes one who is unable to estimate his abilities and who attempts things foolhardy and useless. There is a tendency to irritability and aggressiveness and lack of self-restraint. Thus he will court unpopularity and will suffer from his own actions. It is a symbol of FUTILITY.

♉ 20° *A flight of white eagles.* Denotes one whose thoughts are high and whose ambitions are serenely regulated. He rises in life, gaining command and respect. He is farseeing, and his virtues enable him to accomplish good work in this world. It is a symbol of CELEBRITY.

♉ 21° *A race-horse with the number 3 on his saddle-cloth entering a course.* Denotes one of sporting tendencies who delights in trials of skill and who is generally fortunate. To his nature there is a generous, sympathetic, and interesting side, which gains him many friends and much popularity. It is a symbol of SPORTIVENESS.

♉ 22° *Hand holding a torch amidst the darkness.* Denotes a light bearer whose mission is to guide others and to uplift them. No matter how dark the way, his presence inspires brightness. There is no weakness in this native, who knows just what he is on this world to do and who does it. It is a symbol of DIRECTORSHIP.

♉ 23° *St. Michael slaying the Dragon in a shower of black rain.* Denotes one with strength of purpose and ability to sustain trials. The Dragon is lust, corruption, end the cold moistures of the earth. St. Michael is the life, solar energy, conqueror of decay; the black rain the evil which corruption draws. So when the native realizes his soul force he becomes a veritable victor over the monster into whose jaws so many unwarned and unguarded fall. It is a symbol of VICTORY.

♉ 24° *A prisoner having escaped from his prison is endeavoring to break his fetters with the aid of some large flinty stones.* Denotes one whose life is harassed by other people, and who will be held to a position to his disadvantage from which he will free himself and go where better conditions prevail, and where he will have better opportunities for employing his skill for his own good. Consult the horoscope. It is a symbol of RESTRAINING.

♉ 25° *A dense column of smoke from which issue flashes of lightning.* Denotes one of natural talent who will be beset with difficulties in gaining recognition, but whose mental strength will be the more determined because of them. When his time comes his power will be felt. He will force acknowledgment by sheer ability and energy. It is a symbol of PREMEDITATION.

♉ 26° *A giant of benevolent aspect, with his foot on a broken sword, tearing up the laws of the world by which men have been governed for centuries. Behind him are broken bags of golden coins, which are falling in a shower over a precipice.* Denotes a child of the new age whose thoughts contend against orthodoxy, systems, war, and the accepted justice of the times. He is gifted with a powerful and convincing individuality, strong in wisdom, worth, and excellence. His mind is dominant, and he is morally and mentally brave. It is a symbol of ICONOCLASM.

♉ 27° *An inventor having risen from his bench gazes admiringly at a remarkable engine which he has just completed.* Denotes one who will produce work of value to the race. He is gifted with inventive ability and mind, and will concrete ideas whilst others are but dreaming of them. It is a symbol of INGENUITY.

♉ 28° *A woman looking into a crystal ball in which confused images are reflected.* Denotes a mediumistic person who, for lack of energetic study and cultivation, has difficulty in understanding the true value and meaning of the messages which he receives. To such a one long study and care will bring repayment. But self-sacrifice is demanded. It is a symbol of DISORDER.

♉ 29° *A man at a cross-road. Above him are two spirits, one black and the other white. Each strives to impress him, but his mind is too perplexed to understand either.* Denotes one who is continually beset with difficulties and who finds it hard at all times to decide his course of action. He is ever between forces of opposite natures, and is quite as likely to do the right thing as the wrong one. These conditions must be subdued by the steady cultivation of the will. It is a symbol of EMBARRASSMENT.

♉ 30° *A huge ironstone rolling down a mountain-side strikes a clump of hard flint, causing a bright fiery flash.* Denotes a venturesome and determined spirit who will dare and do much to attain his ambitions. The earlier life will be filled with struggles and beset with difficulties which, as he advances in years, will enable him to gain the experience necessary to make his name known and his ideas respected. It is a symbol of FORCEFULNESS.

GEMINI

♊ 1° *Two Ionic columns adorned with globes—a burst of flame issuing out of clouds behind.* Denotes a double-natured, cultured, and gifted person who gains reputation through his acts. He has great mental energy and will, combined with an impetuosity which directs to good or evil results. His over hastiness may lead him to mistakes which incur displeasure and court danger. It is a symbol of ANIMATION.

♊ 2° *A military officer seated on a heap of arms studying a map which he holds in his hands.* Denotes one of much discrimination and capacity for study, with ability to lead and direct others. His movements are guided by knowledge and molded by study. Danger seems to have a fascination for him; for, conscious of his own ability to surmount difficulties, he has little fear even in the midst of strife. It is a symbol of UN-RAVELING.

♊ 3° *A composer standing before a large organ, with a scroll of music in his hand.* Denotes one who will serve and elevate the public and who will be a master in his own particular work. Gifted with intense idealism and the true understanding of values in his special sphere, he will gain recognition and honors in life. It is a symbol of Elegance.

♊ 4° *A human face, the expression calm and serene, a silvery triangle pointing upwards below, a dark square above.* Denotes one of spirituality and kindness who meets with trials and who is pressed under the rough heel of materialism and the greed of the world. Even so, the serene aura will flow from him as water down a mountain slope, cultivating those

218

who come near. The conscience is strong, and be loathes evil and unworthy actions. This is a peculiar degree, and certain horoscopes will force an entirely opposite interpretation. It is a symbol of Transcendentalism.

♊ 5° *Little children playing near an old wrecked ship on the sea-shore.* Denotes one of gentle and romantic nature who will have many difficulties and troubles, reverses, and hopes destroyed, but who strives in the face of it all, unable to sink into baseness to gain worldly comforts. Later in life the native will have a period of pleasantness, and he passes from earth away from the busy cities of the world. It is a symbol of Concord.

♊ 6° *An analytical chemist holding up to the light a test-tube in which is a dull green liquid.* Denotes one of scientific and cautious mind, fond of experiment and research. Whether recognized by authority or not, this native never leaves his work unfinished, nor will he depart from this planet without adding rays for the progressive enlightenment of its peoples. It is a symbol of Research.

♊ 7° *A white ship with sails set on a peaceful ocean, over which the full moon is throwing a silvery light.* Denotes one of a serenely peaceful temperament, gifted with a fine imagination and creative endowment. His influence is soothing, no matter where he may be, and many are attracted to him. Generally his undertakings are successful, and he may travel much. It is a symbol of Calmness.

♊ 8° *A winged horse in mid-air with the Sun above its head.* Denotes an ambitious person of proud, aspiring nature, who seeks to rise, and who desires honor and reputation. The native has a good grip of human nature, its virtues, and its weaknesses. and he may find a position in some branch of the public service or in the service of his country. It is a symbol of Elevation.

♊ 9° *A hand holding a document on which is a crown and royal seal.* Denotes a judge, magistrate, or one who attains dignity and rank, and who will be entrusted with work of delicacy and responsibility. He will enjoy much favor. and many advantages during a life of more than average span. It is a symbol of Jurisdiction.

♊ 10° *A hospital nurse whose face expresses sympathy and sacrifice, tending a sick man.* Denotes one of sweetness, charity, and worth, who would sacrifice self and self's desires to aid the suffering and unfortunate. Happy and cheerful in the midst of the deepest darkness, this one will be to our race a blessing and an honor. It is a symbol of Cherishing.

♊ 11° *Interior of a stock exchange, a number of men shouting, jostling each other, & holding up papers.* Denotes one of speculative tendency who endures pain for the chance of gain, and who has much fighting and anxiety in the pursuit. He may find that, after all, the "game" is not worth while, and that the energy expended could be more profitably employed in more useful work. It is a symbol of Hazard.

♊ 12° *An accountant puzzling over a ledger, which he is struggling to balance.* Denotes one of mathematical mind who is apt to consider the various questions which arise in everyday life, and to accept nothing without strict examination and thought. He may often be considered stubborn and unyielding, but no one will more readily agree to the truth or falsity of a matter when clear evidence makes it possible for him to do so. It is a symbol of Exactness.

♊ 13° *Two men playing at cards, a man standing behind one player making signs to his opponent.* Denotes one exposed to treachery and deceit who will incline to place too much reliance on those unworthy of his confidence. Care in the choice of friends should be his constant charge, nor should he indulge in ventures of a risky nature at the suggestion of any one, nor put himself in the power of any man. It is a symbol of Deceit.

♊ 14° *A man in a forest handing to another an open box full of jewels which he has just stolen form an adjacent castle.* Denotes one who will be called upon to suffer from the acts of others with whom he is or has been associated. Through taking big risks he may succeed in gaining wealth, but he will be the victim of his own thoughts and the acts of his associates. It is a symbol of Entanglement.

♊ 15° *A wounded soldier drawing an arrow from his arm. A dog is howling near-by.* Denotes one of martial and impulsive nature who is liable to suffer from his restless temperament. His imagination is prolific, but apt to run into wrong grooves and useless pathways. To such, self-restraint and mental training is necessary, and a determination to employ his martial powers for high achievements. It is a symbol of Restlessness.

♊ 16° *A sword lying shattered before a cross of stone.* Denotes one who upholds the doctrine of sacrifice and faith above the boasted influence of force, and who will be enabled or fated to prove of himself that aggression shatters itself, whilst true faith rests unbroken and immovable. It is a symbol of Spiritual Victory.

♊ 17° *A blind giant in full armour hitting out wildly with a huge battle-axe at nothing.* Denotes one who overestimates his power and who rushes into quarrels from which no good can be obtained. After trouble and waste of energy he may find to his chagrin that he has gained nothing by his adventures but the reward of folly. It is a symbol of Blundering.

♊ 18° *An eagle wounded in flight swoops to a mountain ridge, where a brood of young ones rise from the drops of blood.* Denotes one of great bravery who, feeling himself unconquerable, becomes a mark for the attacks of his enemies, who, thinking to smite him at the point of his weakness, raise about themselves the power which arises from his pain. It is a symbol of Invulnerability.

♊ 19° *A mountaineer, climbing in the darkness in a violent storm which has blown away his cloak and hat, saved from falling down a precipice by a flash of lightning.* Denotes one whose vocation is one of danger and technique and who is compelled to labor under most uncomfortable conditions. He will be forced to surrender much, and will often find himself in extremely difficult positions. Eventually he will be enabled to recover himself, and be saved from disaster by a miracle of fortunate happenings. It is a symbol of Interposition.

♊ 20° *A drunken reveler holding a skull in his hands.* Denotes one who is prone to take a fatalistic view of life and to play with it as a cat plays with a mouse. He may perform acts which will cause him suffering and sorrow, and seek to stifle memories in indulgence. Let him transmute himself, and turn his thoughts to the real, fine, and true, and so realize the philosophic power of Saturn when contained in Mercury. It is a symbol of Menace.

♊ 21° *An old man in a graveyard, standing under a cypress-tree, watching a form rising from a tomb.* Denotes one who will be addicted to spiritual phenomena and who will indulge in experiments from which most people would turn away in fear. He will later study closely the higher branches of occult philosophy, for which his peculiar power is well fitted. It is a symbol of Occultism.

♊ 22° *A heap of stones over which ivy is growing.* Denotes one who clings to others for business and advantage, and who will be careful, saving, and given to the accumulation of the riches of the world. He will recognize those useful for his purpose, and recognizing them will secure them. The symbol is not without its danger and its threatening. It is a symbol of Clinging.

♊ 23° *A triangular-shaped hill. On one side the sun is shining on pleasant paths and beautiful foliage—the other side is dark and gloomy.* Denotes one who should make the most of his first half of life, when fortune will favor him, and when the happiest and most useful thoughts will reign supreme. The latter part of life promises nothing. It is a path of a peculiar and mysterious nature, and must be approached with caution. He will possess a love of refinement, especially early in life. It is a symbol of Trial.

♊ 24° *A beautiful woman giving bread to a crowd of starving people. From behind her, showing dimly through a haze of white light, is a high Intelligence placing a crown of a bright strange metal on her head.* Denotes one who accounts charity the highest of the virtues-charity of soul, charity of thought, and charity of action. When a generous act is performed, when charity is given to the opinions of others, and in relieving the sufferings of others, when there is unselfishness in act and judgment, the mystic crown bathed in holy light is on the head. It is a symbol of Glory.

♊ 25° *A hand issuing from the heavens holding a great scroll on which is shining a pentagram.* Denotes one of considerable occult force who has a mission to perform and must do what he is destined to do, no matter how strongly he may be opposed. It will be useless for the native to allow himself to be drawn into the world's gambling and money schemes or towards the lower elements of material life. It is a symbol of Etherealism.

♊ 26° *A broken trident falling into the sea.* Denotes one who will be compelled to face Uncertain and unsettled conditions. Speculations are fatal to him, and should be avoided. He must exercise care in speech and action, and must not be misled by appearances. It is a symbol of Allurement.

♊ 27° *A man seated at a table, gloomily looking at a violin with broken strings before him.* Denotes one of unsettled firmness who allows the remediable ills in life to affect him. He gives way to worry, anxiety, and gloom without any real cause, for the solution is always at hand if he thinks a little-generally it is in himself. Let him exercise his will, and bring into action his fine understanding. Then will even an instrument with broken strings yield music. It is a symbol of Surrender.

♊ 28° *A number of workmen building a railway track through barren country.* Denotes one who through industry and prudence finds ways to aid himself over the greatest difficulties, and in aiding himself he confers lasting benefits on others. He approaches problems with determination and an understanding mind, and grapples until he firmly masters then. It is a symbol of Indefatigableness.

♊ 29° *A child blowing a steel glove from a cube of stone.* Denotes one of simplicity of character, gifted with magnetic fire and knowledge of the power of invisible forces. Against him aggression will avail nothing, and the aggressor will find that he himself is conquered. It is a symbol of Seership.

♊ 30° *A maiden bound to a stake smiling at an angel. Near-by lie three dead bats.* Denotes one who is forced by fate to meet many obstacles, dangers, and deceptions, and whose scope of action is limited and held within bounds. The life is a peculiar one, full of threatenings, dangers, strange feelings, incidents, and uncommon action. It is a symbol of Stumbling.

CANCER

♋ 1° *A curious ring set with a large heart of white onyx.* Denotes one of occult learning and of an extremely sensitive and sympathetic nature who will do much for the pleasure and help of the people. He is gifted with a peculiar power, which produces a feeling of calmness and serenity. He may not be free from his own worries, but the power to cast away such poison is his, and he will find that the rays of good he throws out for others will react with added force on himself. It is a symbol of COMPASSION.

♋ 2° *A labourer leaning against a tree watching a number of others digging in a neighboring field.* Denotes one who lets others do the work which he should do for himself. He is fond of the luxuries of life, but is quite content to receive without the toil of gaining them. He can advance his own philosophy to uphold his actions, and will be supported throughout his present life on earth. It is a symbol of INERTIA.

♋ 3° *A creeping plant, worms eating at the root, growing over a rustic summer-house.* Denotes one who inclines to a quiet and simple life away from the din and struggle of cities. Of a kind and trusting nature, he may leave his vital affairs too in the hands of others, and thus risk danger, trouble, and losses. He will be wise to look to his affairs and to those he trusts to attend to them. It is a symbol of ENTRUSTING.

♋ 4° *A drunken reveler in fancy costume asleep at a table, the contents of his overturned cup of red wine pouring on to the floor.* Denotes a romantic but erratic nature who leads himself to esteem the follies of the world before wisdom. In his pursuit of happiness he will find nothing but exhaustion and fatigue and emptiness. It is a symbol of MISDIRECTION.

♋ 5° *A man seated on a rock on a newly boomed goldfield, a new pick and shovel beside him, looking gloomily at a newspaper containing reports of rich finds in the locality.* Denotes one who takes too much notice of reports and who ventures before he has obtained enough evidence as to the nature of his speculations. This tendency, unless checked, leads him to a land of famine instead of a land of plenty. It is a symbol of PITFALLS.

♋ 6° *A man spending money lavishly entertaining his friends, a clown hidden behind a curtain laughing at him.* Denotes one to whom money comes, but who dissipates it, and falls into need again. He must control an extravagant tendency which can only bring him ephemeral friends and leave him but trouble and misery. It is a symbol of WASTEFULNESS.

♋ 7° *An antique, gold-capped Corinthian column of white marble, slightly crumbling at its base.* Denotes one who strives to stand erect. Time does not cast him down, for grandeur and beauty are his companions; but beauty, however sublime, is never without a flaw, for the flaw intensifies the beauty. The erect column indicates strength, the crumbling at the base fear, which alone can destroy if permitted to infect the whole. Where faith is, then fear will be never. True faith is knowledge absolute, and what knowledge so perfect as the consciousness in man of his own strength? It is a symbol of GRACEFULNESS.

♋ 8° *A newspaper editor at his desk-a mass of proofs before him-parleying with a man who averts his face.* Denotes one whose position in life will enable him to hold many secrets connected with the lives of others and who wields a power which will cause fear to many of position and reputation. A desire for material advantages may cause him to sway in the pursuit of his duty. It is a symbol of MUZZLING.

♋ 9°   *An acrobat performing before a large audience.* Denotes one who comes before the public and whose risky adventures secure him favor. He sees many changes in life, and has a hard struggle at times, but his energy and resourcefulness are great, and his spirits never fail. Great wealth will not fall to the native, but his life will not end for lack of means. It is a symbol of PUBLICITY.

♋ 10° *A painter at his easel in a graceful forest glade. It is the hour of sunset, and strange shadows of unearthly grandeur are falling.* Denotes one of much perseverance and artistic power, to whom the poetry of form and color appeal most magically. He has a love of quiet, and a rustic life will help to draw to his soul a wealth of inspiration and calm. His search is not for immortality, for this is old knowledge to him. He sees deeply into the imperishable paths, tasting of their everlasting grandeur. It is a symbol of SUBLIMITY.

♋ 11° *A number of maidens, crowned with garlands of wild flowers, dancing on a green lawn.* Denotes one of bright and joyous spirit and friendly nature whose desire it is to spread happiness and contentment wherever he goes. The native will always be much loved and popular. He comes to the world with a message of love, life, and hope, and a mind which resists the encroachments of evil. It is a symbol of SIMPLICITY.

♋ 12° *An avenue of trees bending before a destructive wind-storm, the rich golden leaves of autumn falling thickly.* Denotes one whose thoughts will be directed to securing a competency for himself in old age, and who will labor hard to accomplish his desire. His love of quiet is disturbed and outraged, and he will be shaken by storms as a tree in the wind. Still he fights on in gloom or sunshine, passing madness on the way. It is a symbol of BENDING.

♋ 13° *A volcano in active eruption devastating the country for miles around, whilst groups of peasants cling to their little homes.* Denotes one who is born to face danger and to indulge in undertakings of a venturesome nature which yield little profit and entail much trouble. He is rather fixed in his ideas, and may fail to fall in with the views of the majority. Neither will he attempt to escape when the storm is against him. It is a symbol of PERTINACITY.

♋ 14° *A crab climbing up an upright iron spear, above which is a circlet of seven stars.* Denotes one who, never daunted by obstacles, opposition, and hardship, will rise by his own effort to a position of dignity and importance in his special sphere. Uniting an iron will to stubbornness of purpose, the native proves his worth, and triumphs. It is a symbol of IRREFRAGABILITY.

♋ 15° *An auctioneer's hammer lying on a heap of gold money and bank-notes.* Denotes one who acts with craft and sagacity towards his point of attainment and who will ever struggle hard to hold what he gets. His attitude brings material gain, and his methods bring others under his influence. His life will not be without its disappointments, but he is not the man to yield to "set-backs." His philosophy is self preservation. It is a symbol of DISREGARDING.

♋ 16° *A young man standing on the top of a high mountain, the world stretched out below him, grasping a sword which comes from the heavens to his hand.* Denotes one who is entrusted with a high mission and who is deeply inspired, having a spirituality entirely serene. To him has the mandate "Co forth and teach the people" been echoed from the heavens. He will be granted power and influence, so that the people will hear him call. The evidences of this peculiar mission are made manifest in his twelfth year and mature between the twenty-fourth and thirty-sixth years. It is the symbol of the INSPIRED.

♋ 17° *A band of merchants on camels traveling through the wilderness.* Denotes a lover of traveling whose leanings are towards a nomadic life. He is, however, keenly alive to the necessity of material work, and he traffics in stuffs the sale of which is not confined to any one district or country. He will accumulate by or through merchandise, exporting and importing, or through things of universal demand. Sometimes indiscreet, sometimes hasty, the native is always self-possessed. It is a symbol of EXCHANGING.

♋ 18° *A hand grasping gold pieces, some of which are falling through the fingers.* Denotes one who is disposed to place too much value on material things, esteeming them as philosophy and learning, one who will make his days pay him, and who seeks to gain the wealth of the world by all legitimate means. His nature is somewhat hard; he regards his best friends, the friends of his pocket, hence does not know his truest friends at all. He will continue thus to the end of his earth days, when, as the Talmud has it, all that he has gained slips through his fingers. It is a symbol of MATERIALISM.

♋ 19° *An old man sitting alone in semi-darkness with an old book before him, from which emanate bright rays of light.* Denotes one whose whole life is devoted to finding out truth which gives him certainty beyond mere belief. He will never be daunted in his search, no matter how the storms drive round him. As the All-Divine Designer of the Grand Design draws his earth days to a close, he sees Darling of his pilgrimage face to face, and seeing knows. It is a symbol of ESSENTIALS.

♋ 20° *A wounded Bedouin mounted on his horse in the desert.* Denotes one of unsettled tendencies with a strong desire for freedom and liberty of movement who, brave, daring, and adventurous, is ever restless if held to one place for long. He is not well fitted for ordinary life, as his employment changes so much, and some of these changes will be sudden. His nature is willful, erratic, impulsive, and his body is marked naturally or by accident. It is a symbol of LIBERTY.

♋ 21° *A man having jumped over a fence falls into a ditch on the other side of it.* Denotes one who is over venturesome and liable to fall into grave mistakes and errors. He should be exceedingly careful of his conduct and endeavor by strength of will to moderate an impulsiveness which if allowed to grow will bring into form all the threatenings of this peculiar degree. Self-mastery and the forcing of self to obey the power of his spirit should be his chief care in life. It is a symbol of HASTINESS.

♋ 22° *A jeweled crown falling from a height into mud.* Denotes one whose life will have a powerful influence on the people-one who rises to power through no special virtue of his own and who as a consequence of a false education and evil impressions uses his influence badly, going down to a hopeless grave. It is a symbol of EXTINCTION.

♋ 23° *Fishermen pulling in their nets in calm weather.* Denotes one whose business in life is uncertain in its results, but who can calmly go on, contented to take whatever fate sends his way. He is gifted with mediumistic power and his impressions enable him to make but few mistakes in his affairs. It is a symbol of PEACEFULNESS.

♋ 24° *A graceful dancer smilingly receiving applause and floral tributes.* Denotes one of charming manners and graceful style, poetic and artistic, who will be a general favorite. He is fortunate in an artistic or professional career or any calling which brings him in direct touch with the public. The infant life is threatened and should be guarded. It is a symbol of PLEASING.

♋ 25° *The setting Sun reflected from the sea in such a manner that the reflected rays interlace with the solar rays.* Denotes a psychic readily absorbing the thoughts and suggestions of others. He should never permit himself to be hypnotized nor entranced, nor give way to negative states of mind or lowering thoughts. He must absorb noble teachings and eschew unworthy ones. Then as he reaches the latter part of his earth life glories will stream from his soul to unite with the lights of the heaven of aspiration. It is a symbol of IMPRESSIONS.

♋ 26° *A marksman having failed to hit the bull's-eye in eight shots strikes it in the ninth.* Denotes one of a persevering spirit who is not disposed to sink under failures be they ever so frequent, nor will argument turn his mind from a set purpose, for in his soul is the knowledge that success will come to him in the end. In his attempts he is orderly, never undertaking a new thing before he has finished that which he has in hand. It is a symbol of the UNDAUNTED.

♋ 27° *A moth circling a flame.* Denotes one who can be hypnotized by glitter and glare, power and show, and who takes risks which less impulsive people would shrink from. The will is too yielding and the love of pleasure too great. Let him remember that the moth which circles round the flame is ultimately drawn into it and consumed, and that the death of the moth does not trouble the flame. It is a symbol of GLITTER.

♋ 28° *An old mill-wheel lying on the bank of a lily pond, with pretty creepers growing over it.* Denotes one whose life will be peaceful and whose marriage will be blessed. His desires are simple and his talents are natural. He does not wish to rule in the world of men. His mental attitude and manner of living form a magnetic point of help and sympathy where the world-worn may have balm for their wounds. It is a symbol of CHARM.

♋ 29° *A man in a prison cell, a ray of light flowing through the bars, on which a little bird stands singing.* Denotes one liable to be bound soul and body, who will be restricted in action and desire. But even so he may yet release his true self and meet the force flowing from the fountain head. Thus, though one side may frown and obstruct him, the other will smile and release him. It is a symbol of OBSTRUCTION.

♋ 30° *A winged wheel flying across a green field.* Denotes one of character, force, and skill who by the hand of destiny will rise to a position in this world in which he is fitted to play a decided part. He has a keen imagination and considerable constructive ability. He gains from traveling and change. It is a symbol of CONTINUANCE.

LEO

♌ 1°   *A king stepping from his carriage receiving a document from a group of citizens.* Denotes one who will be enabled to grant or to refuse to grant the wishes of others. He will reach a position of importance and will receive many honors, and benefits will accrue to him. The demand is for an understanding of the use, not the abuse, of power. It is a symbol of AUTHORITY.

♌ 2°   *A roll of papers having dropped from the hand of a dying scholar is eagerly caught up by an eminent professor on whose face there is a look of triumph.* Denotes one whose early life is threatened and who in later years will gain possession of material secrets discovered by another which he has long sought to obtain. Having obtained them, he claims the discoveries as his own, gaining thus further professional advancement and reputation. His triumph may last till he breathes his last breath, then he will learn what in spite of all his learning he does not know, and his action of yesterday brings remorse on the morrow. It is a symbol of ARTIFICE.

♌ 3°   *A huge human head. From the left eye emanates a ray of black vapour, from the right a ray of yellow, and from the centre of the forehead a ray of white.* Denotes a remarkable personality who has an understanding of complex subjects. Rich, courted, and strong, he can regulate his forces for the blessing or bane of men. There is also an entirely occult side to this symbol which expresses the same meaning from a spiritual outlook. It is a symbol of LEADERSHIP.

♌ 4°   *An ambassador leaving the presence of a prince who is smiling significantly to his chancellor.* Denotes one who may be deceived by smiles and promises. He should be especially careful of those in power, and should be wary lest in negotiations he betrays his plans and aspirations to keen and subtle adversaries. Wisdom is in silence. It is a symbol of TREACHERY.

♌ 5° *A lawyer placing a document before a client, who signs it. His eyes are bandaged.* Denotes one who should be critically careful of attaching his name to papers and in putting absolute trust in interested advisers. In all writings, care should be taken if the native would save himself sorrow, suffering, and the results of impulsive action. He should look many times at a pen before he dips it in the ink. It is a symbol of COMPLICATIONS.

♌ 6° *A lion crouching in a jungle with a large bird of the eagle type in his mouth.* Denotes one who will be compelled to fight and struggle during a great part of his life and who will often have to use his ingenuity to release himself from entanglements and troubles. He may have financial difficulties or difficulties over property or estates. In the end-perhaps even in the midst of worry-his star rises and he triumphs over enemies and evil conditions. It is a symbol of STRATEGY.

♌ 7° *A book, on which is a crown, resting on a golden throne.* Denotes one who will by his own skill and ability receive and profit by impressions and reach a position which gains him the recognition due to him. To such, perseverance and faith are the essentials, and if he regards the meaning of these two words apart from the words themselves he will crown his labors with success. It is a symbol of FAME.

♌ 8° *Two lovers walking in a forest glade. Before them are two doves and a brilliantly coloured butterfly.* Denotes one of an idealistic and affectionate disposition whose poetic nature will at times put him out of touch with the world of men, its false ideas of justice, and its oceans of pain. Then should he "seek the forest lands for peace and heaven." He is himself a happy influence and generally he will be favored. Should the horoscope show marriage it will be a union of souls. It is a symbol of AFFECTION.

♌ 9° *A lady, elegantly dressed and bedecked with many jewels, standing before a mirror.* Denotes one fortunate, but some-what vain, whose desire it is "to make a good appearance' and who expends much money for this purpose. But the glories which shine forth from a great soul glitter more than the choicest diamond in the daintiest setting, giving a lasting beauty which age cannot change nor time obliterate. There are two sides to this symbol, and both reflect, for it is a symbol of REFLECTION.

♌ 10° *A soldier rescuing a wounded comrade on a field of battle-a dark, sinister figure rising behind him.* Denotes one of brave, fearless, and noble disposition whose natural greatness of soul is moved by the necessities of others, and who always puts the well-being of another before his own comforts. Envy is directed against him and malice turns her evil eyes on him. He will be exposed to many and grave dangers, for duty to him is ever the first thought. It is a symbol of DARING.

♌ 11° *A troop of old barbarian soldiers carrying off struggling women.* Denotes one over whom the wild senses strive for mastery, whose philosophy of force crumbles before what is truly real. The time may come when he will be forced to pause, when he will be made to see the uselessness of it all, and how strangely things are mirrored in the world of illusion. He must strive lest he become the slave of his lower self and the inducer of his own dangers. It is a symbol of INDULGENCE.

♌ 12° *A man of martial and distinguished bearing giving alms to the poor.* Denotes one of brave and generous disposition who is an earnest and sincere champion of the oppressed and who is one of that great band who cannot be deaf to the moans of the suffering many. He is a militant, generous force, and in his philosophy "charity covereth a multitude of sins." It is a symbol of HUMANITY.

♌ 13° *An old oak-tree over which shines the noonday sun in a clear sky.* Denotes one of rugged, conservative, and patriotic nature who will be blessed with the goods of the world and who will use his blessings well. His position in life will be distinguished and his sincerity will command respect even from his enemies. He carries about him a fine and pure aura which benefits all who come within its radiations. It is a symbol of EXALTATION.

♌ 14° *Two men tossing coins whilst another looks on.* Denotes one of a sporting nature whose instincts are keenly set on those things which the world is content to regard as chance happenings. The native will not be greatly interested in chance as a problem amenable to scientific treatment. He prefers to ever regard it as the absolute unknown and to let its solution be a matter of risk. It is a symbol of GAMING.

♌ 15° *A mass of black rock in the centre of which is a large diamond.* Denotes one who is forced to labor hard for the greater part of his life, but who contains within himself some brilliant gifts, one of which will progress and bring him into fame. It is a symbol of CREEPING.

♌ 16° *A pyramid in the midst of a sand waste, with lowering black clouds about it.* Denotes one who in the midst of threats, difficulties, and oppositions raises himself to a position of dignity and responsibility, and the stings of envy will follow him. He will see many pass through this world of matter before he receives the call, and will keenly feel and deplore his errors. He may find that the road to power is not the road to happiness. It is a symbol of VEXATION.

♌ 17° *An architect standing by a desk with the plans of a building before him.* Denotes one of understanding and power of purpose who is gifted with fine perception and a lively imagination. As a theorist he is generally correct in his deductions and he can quickly clothe his thoughts in material dress. It is a symbol of KNOWLEDGE.

♌ 18° *Two gold-miners seated near mining machinery examining a strange metal unknown to modern science, which they have found amongst the quartz.* Denotes one of a peculiar and original mind with a strong leaning towards the unraveling of the many mysteries of science. Entirely unorthodox in his methods of research, he is not likely to obtain recognition from book-drilled students, but people of true learning will always be attracted to him. The personality is double, and he is able to carry on two lines of investigation at the same time. It is a symbol of INTROSPECTION.

♌ 19° *A giant holding a number of bleeding hearts pierced on his sword.* Denotes a man of compelling will and magnetic force who stops at nothing to carry out his ambitions. He rises to power through blood or tears or both. He wields and binds, and those whom he binds will bleed, for his work is the work of materialistic pride which dissolves in the fires of hate. It is a symbol of COMPULSION.

♌ 20° *A violin and bow lying on some sheets of music.* Denotes one of a refined and harmonious nature, skilful in one of the entertaining arts, and a psychic of some ability. He is gifted as a composer either of music or some allied art. It is a symbol of REFINEMENT.

♌ 21° *A man in the robes of a magician tracing mystic signs on the sands of the seashore in the silence of night.* Denotes one of mystical mind who is attracted to the ritualistic and ceremonial. The mind is capable of serious thought, seeing miracles in actions which to others seem quite commonplace. With him romance, poetry, and wonderment travel. It is a symbol of MYSTICISM.

♌ 22° *A man carrying a bird in a golden cage.* Denotes one who is in danger of being held in restraint of some kind and of being moved to different places at the will of others. There is no suggestion of unkind treatment, but there is that the native is not a free agent. He should never permit others to gain an influence over him in any way. He is very mediumistic, but can be controlled from the visible as he can from the invisible. It is a symbol of RESTRICTION.

♌ 23° *A trumpet made from a ram's horn bathed in the sun's rays.* Denotes a rouser of men, one destined for action, who will bring light and benefit to mankind. His way will not be without its roughness, and many times he will be weary. Then the sound of the horn will rouse him to an understanding of his work and he will see the light. It is a symbol of INCITEMENT.

♌ 24° *An old rusty sword, over which grass is growing, outside a rustic cottage.* Denotes one who, after struggling and fighting to gain ascendancy in the world of illusion, realizes in his later life the futility of it all, and throwing away his aggressive sword he retires to a life of peace and simplicity, whilst the sword rots to decay and the tender grass covers it as the flowers over a grave. It is a symbol of RENUNCIATION.

♌ 25° *A poet reading his verses to a group of ladies in an old castle garden.* Denotes one whose influence will be ideal and cultivating, and who, notwithstanding his simplicity of character, is not without a degree of pride. This alloy but serves to show the points of artistic excellence, and will not prejudice him if kept within bounds. It is a symbol of PROPORTION.

♌ 26° *Two hands clasped under a floral crown.* Denotes one talented, poetic, and scientific who gains much through the quiet influence of helpful friends. He himself is true and peaceful. He dislikes quarrels and disturbed conditions. He is considerate in his dealings with others, and can be relied on to keep a secret. It is a symbol of COMRADESHIP.

♌ 27° *A bleeding hand holding a thorny orange branch on which the fruit is growing.* Denotes one who will be compelled to gain experience through suffering, losses, and deceit. He is sincere and affectionate, and will sacrifice much to help another. He is aided, patronized, and advanced, and from his former sufferings his fame springs. It is a symbol of APPROVAL.

♌ 28° *A stream of oil falling from mid-air upon the troubled waters beneath.* Denotes one who will exercise discrimination in the affairs of daily life; one who will possess tact, understanding, and diplomacy, and a peculiar magnetic aura which enables him to bring quarrelling units to a peaceful union. It is a symbol of CONCILIATION.

♌ 29° *A man climbing a ladder and helping others who strive be-hind him. At the top, a veiled figure holds out to him a wreath of stars.* Denotes one who has power enough to rise in the world and heart enough to help others to rise. His destiny is to rise. It is his soul of sympathy and justice which merits the victor's wreath, and his every action of kindness to the struggling and to the suffering brings to him blessings of power, adding heavenly glory to the rewards awaiting him. It is a symbol of REWARDING.

♌ 30° *A ship's steward carrying a bowl of enchanting white lilies.* Denotes a changeable person, loving to journey about. He gains much benefit from ships, shipping, means of transit, and the public. While on a journey he meets his greatest happiness. He is generally fortunate with his friends and in all his affairs of life. It is a symbol of VOYAGING.

VIRGO

♍ 1° *A traveling pilgrim leaning on his staff, which he holds in his left hand, addressing a small band of men & women.* Denotes one whose early life is threatened by the elements and who will be compelled to endure sufferings, hardships, and trials as an atonement for remote past acts. If his destiny is to live, his destiny is to overcome, and he will be a wise instructor and guide to his fellow-men. It is a symbol of REPAYING.

♍ 2° *A waning moon in a sky, half of which is clear and studded with stars, and half of which is covered with dark clouds which herald an approaching storm.* Denotes one of considerable ability who, as his life grows older, will be plunged into difficulties and trouble. It is well for one born in this degree to study his actions and to be scrupulously cautious as to his plans and movements. He should avoid speculative ventures, guard against deceit and treachery, and do all that is possible to lead an even, temperate life. It is a symbol of THREATENINGS.

♍ 3° *A young woman working at a spinning-wheel by a cottage window, which opens on a smiling garden in which bees are flying amongst the flowers.* Denotes one who is gifted with a sunny nature, patience, and the ability to labor hard and to endure. He will produce works of benefit and charm, and experience will expand his soul and teach him the truth which he values as a companion to beauty. It is a symbol of PERSISTENCY.

♍ 4° *A bookbinder fastening covers on a number of unbound books.* Denotes one who spreads knowledge of some special nature whose position in life will be one of trust and responsibility. His mind is analytical and exact, and his actions are regulated by necessity and the acts of others. "Safe bind, safe find," is his motto, and carelessness does not enter into his nature. It is a symbol of PROTECTING.

♍ 5° *An artist working at a large piece of tapestry of charming design, which he has almost completed.* Denotes one of a constructive and artistic mind, a lover of art, and quaint but picturesque philosophies; one who perceives the exquisite loveliness of an old garden, a moss-covered wall, a running brook, and nature's changing moods, and who is attracted to old-world lores. It is a symbol of CONSERVATISM.

♍ 6° *A large ballroom in which men and women are dancing.* Denotes one of light and free mind who allows nothing to oppress him. He meets with favors and enjoys gifts. He loves the beautiful in form and color. Scents and perfumes fascinate him. It is a symbol of ELEGANCE.

♍ 7° *A man in ceremonial robes, with a circlet about his brow, holding the emblem of life—the Crux ansata—in the air.* Denotes one who finds in the philosophies of the ancient masters the true knowledge of life, whose search for the truth is rewarded, and who, an consequence of his dread of doing wrong, has the power of drawing the greatness of right towards him. It is a symbol of PHILOSOPHY.

♍ 8° *A man, holding a pen in his right hand and a sword in his left, standing at the entrance to a palace.* Denotes one of forceful and aggressive mind who presses onwards with energy and determination. His assertiveness will not easily be opposed, and in all his dealings with others he demands the answer to be "Yes" or "No," for to his mind there is no middle course. He will draw to himself great responsibilities and will ever be involved in argument and dispute. It is a symbol of ASSERTION.

♍ 9° *A sack of corn, from a hole in which the grain is falling out.* Denotes one who through neglect and want of caution is likely to risk too much. To him speculation and gambling will only mean gradual ruin. He should be careful of his associations and dealings with other people, of his business transactions, and his manner of life. It is a symbol of CARELESSNESS.

♍ 10° *A sibyl in a cave, seated on a tripod beneath which is a cloud of smoke. The leaves of fate are flying into the open air through the mouth of the cavern.* Denotes one of a fatalistic mind who sees in the operations of nature, the actions of men, the habits of animals, and the growth of plants the direct manifestations of the Divine Mind; and who holds that what is laid down must ever be, for the Will of God cannot be changed, and man and nature are but allies in the fulfillment of it. It is a symbol of FATALISM.

♍ 11° *A king, seated in a chariot drawn by two stags, throwing coins to some peasants who are singing on the roadside.* Denotes one who is born to honor and who will be esteemed for his goodness of heart and appreciation of effort. The position he gains by perseverance will enable him to do well for the world in many ways. He receives more than he gives, and for all he gives he receives blessings which carry to him a strong and subtle spiritual force which clings to him for eternity, whilst what he has given mixes with the elements. It is a symbol of CHARITY.

♍ 12° *A horseman holding with difficulty a rearing horse.* Denotes one who is drawn into rash ventures and who will be forced to work hard to save those things truly his own. He may be too dependent on his strength, which he overtaxes, or on his resources, which he overstrains. The rising planet contains the warning. It is a symbol of GRAPPLING.

♍ 13° *A large black cloud, around which are bright silver lights.* Denotes one who will endure much sorrow and strange experiences. He is well and strangely gifted, and will leave his mark on the world. He should be cautious in his choice of companions, and should not allow fading, falling allurement, to threaten him on the way. It is a symbol of TRIBULATION.

♍ 14° *A torn document, old and crinkled, on which is a large black seal.* Denotes one a conservative and old-world mind who talks little, but to the point. He will be out of touch with modem society, leaning neither to their teachings nor ideals. He will have struggles and hard climbs, and does not think enough of possessions ever to become wealthy. He holds what he possesses and lives quietly. It is a symbol of CONSCIENTIOUSNESS.

♍ 15° *A radiant rainbow, in the centre of which is the sun in its brightness.* Denotes a lover of nature in her grandeur, one of artistic, mystic, and philosophic mind, who will move about a great deal and travel to various places. He is capable of spreading the light of truth and of helping many to see and appreciate its marvels. This degree is a fortunate one and promises much. It is a symbol of ARISING.

♍ 16° *A fire emitting flames of beautiful colour-blends.* Denotes a thinker of thoughts, but slightly regarded by the mass of present-day earth men, who seeks for right, feeling the silent appeal of beauty and the cry of oppressed humanity. His is a deep, sensitive nature-poetic, romantic, and full of action. It is a symbol of LUMINOSITY.

♍ 17°   *An astrologer seated at a desk, his head resting on his left hand, judging a nativity.* Denotes a student of the prophetic and curious arts who will command respect, one of skilled judgment and dignified bearing, devoid of pride and littleness. He will prove a trusted guide, especially to the masses, from whom he benefits. It is a symbol of FOREKNOWING.

♍ 18°   *A man, supporting a little girl, swimming towards the shore in a rough sea.* Denotes one whose mission it is to serve his fellow-men. He will perform acts which will win him approval and honor. Life will not be always smooth with him, and he will have his part of sorrow and pain in this world of matter; but ever near him are the protecting forces, and he cannot fail, no matter how fierce the waves. It is a symbol of SERVING.

♍ 19°   *A rough fire mountain, from several parts of which smoke is rising. On one of the slopes laborers are working.* Denotes one who exercises patience and persistence in his life's work, and whose position is oft attended with much worry and personal danger. His soul is full of enterprise. He is magnetic, psychic, and extremely active. It is a symbol of ENDEAVOR.

♍ 20°   *A great grey warship with her decks cleared ready for action.* Denotes one of pugnacious nature who forces his demands and ideas by sheer power of mind. He has strong magnetic force and knows when to use it. He travels much in search of adventure and gain, and holds the fruits of his labors. It is a symbol of PURPOSE.

♍ 21°   *A man burning a will as he triumphantly looks towards an-*

other lying on a table. Denotes one of resourcefulness and determination who can be trusted to protect and safeguard his vital interests. Others, perhaps even amongst his own kinsmen, may interfere or attempt to interfere with the liberty of the native and prevent his free actions, and he may have to use craft to protect his rights and himself. It is a symbol of FINESSE.

♍ 22° *Nymphs and fauns in the midst of Bacchanalian orgies in the woods.* Denotes one of an artistic and sensuous nature who may be misled by the allurement of passion and desire. He is always a true friend, but may put his trust in the hands of those who are unworthy to hold it. He should be careful lest the awakening brings suffering. Under certain horoscopical conditions this degree can denote one of an entirely opposite nature, but with it there is always some degree of binding. It is a symbol of SEDUCTION.

♍ 23 ° *The Virgin Astraea, with bandaged eyes, being led away by the angels from the world flooded with blood, misery, injustice, and crime.* Denotes one of a refined and sweet nature who keenly feels the wickedness of this wrongly taught world, which would be God's own paradise were men fair and kind to one another. The native should not allow others to lead him into speculation or any form of gambling or chance. He is ideal in thought, and seer enough to see what might have been. It is a symbol of SYMPATHY.

♍ 24° *A colossal giant holding a woman in his hand.* Denotes one who may become vain of his earthly power and may use it for purposes which can be of no real benefit to him and no real gratification. Suffering may force him to hold himself in check and to understand that" he who conquers himself is greater than he who conquers a kingdom." It is a symbol of VIOLENCE.

♍ 25° *A man, from whose forehead streams a dazzling white light, passing through a fiery valley, at the end of which are beautiful lawns, flowers, and trees bathed in brilliant sunlight.* Denotes one of an affectionate, hopeful, and sincere nature who endeavors to do by love alone what others are attempting to do by force. Gifted with a will of strength, he is able to resist and subdue all the demons which rise against him; thus is his spiritual nature uplifted, and he is inspired and helped from occult sources. He will have struggles in life and difficulties which seem insurmountable, but he knows he will overcome them, and he overcomes them all, for they are but sent to teach him what world-life is and what it may be. It is a symbol of OVERCOMING.

♍ 26° *An antique temple of the Muses built on a rock, over which flows an enchanting fall of clear sparkling water.* Denotes one who would seek the ideal in all things, even amidst the hell of war and the fires of destruction. One of a strange, happy, though wise philosophy of thought. He is a votary of art, music, culture, and all uplifting studies. It is a symbol of CULTIVATION.

♍ 27° *A newspaper critic seated in a theater watching a performance.* Denotes one of a quick and critical mind who is gifted with powers of observation and discrimination He is able to turn points to his advantage, and does not hesitate to push forward with energy and activity to gain his desires. It is a symbol of KEENNESS.

♍ 28° *A gang of stevedores loading a vessel with product.* Denotes one who works hard and denies himself much. He is

entrusted with delicate missions and satisfactory commis-
sions. Work to him is prayer, and he never grumbles at its
demands. It is a symbol of LABOR.

♍ 29° *A crescent moon shining with especial brightness in a blue, star-crowded sky.* Denotes one of some especial genius and extremely artistic who is restless under restraint and who loves to roam about. He roams for a purpose and not for idle pleasure, for this native never idles. He has great faith and obtains recognition and success. It is a symbol of BRIGHTNESS.

♍ 30° *A heap of bright yellow oranges blown from the tree by the wind.* Denotes one who suffers much deceit and whose hopes are threatened. Himself of a sincere and spiritual nature, he dislike, to find fault with the actions of others, and he goes his own way whether they hurt him or no. Fate is strong in his life, and he is forced by circumstances to accept its ruling. It is a symbol of CIRCUMSTANCES.

LIBRA

♎ 1° *A lion with his paw upon a heart, above a square.* Denotes one of a highly magnetic and affectionate disposition combined with mental firmness and endurance. The life will be filled with strange happenings, obstacles, and sorrows. The affairs of his heart bring bitterness, but sweetness may come from pain. It is a symbol of THWARTING.

♎ 2° *A gold-covered book, on which is cut a Crux ansata crowned, floating in the misty air.* Denotes one of psychic understanding, peculiar knowledge, and inspiration, who will produce work of use or distinct beauty. Particularly is his understanding directed to certain knowledge of the continuity of life, especially as regards individual existence. Within himself rages the eternal contest between spirit and matter. At one time matter is triumphant, at another spirit, but spirit will gain in the end. It is a symbol of FORESEEING.

♎ 3° *A young girl striving to escape from immaterial, but visible cords which surround her; the more she struggles the more they increase.* Denotes one who is in danger of being drawn into psychic conditions from which escape is difficult. Such a one should refrain from dabbling in matters he does not thoroughly understand. Danger in connection with occult or psychic matters is threatened and much suffering there from. Love affairs may embarrass, especially if intertwined with occult practices. The native will be gifted in some branch of art or science, but there is a peculiar force fighting against his success and against which a calm placidity is the only protection. It is a symbol of INVOLVING.

♎ 4°   *A broken wedding-ring lying on a table.* Denotes one whose path will be filled with bitterness, whose affections are enduring, but lacking in the principle of true love. He is fated to suffer in order to attain development and mind expansion, for his mistakes are many. The experiences of the native will force him to understand the purpose of life. It is a symbol of ISOLATION.

♎ 5°   *A naked arm and hand, from which blood is flowing. Above, a sword.* Denotes one who attains influence and a degree of power through aggression, forcefulness, and fighting. He is of an adventurous nature and endures a wound for the glory of getting it and the honor it gains him, and he will have many wounds. It is a symbol of ENCROACHMENT.

♎ 6°   *A traction engine traveling along a newly made road in very charming country.* Denotes one of an artistic nature and a plodding but powerful disposition who is called to do work of a pioneering nature. He is an advocate of force, and the discipline with which he has been bended he would use on others. It is a symbol PIONEERING.

♎ 7°   *A winged globe on the back of a sporting dolphin.* Denotes one with a great message who will travel everywhere and whose thoughts and feelings are expanded and uplifted thereby. His wanderings are often directed beyond this earth to the heavenly fields and, to the lands dosed to those held in material bodies. He is capable of performing many good acts for others and is ever ready to resist actions unworthy of a true man, holding meanness in contempt. It is a symbol of MOVEMENT.

♎ 8°   *A group of people standing dejectedly outside the closed doors of a big financial institution.* Denotes one who will have need to exercise very great caution as to the safe keeping of his worldly possessions. Such a one should keep away from speculations, ventures, and crafty people, and undertake nothing of a nature involving risk. It is a symbol of FORFEITING.

♎ 9° *A large pair of scales. Two men quarreling behind.* Denotes one who should avoid law and disputes. Inharmony is to him a state of evil which forces him into a groove of fate and holds him in bondage. He should endeavor by the power of his soul to keep the scales even and do nothing to prejudice his peace. It is a symbol of UNEVENNESS.

♎ 10° *An old hermit, in a cave, grasping a crucifix.* Denotes one of a conservative and religious mind who is drawn towards solitude. He has many troubles, and endures mortification and suffering, but he directs his thoughts to the grand ideal which materializes as life advances, and this to is happiness. It is a symbol of SOLITUDE.

♎ 11° *A crow with a large rat in its beak.* Denotes one who is liable to be assailed by enemies, but who, being conscious of his own strength, is content to wait patiently until by frequent attacks they fall at last into his power. He is gifted with patience and sagacity, understanding and diplomacy. It is a symbol of DEFIANCE.

♎ 12° *A man falling from an insecure and broken bridge into a dark pit below.* Denotes one who will suffer chiefly from a lack of confidence in self and ability to realize his own powers and limitations. Evils may assail his health or financial position, and place him in positions of danger from which he can only escape by the power of a resisting will. It is a symbol of TIMIDITY.

♎ 13° *A woman in a dark blue costume entering a convent door; her head is erect, her arms raised, and she heeds not a handsome cavalier who is offering her fruits and flowers.* Denotes one of a refined and highly sensitive nature, religious and disposed to self-immolation. He will be blessed with worldly gifts, but will in the midway of his life know how really weak worldly wealth is, and how impotent to satisfy the cravings of the spirit. It is a symbol of ABDICATION.

♎ 14° *A brilliantly plumaged peacock strutting towards a wall, behind which are two men unwinding a net.* Denotes one who if not born into worldly wealth will obtain it in another way. He will have much "good luck" and in consequence will feel unduly elated and proud. Then is it that danger is near. He may be snared into a false investment and lose in a night all he has gained in years. It is a symbol of SNARING.

♎ 15° *A man who has just left the banquet table in a dazed condition, holding his hand to his head as if trying to remember something.* Denotes one who is too psychic for strong drink and strong food, which throw him off his balance and injure the fine machinery of his extremely sensitive brain. It is when hurt by any form of overindulgence that he renders himself liable to obsession or evil suggestion. If he resists these evils his gifts will manifest and bring him honor. It is a symbol of OBSESSION.

♎ 16° *A large hole out of which gases are rising. A number of birds seeking to cross are overcome by the fumes and are falling into the gap, over which only one has passed safely.* Denotes one who will take many risks and expose himself to needless dangers. He should be especially careful when near subtile substances, gases, poisons, etc., and should always strive prevent others obtaining an undue influence him. Many traveling with him will fall by way, being ignorant of approaching dangers, he will perceive-let him regard his perception. It is a symbol of SUBTILTY.

♎ 17° *A beautifully formed foot rising from a haze of colour-waves.* Denotes one artistic, thoughtful, and able, an idealist of a highly sensuous nature whose it is to blend material thought with spiritual understanding, who perceives that beauty of form must melt into the sublimity of spirit. He will have powers as an inventor, for his inspirations are of a highly utilitarian nature, despite the Neptunian flights to which they ascend. It is a symbol of SENSIBILITY.

♎ 18° *A fireman rescuing a little child from a burning house.* Denotes one of a simple nature who is gifted with a strong spirit of self-sacrifice and endowed with inherent bravery. His way in life will be tangled at times, and he will need his energy to set it right again. He is a helper of himself and of others, and he does not count his own needs first. It is a symbol of SELF-SACRIFICE.

♎ 19° *A lion rising from the blood of a wounded soldier.* Denotes one of powerful and active mind and magical knowledge who knows the extent of his own force and ability, and, knowing it, he concentrates and suffers to give birth to an ideal of strength and nobleness combined-a strength and nobleness fitted to govern men and to demonstrate even to the weak that the concretion of abilities is the key to individual greatness. It is a symbol of MASTERY.

♎ 20° *A young girl amidst the flowers in the sunlight wearing a garland of roses and weaving others.* Denotes one to whom natural beauty offers the strongest appeal, whose happiness is in simple things, in art, literature, and science. Pleasure claims him only when pleasure is connected with the artistic. He can keep a secret better than he can keep his money and possessions, and he must be careful lest he be led into extravagances which can never appeal to his plain philosophy. It is a symbol of GENTLENESS.

♎ 21° *A flashily dressed woman singing, with a glass of wine raised in her right hand. On one side of her is the spirit of Mirth, on the other the spirit of Sorrow.* Denotes one who is liable to be led astray by externalities, who grasps at the shadow and misses the substance. Ornaments and the things which gratify the demanding senses only allure, but never satisfy, the continued demand for more. If in the government of himself he does not employ care and intelligence, he will find himself stung by a serpent, and the wound can never be healed. It is a symbol of RETRIBUTION.

♎ 22° *A youth searching for a jeweled ring which he has on his finger.* Denotes one who will waste time which, if he uses his mind and senses, he can save. He will be fairly favored by fortune, will possess a dainty mind with an appreciation for all that is enlightening and charming, but there is a danger of negligence and lack of caution which will hurt him if he lets it. It is a symbol of THOUGHTLESSNESS.

♎ 23° *A pair of compasses lying on a map of the world.* Denotes one whose business will demand movement and journeying. The native is a lover of ill traveling, for with him the rolling stone does gather moss and the still one but stagnation. He is a traveler and a searcher, seeking to know, not only this world, but that great beyond into which he also travels when sleep holds his mortal body. It is a symbol of OUTREACHING.

♎ 24° *A whirlwind scattering a mass of papers into the air.* Denotes one who will suffer from an overconfident nature that neglects those details which, insignificant as they may appear, are as necessary for the safeguarding of his interests as water is to earth. His mentality is good, and he is capable of useful mental work, but he may lose the results of his labor. and suffer thereby in many ways. It is a symbol of ENTRAPPING.

♎ 25° *A woman naked standing on a crescent moon, the stars glittering behind her in a sky of blue.* Denotes an attractive person who is in danger of being held in the chains of sense and at the will of others. His nature is impulsive and artistic, restless and pleasure-loving. His desires are strong and may run riot with his reason. There is a leaning to the artificial, the theatre, and the dance, and a very sensuous love of earth life. It is a symbol of VACILLATION.

♎ 26° *A successful candidate for Parliament addressing the people after an election.* Denotes one who will gain from the masses. He is subtle, diplomatic, and capable of handling subjects from different view-points and in adhering to that interpretation which the majority believe to be correct. His philosophy teaches him to subordinate his ideas to the wills of those whose cause he champions. It is a symbol of DIPLOMACY.

♎ 27° *The moon throwing its beams on a little bush hut amidst forest trees. A storm has just passed.* Denotes one who if saved from malefic planetary action is contented with little and is pleasant and kind to men and animals. His nature is devotional and sensitive, and is capable of obtaining knowledge from astral sources and atmospheric conditions. He influences others for good, spreading content in the halls of inharmony. It is a symbol of HARMONY.

♎ 28° *A mass of quartz through which veins of fine gold can be traced.* Denotes one to whom bard work appears to be the only thing worth while in this world, and who carries out his belief with himself as subject. He is conservative in his ideas and fights to uphold the landmarks of the fathers. It is a symbol of EXERTION.

♎ 29° *An eclipse of the sun.* Denotes one who will have to be guarded in his dealings. With financial affairs great caution is necessary, for losses may occur of a serious nature, involving the native in much responsibility. He should never become surety for others, and should endeavor to realize himself and hold his earthly possession. Death will make inroads into his family circles and amongst near friends. It is a symbol of FADING.

♎ 30° *A boy moping over his book in a schoolroom.* Denotes one who will have to wake up else he will be elbowed out of everything by others more vigorous. He is possessed of good mental qualities, is well-mannered and good-natured, but he allows others to take advantage of him, and he will suffer from deceit and unfairness. It is a symbol of SLUGGISHNESS.

SCORPIO

♏ 1°   *A man, enraged, tearing a book in pieces.* Denotes one of a passionate and determined nature. The personality is forceful and magnetic, but there is a lack of those fine feelings which render life something greater than a mere mass of disruption. It is difficult for the native to discipline and control himself, but his will is strong, and what is a fractious horse to a determined master! It is a symbol of IRRITATION.

♏ 2°   *Two men deeply engrossed in a game of chess.* Denotes one of excellent and discriminative brain who is capable of firm and continued concentration. The mind is intensely mercurial and penetrative, mastering difficult problems with comparative ease. It is a symbol of COMPREHENSION.

♏ 3°   *Blacksmith striking anvil, the impact causing a dazzling display of bright light.* Denotes one who strives to bring the light of truth into a world of darkness. It is not enough for him gradually to secure acknowledgments- individual minds won over, whilst useful, are not what he most desires. He must arouse the masses from their sleep, and the blow he strikes on inert materialism will bring into action a light more brilliant than the stars. It is a symbol of PENETRATION.

♏ 4°   *Sword maker tempering a sword.* Denotes one of skilful mind and aggressive nature who desires to rise in life and lead, but who recognizes the need of careful preparation and planning before he ventures out. When fortified, he uses his inborn nature and tact, making sure his weapons are keen and capable. It is a symbol of PREPAREDNESS.

♏ 5°   *An ancient temple from which shoot forth forks of electricity.*

Denotes one singularly gifted and of great power of observation who has ability to turn even the thoughts of old-world philosophies into forms of materialistic triumph. He is disposed to regard the thoughts of men and to ponder over, consider, and utilize what most people would cast aside as useless. Failures do not daunt his spirit, for he knows that success comes from repeated failures. He "attempts the end and does not stand to doubt." It is a symbol of ACHIEVEMENT.

♏ 6° *An eagle with a snake in its beak.* Denotes a forceful, determined character who will not be easily imposed on. A hater of deceit and mean actions, he silences the deception by crushing the deceiver. With himself he is continually at war, being swayed by two emotions, one uplifting, the other degrading. What he wishes to remain in mastery will remain. It is a symbol of WATCHFULNESS.

♏ 7° *A winged horse flying over a fortress.* Denotes one whose destiny is to triumph over mere material force. One of great spirit, who will be enabled to demonstrate how much grander and how much more uplifting are the applied thoughts of man than the crude assertions and denials of materialism, no matter in what garb it may appear. His nature is free, his thoughts are free, and he desires to see all men aspire to true freedom and understanding. It is a symbol of RAISING.

♏ 8° *A bundle of papers floating down a dark winding river under a starlit sky.* Denotes one whose object is to gain knowledge and who strives hard to attain his desires. In his dealings with others he holds the thought uppermost, and endeavors to turn the light of his acquirements on to material things. He has the ability to make his work on earth interesting and popular. He gains by deaths and certain work with others, but happiness will not be his so long as he holds the false light of materialism before his eyes. His happiness is in the ideal, the true and only real. It is a symbol of EAGERNESS.

♏ 9°   *An ancient Hellenistic warship lying on the seashore.* Denotes one to whom ancient lore, poetry, and life strongly appeal, and whose soul goes back to those old days often in thought, often in sleep. But his nature is more positive than negative, and he can exhibit an aggressive or warlike front. He would do well to yield to his artistic nature and not allow the rustling of the wind to disturb his higher dreams. Let him let war rest like the old ship of the Greeks in the symbol, for the cruel days of war are passing. It is a symbol of ANTIQUENESS.

♏ 10° *A revolving star which throws off many colors and shades of color.* Denotes one capable of receiving, translating, and presenting many shades of opinion, chiefly as regards philosophies or sciences with which he is identified. He is unorthodox in thought, but reasonable, desiring not to condemn, but rather to enlighten, others. He may travel a great deal, but money does not cling to him, and he must avoid risks of all sorts. His wealth is in himself. It is a symbol of DISCRIMINATION.

♏ 11° *Pretty little flowers growing on an old moss covered wall in an old green country lane.* Denotes one poetical, intense, conservative, imaginative, idealistic, and artistic, one for whom simple beauty has a lasting and long appeal. His thoughts are above the narrow limits of form, creed, and custom, and his actions are marked by gentleness and feeling. The scientific vein in his nature is nurtured with the blood of Uranian science, and he is held but little to the wilder theories of some modern materialistic speculations. Whatever he handles must be dainty, sweet, and artistic. He loves children, flowers, the country, and all those things which lend grace and charm to earth life. It is a symbol of SERENITY.

♏ 12° *A galvanic battery resting on a rust iron stand.* Denotes one of a strange and sensitive temperament occult, thoughtful, and original. One who, like the battery in the symbol, will give shocks to many. He will have peculiarities and eccentricities, and will not be altogether easy to pull with, not that his temper is unkind, but that his vibrations are so fervent and his emotions so powerful. He is disposed to austerities and rigid rules of living which greatly influence others. It is a symbol of IMMOLATION.

♏ 13° *Water bubbling over rocks and flowing into a large river.* Denotes one whose work is destined to live and influence men long after he has left the earth, one of an intensely psychic nature, sensitive, and mediumistic. He will have many earthly struggles and will find many sharp rocks in the way of his progress. He suffers more from his absolute lack of sympathy with earth matters as they are at present. His wanderings in the summer lands, however, bring him infinite peace and joy in the midst of pain. It is a symbol of REVERIES.

♏ 14° *A lad pouring water into a sieve instead of a large jug and watching two others fighting.* Denotes one whose mind is disposed to wander to be distracted by the events of the moment. He needs to concentrate and to fight against the scattering of his thoughts. Ability he has, and can do well enough if he attends to one thing at a time. The tendency is to lose by carelessness what he earns by labor. It is a symbol of DISTRACTION.

♏ 15° *A large ship ashore on an ironstone coast, waves dashing over her.* Denotes one disposed to travel and to delight in adventure and change. He has a vigorous personality, but is inclined to take from others more he is willing to give. He will possibly attain a position, and his influence will sway many, it let him learn when to fall back into a more peaceful life, else will the great ship be cast on a dangerous coast by reason of strange influences, and disaster will be the end. It is a symbol of CONFLICT.

♏ 16° *An ancient warrior on his knees, with a cross-sword stuck in the ground before him, praying.* Denotes one who is mixed up in life's battles and fights for every advantage. Gifted with endurance and a penetrative mind, he wins his way through obstacles only to meet more obstacles later on. But he knows, for all this, that the Power sustaining him is faithful, and he prays for peace in the midst of war. It is a symbol of CONTRITION.

♏ 17° *A dagger with a jeweled hilt, stuck in a document.* Denotes peculiar birth conditions, but a gifted person who, though threatened with danger, overcomes and produces worthy works. His powerful and energetic soul is blended with idealism, poetry, and beauty. There is firmness in all he does, and a power which gives it penetrative force and excellence. It is a symbol of ROMANCE.

♏ 18° *A ballet dancer who has just left the stage talking to some men who are flattering her.* Denotes one for whom pleasure hides danger. His passions are high and not easy to control, and his appetites tend to follow his desires. There is a love of grace in art, movement, and sound which impels him to excitement and sensation. He attempts to influence and control, but is liable to be deceived himself in the end. Let him be warned. It is a symbol of INFLAMING.

♏ 19° *A woman flashily dressed and adorned with rings, bracelets, and numerous glittering jewels, looking with longing eyes in a jeweler's window.* Denotes one who is allured by the glitter of earth as a moth is by the lamp glare. He finds it hard to satisfy the yearning desire to possess and still possess, like one of abnormal hunger who is never satisfied. Let him take care lest this craze grasp him body and soul, and grasping him makes him the slave-victim of his passions. It is a symbol of RETROGRADING.

♏ 20° *A handsome boy, climbing up a ladder, looking upwards to the heavens.* Denotes one especially favored and of magnetic personality who raises himself by his own efforts and indomitable mind. He gains by right, scorning base and unworthy actions, and gains in spite of obstacles which are raised against him. He brings to others pleasure and help. It is a symbol of DETERMINATION.

♏ 21° *A double headed giant, in his right hand a club, in his left a tree, roots and foliage.* Denotes one who conceives the dualistic nature of man. He holds that the connexion of spirit and matter is the initial force from which all other forces are brought into being. He admits no intermediate force, pressing home his beliefs with all the certainty of proven facts and with all the vehemence his powerful nature is capable of. It is a symbol of FORCING.

♏ 22° *A tax gatherer demanding dues from a poor poet.* Denotes one who is forced by circumstances to undertake duties which are not always of a pleasant nature. His destiny is to adjust and to demand, and the necessities of his life are opposed to investigations of an ideal or psychic character.

It is a symbol of GATHERING.

♏ 23° *A man blowing bubbles, a ledger at his feet.* Denotes one who is in danger of being misguided and led into undertakings which can only result in failure and regret. Should he attempt to initiate any scheme himself, he will feel the mortification of seeing his hopes shattered. He should be content to take no risks. It is a symbol of UNCERTAINTIES.

♏ 24° *A wearied traveler on a wet dusty road obtaining a drink of water from a peasant girl.* Denotes one who gives and receives, who loves a roving life, and faces trials and hardships. But no matter how hard the road may be protection comes before the journey's end. It is a symbol of RECIPROCITY.

♏ 25° *A moneylender counting his gains in front of a safe crowded with valuables.* Denotes one who is lost in the maze of worldly gain and whose sole happiness is in his ever-increasing wealth. His nature is hard and his estimate of his fellow-creatures is judged by his own standard. His motto is: Treat every man as a rogue until you find him out to be honest, and when you find him out to be honest, think again before you trust him. It is a symbol of HARDNESS.

♏ 26° *A pretty little bird standing on the back of a lion, singing.* Denotes one of charming fancy, a singer of sweet songs, one of creative energy and personality. He is exposed to the craft of those in whom he has aroused feelings of envy, but he is under powerful protection and has little to fear. Let him sow seeds at the sun-rising part of life and be ready to gather the harvest in the setting. It us a symbol of POESY.

♏ 27° *A king, holding an illuminated sun's disk on a spearhead, speaking to his ministers.* Denotes one capable of lofty thoughts and high mental flights. There is a subtle, strong diplomacy about this native which cannot be easily gauged by others, but he knows himself, his own ambitious spirit, and his ever-growing faith-a faith which never wavers, no matter if he basks in favors or shields himself from frowns. It is a symbol of DISTINCTION.

♏ 28° *A sailor steering a ship in a rough sea, looking anxiously ahead.* Denotes one of brave, adventurous, and scientific mind who will dare and do much to satisfy the demands of the curious. His life will be exposed to many dangers, most of which he will be prepared to meet, for he is the helmsman, and rough seas do not cause fear to him. It is a symbol of ADVENTURE.

♏ 29° *A university professor lecturing to his students.* Denotes one of an entirely capable and trained mind who is enabled to throw some little light on the darker problems of life. He is fearless and cultivated, expressing theories and sticking to facts. His influence will sway many and his personality will win him confidence. It is a symbol of PERFORMANCE.

♏ 30° *A hand coming out from the heavens holding a pair of per-fectly balanced scales, the star Venus glittering beneath.* Denotes one with a high ideal of true justice which to his mind is not possible without pure love. He is destined to send forth knowledge of a practical and philosophical kind which will help many along the stony way of life. He himself is a just and generous person, his principles guiding his acts in life. It is a symbol of JUSTICE.

SAGITTARIUS

♐ 1° *A woman in the dress of a religious order struggling through a dark and storm-swept valley, a luminous anchor above her.* Denotes one of fine intellect who is gifted with persuasive eloquence. The native is poetic, reverential, and inspiring. He reaches a certain power and dignity after striving through worries and inharmonious. His will is firmly directed and cannot be broken, for above all he has faith in self and knows his own powers. It is a symbol of TRIUMPH.

♐ 2° *A woman of angry countenance holding a dagger in her hand.* Denotes one strongly passionate and well favored who finds it difficult to subdue and control the forces by which he is swayed. Hence there is a tendency to do many regrettable things. He may be drawn into litigation and quarrels of various kinds, and may be tempted to aggressive action and threatening attitudes. Gradually, then, the finer side of his character will be hidden if not corrupted by the employment of the grosser. It is a symbol of MUTINY.

♐ 3° *A man of scornful face with a big sword in one hand, carrying a child.* Denotes one over whose early life darkness hangs and who, if he escapes, will be involved in dangerous undertakings from which he will emerge triumphant or fall, perhaps not in vain. The mind is roused to intensity, and the native feels himself called to champion a great cause. He will follow with many followers. It is a symbol of REDRESSING.

♐ 4° *Two arrows crossed and surrounded by zones of glistening white light.* Denotes one who has a tendency to pull in opposite directions. The struggle between the desires and right will be constant, and an act of hostility will be followed by deep remorse. It is a fight between the world of matter and the world of spirit. There may be peculiar changes in life, and that which is most unexpected is that which is most likely to happen. It is a symbol of WAVERING.

♐ 5° *A dark bank of cloud passing in front of the sun, cutting its rays from the earth.* Denotes one of a melancholic, retiring, and occult nature who is drawn to a life of austerity, and whose search is for that hidden grail which holds the nectar of life and supreme knowledge. He is religious and sincere, but he should be careful lest his peculiar attitude or method of approaching the secret should hide it from his view, as the dark cloud-bank hides the rays of the sun. It is a symbol of MONASTICISM.

♐ 6° *A man in a black robe carrying a black rod, on the top of which is a hand, the thumb held between the fingers of Jupiter and Saturn, whilst the fingers of the Sun and Mercury are pointed upwards.* Denotes a powerful character of a religious and penetrating mind, by the virtue of which he rises to a position of enduring fame. Force, riches, and treachery oppose his power and influence, and may ultimately check, if not end, his career. But his actions will live and his spirit will rise above the power of reverses. It is a symbol of VALOR.

♐ 7° *A large ship on a calm sea in a dark starless night, a black bird of the raven order sitting on the mainmast top.* Denotes one whose position may be of some importance, but whose life will not be of any particular note, except in the manner of leaving it. He is not gifted with exceptional energy, nor with any particular ambitions, but he will meet with envy and hatred, from which he may suffer. He is by nature con-

servative, and will not easily yield to others. It is a symbol
of RETALIATION.

♐ 8°   *Draught horse pulling a load of chains up a hill, at the top of
which is a great revolving wheel.* Denotes one who is limited,
edged in, bound. and restricted, whose way is paved with
difficulties which threaten and torment. He is exposed to
dangers until after his seventh year, and if these are passed
he is faced with a narrow way. He might remember the old
Talmudic maxim, Those whom God loves He oppresses with
suffering, and endeavor to grasp the purpose of his life. It is
a symbol of OPPRESSION.

♐ 9°   *A burning oil well into which men are pouring quantities
of water.* Denotes one gifted with a degree of mental rich-
ness, but who is somewhat diffusive and irregular. He has
some remarkable qualities and good intellectual power, but
is weak in application and method. Still he has wisdom, and
can direct with magnetic forcefulness and purpose. It is a
symbol of RETAINING.

♐ 10° *A large metallic ball reflecting various colors.* Denotes one
of a high order of intellect. He is naturally scientific, and
gains recognition and esteem. He will be enabled to throw
much light on obscure subjects and complex problems, and
will win respect for his labors. He is highly inspirational, and
embraces some school of occultism or uncommon thought.
It is a symbol of GROWTH.

♐ 11° *A fisherman with a net over his shoulder sitting on a bas-
ket, a group of people advancing towards him.* Denotes a
psychic of ability and reputation. He may hold some public
position or come before the public in some way. The temper
is somewhat jerky and the nature a little irritable, but he has

good controlling power and a firm will. As a collector and publisher of knowledge this native has special genius. It is a symbol of PROJECTION.

♐ 12° *A coiled serpent, above which is a grinning skull.* Denotes one of a vicious temperament who is liable to be obsessed and used by the dark forces. A strong and beneficent power over him may transmute his nature and aid him to overcome ill fate, but evil is more likely to attend him and make him her victim. It is a symbol of OVERTHROWING.

♐ 13° *An archer, with bloodstained dress, shooting at a stag.* Denotes one of very strong vibrations and martial nature who will have responsibilities and power to fulfill them. He will meet with oppositions and be exposed to considerable danger, especially in the latter part of life. He is prophetic and gifted in certain directions, but he must control irritation in himself and soothe it in others. It is a symbol of PROVOCATION.

♐ 14° *A human eye surrounded by a circle of flames.* Denotes one of penetrative power and clairvoyant gifts who will be well regarded by his associates and selected for positions of influence. He is naturally attracted to occult philosophy, uncommon learning, and that knowledge which concerns the coming into and going out of earth conditions. Peculiar magnetic and intensely active forces are associated with this degree. It is a symbol of KNOWING.

♐ 15° *A painter at his easel in a forest upland, observing not the heavy black clouds which betray an approaching storm.* Denotes one of a refined and sensitive spirit capable of becoming so absorbed in his studies that he detaches himself from the world and its peoples. The love of nature and the beautiful is very great and may sever his sympathy from the ordinary routine of earthly desires and ambitions. He may obtain excellence in his sphere and some degree of honor, but there is a fatality connected with this degree which will claim him sooner or later. It is a symbol of RADIATION.

♐ 16° *A woman outside an old ruin under a starlit sky, a white angel on her right, a dark angel on her left. The stars — the lamps outside the palaces of the Holy Ones — are shining.* Denotes one of intense mind capable of great acts. Very mediumistic, he is greatly influenced by his impressions and impulses. His path throughout his life is full of varied dangers, and he must be careful lest he miss the way. Let him often look up to the stars and pray for the guidance of the Good. It is a symbol of RESTRAINT.

♐ 17° *Cupid holding a broken arrow in his right hand and a miniature anchor in his left.* Denotes one of an artistic and romantic temperament, fond of the poetic and beautiful and of that branch of science which lifts the soul of man beyond mere worldly limits up to the star-lands and the mountains of the moon. He may leave an enduring work of science, poetry, or romance. Whatever he does he has faith in, and whatever he does hits the mark. It is a symbol of IMPARTING.

♐ 18° *A horse's hoof, winged, crushing a butterfly.* Denotes one of great power of mind whose external thoughts threaten the glory of his soul. For his thoughts are powers which are ever striving to blend the spiritual and material in one great mould. He realizes to a great degree the potency of small things, and he is sensitive enough to feel acutely for suffering and to do all in his power to repel cruelty. It is a symbol of SUBDUING.

♐ 19° *A wand divided by a star.* Denotes one of philosophical force capable of manifesting from the silent hidden into the outer. Therefore his quality is explained in no ordinary terms. He has much personal force and magnetism which, if exerted for high ends, will become a harbinger for peace on this planet of experience and suffering. It is a symbol of the AWAKENING.

♐ 20° *A pleasure-boat on a picturesque river.* Denotes one who delights in the best the world can give and who strives to keep worry and trouble away at all costs. All that is beautiful in form, color, and sound attracts him. He is a lover of ceremony and peaceful reveries, and his reputation in the arts that cultivate will be recognized, not, however, through any special power in himself, but just because it has to be. It is a symbol of EASE.

♐ 21° *A giant tidal wave.* Denotes one who from comparative obscurity raises himself to a position of influence. He is somewhat inconstant and uncertain, but he crushes opposition and all who challenge his way. He should be careful lest the force he uses be turned against himself, no matter how powerful he may be. It is a symbol of ONRUSHING.

♐ 22° *A dog on a wall baying the moon.* Denotes one restless in manner and uncertain in temperament who ever seeks for the unattainable and worries himself because he cannot get it. In his cry, however, there is poetry; poetry of a sad, hopeless strain as if foreboding some forlorn end to ambition, power, and aspiration. It is a symbol of SIGHING.

♐ 23° *A bee stinging a roaring lion.* Denotes one of sharp, stinging wit, of democratic feeling, and a fine order of intellect, who is bound to gain distinction of some kind. He will take a clear and extremely sensible view of things, and will be able to gauge and construct. The note of his sarcasm is directed against certain authority, and forces action when passivity seems firmly fixed. It is a symbol of STIMULATION.

♐ 24° *A bag of gold money falling into the ocean.* Denotes one who holds to the philosophy of fate and who will listen to no other. He makes mistakes and performs erratic actions. In money matters he should be extremely cautious, and he must not enter speculative fields, for heavy losses threaten him. He should hold what he can and trust in God and himself. It is a symbol of MISTAKES.

♐ 25° *A ruined castle by a waterfall, near which is a naked woman holding a bunch of grapes to an old philosopher who, seated on a rock, is studying a manuscript.* Denotes one of romantic mind, loving and leaning to the philosophy and thought of other days, in which he is a master. The forces play around him and attempts from the two worlds will be made to draw him from his deeper thoughts to the frivolity, folly, and transitory joys of earth. Many times will he be shaken, but his power is too great for sensual over comings. Instead he throws to the world the wine of life that those who are able may drink. It is a symbol of Spiritual STRUGGLES.

♐ 26° *Two girls on a seesaw gaily dressed, a man in motley in the center holding a cup of wine in his hand.* Denotes one who is attracted to the sport and gaieties of life, and to whom physical pleasures constitute the essence of existence. The native may indulge in extravagances and will feel the ups and downs of life. His philosophy favors the pursuit of happiness, and his mental gifts will be directed to the furtherance of his thoughts. It is a symbol of PLEASURE.

♐ 27° *Mercury holding up his caduceus in his right hand and with his left helping a fallen man to rise.* Denotes one inspired and gifted, one prophetic, poetic, and artistic, whose mission it is to raise and uplift the race. He brings through the dark paths light and ecstasy, and those who hear the music will have their wounds healed. To see nature is with him to know nature, and the honey of wisdom flows from his mouth. It is a symbol of ELOQUENCE.

♐ 28° *A simply dressed woman breaking a sword over her knee. In the heavens above, masses of dark clouds are scudding before the rising sun.* Denotes one possessing power, but utterly without bombast. To him war, quarrelling, and all forms of inharmony, while abhorrent, are well inside the power of remedy. His nature inspires hope and security, and the dark threatenings of evil fly before this rising sun. It is a symbol of BENEVOLENCE.

♐ 29° *A chariot decorated with garlands of flowers, broken down on the roadway.* Denotes one to whom pomp, glitter, and show strongly appeal, combined with a love of traveling and pleasure. To such a one caution cannot be too strongly rec-ommended. It is not a chariot gaily decorated which aids his power. Wealth combined with strength tells. It is a symbol of VANITY.

♐ 30° *A shield, with a gorgon's head embossed on it, attached to a column.* Denotes one of active mental power who is indis-pensable to his friends and a thorn to his enemies. He is ca-pable of seeing events far in advance of their materialization and counts the years of human progress in its pendulum-like motion. He has in him a strong spirit of fight and a feeling of naught else but victory. It is a symbol of SUPREMACY.

CAPRICORN

♑ 1°   *A man, armed , rising out of the earth.* Denotes one to whom power is given, especially connected with earthly science and knowledge. His passage through life will not be pleasured by calm and perfect peace. Rough seas and angry rocks will threaten him. As he grows older in years and experience he will know that combative science and theory but lead to unrest and fear. When this time comes he will truly arise out of the earth. It is a symbol of DISPUTING.

♑ 2°   *A revolving disc of light, red centre surrounded by a black rim. The colours are pure and distinct.* Denotes a distinct personality of a martial, philosophic type, whose destiny it is to leave his mark on the world's tablet. The influence favors elevation to a certain position of responsibility, but having reached this it is difficult for the native to retain it, and his restless spirit brings him into conflict with enemies of power who, if he be not cautious, will overthrow him. It is a symbol of WRESTLING.

♑ 3°   *An old man seated on a throne in the clouds with his right foot on a sword. A large bright star is above his head and two pillars of light are on either side.* Denotes one of genius whose gifts raise him far above the common things of earth, enabling him to comprehend sublimities. What he feels and knows he endeavors to clothe in a dress of vibrating colors to charm the children of earth and to raise them to dreams and contemplations of a glory beyond all material thought and understanding. It is a symbol of IMMORTALITY.

♑ 4°   *Persephone rising gracefully from the under to the upper world. The sun is shining, and the surrounding country is rich in fields of corn, fruits, birds, and flowers, whilst butterflies are sporting round her head.* Denotes one of great power of endurance who forces himself, ill or well, to brush away obstacles in the way of his desires. There is here a combination of mental, moral, and physical force, a trinity which carries the native through danger and conditions the most adverse. At birth the soul is rising from the shadows, and as life advances the temples of enchanting lights are reached, sand constancy begets deathlessness. It is a symbol of PERSEVERANCE.

♑ 5° *A winged urn from which water is pouring on to the parched earth. Where the water falls vegetation springs forth luxuriantly.* Denotes one of sympathetic and charitable nature, simple and charming, unorthodox, and free of religious and racial prejudice. The sordid fields of life have little hold on him, for his soul is expansive, eccentric even, and he hates pettiness. It is a symbol of KINDNESS.

♑ 6° *A traveler walking up a long forest rise, the path surrounded by dense gnarled trees. It is approaching evening, and the way is long and gloomy, but at the top can be seen a star within a wreath of fine clouds illuminating a beautiful blue sky.* Denotes one destined to lead in one of the great departments of life, but whose way will be threatened and whose heart will sometimes be faint. But even in the darkest times the light. of heaven will shine on him, stimulating him to action and accomplishment. His latter days may be days of faded flowers, but he will reach his star before his journey ends. It is a symbol of MANIFESTATION.

♑ 7° *A harp with broken strings, a scowling face above it.* Denotes one of ability whose career will be full of difficulties, mistakes, and threatenings. He is somewhat eccentric in manner, and will be led into action and argument from which he will gain no credit. He is susceptible in heart affairs is cultured, and loves the beautiful in its many forms. If he would produce music, let him first string his harp. It is a symbol of JEOPARDY.

♑ 8° *A woman looking on an empty cradle in an attitude of deep grief, the figure of a child near her, surrounded by a bright light, striving to pierce the gloom of her atmosphere.* Denotes one whose life will be one of experience and who will suffer greatly through ignorance of certain knowledge which would free him if he knew it. He should try and comprehend that the deeper the expressed grief, the harder it is for the truth to be known; the blacker the darkness, the greater the danger into which he may walk. It is a symbol of ADMONITION.

♑ 9° *A man lying half asleep in a field, a veiled figure behind him with upraised hand.* Denotes one born for great deeds whose work will be regarded many, many years after his exit from the narrow conditions of mortal life. Gifted with inspirational powers and strongly impressed by powerful invisible forces, the native will be one of the many lanterns destined to throw light on this dark world. It is a symbol of ENLIGHTENING.

♑ 10° *A glimmering light stealing into an armory, on the walls of which hang polished implements of war.* Denotes one, active, ardent, and militant, whose enthusiasm will lead him into trouble or danger, and who is capable of heroic effort for an espoused cause. The nature is by no means selfish, indeed the native would lay down his life for that which to him is right. It is a symbol of MILITARISM.

♑ 11° *An armed man riding on a lion, below him a scarabaeus; above, a mailed hand grasping an iron rod.* Denotes one who by force and aggression gains position above his fellows, and holds it. He will rise above the proud and force them to raise him higher, and his life and influence will be long. There is much materialism in this native and much disregard for others. If he does not let the light enter his soul he may suffer from the force typified as an iron rod. It is a symbol of UNDERTAKINGS.

♑ 12° *A man in full armour, visor up, holding his two hands on the hilt of his sword, the point of which pierces the ground.* Denotes courage and self-confidence. The native often meets danger or anxiety face to face, and is ever prepared to repel it when it comes. His sword is always ready, but he presses the point to earth, for he knows the power of the spirit, above all material force. It is a symbol of STRIVING.

♑ 13° *A sublime spirit of female form holding by the hand a poorly attired child coming from the darkness into the mists and ascending from the mists into the light.* Denotes one who without regard to worldly condition will be aided and advanced to super-earth state by a great protective agency, and the more the mind is raised to glorious contemplation the more closely will the heavenly cloak fall about his shoulders. It is a symbol of GUARDIANSHIP.

♑ 14° *A woman in a drapery establishment, the table crowded with articles of dress, none of which please her.* Denotes one not easily satisfied and who is not always conscious of the feelings of others. He is not deficient in taste, but he allows his mind to be so affected by varied desires and feelings that it is difficult for him to preserve firmness. He should ever strive to encourage the positive and to cultivate fixity of mind. It is a symbol of DISSATISFACTION.

♑ 15° *A hand extended, on which is resting a triangle, from which rays of light are issuing.* Denotes one of fine comprehension and intellectuality, essentially fitted for very special world work. He is ever searching for the truth in art, science, and life, and has a mind powerful enough to withstand criticism from the ignorantly learned. Reward comes to him. At the close of earth life he sees the light. It is a symbol of TRAN-SITION.

♑ 16° *A number of books floating near a coast land rich in vegetation and floral charm, with beautiful grottos rising from the blue sea.* Denotes one, artistic and nature-loving, who has a rapturous appreciation for the grandeur of creation and endeavors by some media-art, letters, or song-to express it. He has a strong affinity with nature, and her many moods will act and react on his sensitive soul. It is a symbol of EXPRESSION.

♑ 17° *A flood of deep blue light which, gradually becoming more and more refined, fades away altogether.* Denotes one of sublime aspirations. To him the spiritual is ever more attractive than the material. The more life advances, the more refined his philosophy becomes until its rays fade from earth with the soul so well expressing it. It is a symbol of SUPERSENSUALISM.

♑ 18° *A silver-hued garment lying in the mud. Overhead are the dark clouds of an approaching storm.* Denotes one whose fate is greatly influenced by the acts of others, and whose life is blended with the hopes and ambitions of the many. He will have trials and temptations, and can only defend himself and his honor by firmly refusing to be drawn into affairs of an unworthy nature. It is a symbol of CHANGES.

♑ 19° *A large crab with its claws imbedded in a seal.* Denotes one of a vigorous and determined nature and great stubbornness of character who holds strongly to pronounced opinions and ideas. If he is thrown into political life he becomes a statesman whose firmness will be appreciated by his friends and regretted by his enemies It is a symbol of HOLDING.

♑ 20° *A girl carrying a bowl of water into which are reflected the rays of the setting sun. All around is darkness* Denotes one whose spirituality shines amidst the intensity of the darkness of materialism, a seer whose destiny it is to raise the fallen to a realization of the divine excellence of man and to warn off the dark and opposing enemies. It is a symbol of EVOLUTION.

♑ 21° *The head of a goat with the solar disc between its horns.* Denotes an extremely sensitive and impressionable nature of romantic and strange fancies. If the sun is afflicted at birth or if the moon is changing from old to new, the native is liable to obsession or evil company, which threaten his honor, and he will have to seek help from more positive minds. But if the orbs be in good aspect and the moon be elevated, strong, advancing from new to full, advancement will be the native's destiny. It is a symbol of PERPLEXITY.

♑ 22° *A hawk standing on a square black rock bathed in the rays of the rising sun.* Denotes one whose power is directed to the uplifting and advancement of his race-a stayer of war and strife, of plague and riot. He looks directly ahead, far ahead into the years to come when the new sun will illuminate the glory of a new age of gold. It is a symbol of RENEWING.

♑ 23° *A dog, holding a bird in his mouth, running across a field of daisies.* Denotes a far-seeing person with a fine appreciation of poetry and the arts and a well-endowed mind capable of delving deeply into obscure subjects. Should Mercury be afflicted in the horoscope, especially by Saturn, the native will incline to exercise his powers in a wrong direction and to seek to restrain to his advantage the rights of others. It is a symbol of SAGACITY.

♑ 24° *Three quivering arrows speeding towards a kneeling maiden, but before they reach her they crumble to atoms against a mighty hand which suddenly descends from the heavens.* Denotes one who will escape three great dangers by reason of a faith which draws to him the protection of the higher Powers. The most threatening is the third danger, but his faith is proof against this also. He will have moments of intense feeling and will not permit others to usurp his position nor rob him of the fruits of his toil. He is a peculiar child of destiny, and destiny does not design him for a low position in earth life. It is a symbol of FAVOR.

♑ 25° *A man, gaudily attired, opening a document in the centre of which is a dagger.* Denotes one who will hold positions of responsibility and advantage. He has an inborn love of show and glitter, pomp and ceremony. He will be endowed with much mental ability and powers of persuasion, but is not free from secret enemies who seek to end his career by craft or violence. It is a symbol of UNREST.

♑ 26° *A woman lifting from the ground an injured child.* Denotes one whose ruling impulse is for the protection and comfort of mankind and who will put this into practice; in fact he will be called upon to do so by the influence of that Power who sent him to earth as a defender of the weak. He will find himself in the midst of various aiding and opposing forces, but so deep is his sympathy with the oppressed that conquest as sure unto him. It is a symbol of TENDING.

♑ 27° *A woman, neatly dressed, seated on an old-fashioned chair, looking out of a cottage window on to a pretty little garden. Her face expresses pleasant contemplation.* Denotes one of a particularly kind and temperament, extremely thoughtful and a lover of men, animals, and nature, of sin-tastes and careful judgment. The native psychic powers and prophetic foresight regarding future events. It is a symbol of MEDITATING.

♑ 28° *An athlete throwing a large iron quoit and disregarding a wild, ill-conditioned dog who is barking at him.* Denotes one, vigorous in mind and body, who advances in his special sphere through his energy and by virtue of his destiny. He is sure to meet with enemies and opponents in life, and his way will be frequently threatened and challenged. But he is mysteriously protected. and so long as his intentions and actions are not stayed by the envy and criticisms of others all will be well with him. It is a symbol of PARRYING.

♑ 29° *A dismantled fortress in ruins; near-by, an old man sitting on the ground, his back resting against a rock, with a sacred book beside him. His face expresses great sadness.* Denotes one of conservative and contemplative mind, aspiring, purposeful, and retentive, who mends the broken chains which link the past to the present, and who sees in the coming dawn a reflection of the remote past. He gains honor and esteem, but is not free from sadness. His ideals will be injured by events, expected perhaps in all but intensity. It is a symbol of COMPARISON.

♑ 30° *A meteorite falling on a mountain-top.* Denotes one who is cautious and generally fortunate, and who nevertheless may be subjected to sudden attacks on his name and possessions He should avoid law and legal tribunals, and always fix agreements by writing, in order prevent future disputes. He may gain a position of importance, but will not be able to hold it, he may be elected to a position which can only be held for a limited term. The higher he aims the more he renders himself vulnerable to shafts of those above him. It is a symbol STRENGTHENING.

AQUARIUS

♒ 1°   *A human head in a mass of clouds, which are rose-tinted by the rising sun.* Denotes one of sensitive and poetic imagination who is capable of sublime flights of fancy. He is somewhat easily swayed by others, although himself capable of showing the way. He is a dreamer of dreams and a man of action, and many will have cause to honor his name. It is a symbol of DOING.

♒ 2°   *A large mulberry-tree laden with fruit, around which are many birds.* Denotes one of romantic disposition and fine taste who will be favored by fortune and who will attract many friends. There is benevolence and sympathy in this nature, and prophetic ability also. He is generally successful in the attainment of his desires. It is a symbol of CONTENTMENT.

♒ 3°   *A white-haired man, holding a cross before him, walking over a mosaic pavement.* Denotes one of a truly religious mind whose career will be as full of incident as the many pieces which go to make a mosaic pavement are full of color. Material life is not without its dangers-moral and physical-but the native is not born under the heel of fear. He sees beyond his times and bears his cross. It is a symbol of FAITHFULNESS.

♒ 4°   *A beautiful fountain throwing upwards delicate sprays of yellow-tinted water, a jeweled crown showing in the mists.* Denotes one of refined mind who is destined to advance and gain power and influence over others. He will bring relief to many a thirsty soul, and many will bless him as he passes by the way. He is humanitarian, sincere, romantic, and harmonious. The life is not free from danger until after the thirtieth year has passed. Thence his way is elevation and peace. It is a symbol of DEFENDING.

♒ 5°   *A nautilus shell being driven, on the sea, before the wind towards a rocky shore.* Denotes one who reaches fame fitting his rank. He will have elegant tastes arid a love of luxury, but is liable to be imposed on or wrongly advised. He can quickly grasp impressions and set his thoughts into activity, but he should direct his will unto himself and watch the threatening rock shore with his eyes well opened. It is a symbol of INCLINING.

♒ 6°   *A lady raising her white-gloved hand to receive a jeweled crown surrounded by a strange light which is floating towards her.* Denotes one on whom Fame smiles and who is fitted to receive her favor. For this native there is dignity and honor, which follows a degree of struggle, disappointment, and comparative obscurity. He is moved by many and varied feelings and is blessed with a vivid and fine imagination. He is cultured, neat in style, and artistic, with considerable psychic ability and occult understanding. It is a symbol of ASCENDING.

♒ 7°   *A naked foot bleeding; above, a burning lamp.* Denotes one whose path in life will be filled with rocks and roughness, whose soul will be directed to the secret of the Holy Truth. He is liable to assaults, injuries, and the stings of jealous hate. Still he goes forward, forward like a conquering hero with light to lift the darkness and pain. He may falter, but he will not fall by the way. It is a symbol of SUFFERING.

♒ 8°   *A soldier endeavoring to escape from a prison cell through a barred window.* Denotes one of a vital, vigorous, and martial disposition who endeavors to cut his way by mind or sword. Danger in early childhood may be overcome according to the power of the horoscope, but danger is never absent from him, and he is liable to be constrained or oppressed with enemies of his own making or he may be a dangerous enemy to himself. To pass through a barred window self-conquest alone knows the way. It is a symbol of LIMITATION.

♒ 9° *A large, bright, military shield lying on a mountain, from which stream rays reflecting shafts of brilliant light.* Denotes one of powerful energy and firmness of purpose who in the second half of his life attains the reward of his labors and the gratification of his ambitions. He then attracts fame, drawing it unto himself as the loadstone draws steel. From his wisdom come rays which dazzle men by their brilliancy. It is a symbol of REPUTATION.

♒ 10° *A woman, blind and in chains, in a magnificent and brilliantly lighted room.* Denotes one fated in the strongest sense of the term. If Venus is afflicted in the horoscope the native will be liable to suffer from overindulgence of some kind or from some trouble indicated by the Venusian position in the natal chart. He may do things he will regret and from which suffering may come. He should take hold of himself as a rider does a restless horse. Let him learn to open his eyes and to strike off his chains, and he will know the beauty which surrounds him. It is a symbol of NARROWNESS.

♒ 11° *Flowers twined round a scepter.* Denotes one of gifted mind and exceptional qualities, a singer of songs and a bearer of light, whose works gain for him respect and dignity, and whose name will be remembered long after his form has left this earth. Beautiful thoughts will cling to him as the ivy clings to the garden wall, and pleasant minds will come to him as the flowers which entwine the scepter. It is a symbol of TASTE.

♒ 12° *A beautiful woman tending a dove with injured wing. On a table a manuscript, a bundle of letters, and an open book.* Denotes one of sympathy and feeling who thinks deeply because he feels deeply, and whose ideas, entirely utilitarian, find the ready acceptance of is will have much to do with the majority. He launching of beneficial reforms, and will ever be striving to heal the wounds of others and point a way to go. It is a symbol of REFORMING.

♒ 13° *A veiled figure, seated on a rock, pointing to a radiated human eye in mid-air.* Denotes one of occult understanding and a deep, feeling nature who will often be alone or apart from busy centers. Wherever he may be he never can feel really alone, for there is a power of seership bestowed on him which enables him to see the true, the beautiful, and the sublime in a form unknown to the masses of humanity. His is the eye that sees. It is a symbol of DISCERNMENT.

♒ 14° *Man writing, with a quill pen in each hand, in front of him a flickering oil-lamp. His face betrays anxiety.* Denotes one who strives to do more than he can accomplish, who has " too many irons in the fire," and, while thinking to accomplish much, does but little. He may be two-sided or have two philosophies obtruding themselves at the same time. The life is restless, anxious, and over it hangs a threatening hand. Peace comes from the cultivation of the higher and the rejection of the lower. It is a symbol of DIFFICULTIES.

♒ 15° *A woman seated on an anchor, a rudder in her hand and an opened book at her feet.* Denotes one who is guided through the many intricacies of life by a faith which cannot be shaken, being born of a philosophy or understanding which sinks deeply into a receptive nature. The mind is broad and wide in its sympathies, and the native feels and knows the reality of the way immortal, even though he may not be able to express it in mere words. It is a symbol of GUIDANCE.

♒ 16° *A ship running before the wind with bare poles. The sea, black and angry, is illumined by a ray of moonlight which shines through a break in the heavy clouds.* Denotes one of a trusting spiritual nature who will have trials in life threatening and bitter, and who will often be storm-driven and held in the grip of hard circumstances. Now and then there are breaks in the storms of life which bring relief, no matter how small. But he must go on; his way is difficult and the night is dark, but in the morning light will come. It is a symbol of EXPERIENCE.

♒ 17° *A crab on an inverted triangle, above which are two hands tugging at a laurel wreath.* Denotes one of great perseverance who clings on to his ideas with a tenacity which forces respect. Things of earth worry him; he will have to bear his cross, and he bears it without protest. He will not surrender, no matter how hard he may be pressed. He gains the victor's wreath in the teeth of opposition. It is a symbol of STRIFE.

♒ 18° *A lion running down a dreary and barren field at the end of which is a V-shaped road. On the one side are hunters armed, on the other a rocky entrance leads to sunlit lawns.* Denotes a strong nature, capable of good or evil, who, after early struggles amidst uncongenial surroundings, begins to perceive roads leading to some definite goal. According to the portents in the horoscope will the selected way be one of tears or smiles. There will be achievement of benefit or otherwise, and the earth end will be violent or peaceful as it is willed. It is a symbol of DOUBTING.

♒ 19° *Setting sun shining on a waterfall, giving it the appearance of golden water.* Denotes one who has a graceful method of expressing his thoughts and who will reach his place when life's midway has passed. He will accomplish much, and his words will ring so that many will stop to listen. His actions harmonize with his beliefs, and his soul is serene. It is a symbol of PROCLAIMING.

♒ 20° *A quaint old chest standing in an old hall, a large key on the floor before it. Around are pieces of armour and old instruments of music. On the top of the chest is a dog asleep.* Denotes one of a somewhat conservative nature, thoughtful, studious, and serious, by whom the training of the mind is placed before all else and whose soul is set on works of cultivation. He may show special genius in some section of art or music, or he may be in a position to advance them. He is a seeker after truth and the key is near for him to use when the guardian has slumbered. It is a symbol of SKILLFULNESS.

♒ 21° *A man with chains on his wrists appealing to a crowd of people.* Denotes one whose life is set on the eradication of injustice and whose advocacy of what he considers right brings on him pain, ridicule, and misrepresentation. He is limited, chained, constrained, opposed, and oppressed, and will suffer hurt even from those for whom he gives up his comfort and ease. But the seal is set, and he will see the tree which many considered barren bearing fruit. It is a symbol of HERALDING.

♒ 22° *A number of men saving volumes of books from the flames which are enveloping a library building.* Denotes one of a literary and scholastic mind to whom the pen is truly "mightier than the sword," and who inclines to the production of original works, whilst carefully preserving those that have gone before. In other ways he is a patron of literature and redeems much of value to the world. He may find himself in the midst of conflicting forces and be compelled to actions which may cause pain. It is a symbol of CONSERVING.

♒ 23° *A musician playing a curious instrument of the organ type. In the foreground a large St. Andrew's cross, one limb of a dark, cloudy substance, the other white.* Denotes one over whose early life a shadow hangs, of original mind, unorthodox and artistic. He is strangely moved by beauty and grace, blending loveliness of form with the seductive invisibility of sweet sounds. Living in the midst of high vibrations, the native is in danger of being drawn into the vortex of oppositions. Then the evil crosses the good and the devil wrestles with the man. It is a symbol of CROSSING.

♒ 24° *A woman neatly attired, with her hand on a tomb, looking sorrowfully on a flower-covered grave.* Denotes a refined person forced to meet sorrow face to face. According to the degree of experience to be learned, so will be the degree of sorrow to be endured. Passion is not apart from this degree, but passion leads to pain, whilst subjugation leads to mastery. It is a symbol of TRIBUTE.

♒ 25° *A victor in a duel with a look of agony breaking his sword over his knee.* Denotes one born to conquer, but whose material conquests bring him pain and grief. As he advances in life and the sun of his soul throws brighter lights before him, he will realize how worthless aggression really is and how much grander is a word spoken in kindness than one spoken in anger, how much sweeter a kind face than one made hideous by the poison of hate. Then he will break his sword. It is a symbol of REACTION.

♒ 26° *Three fires blazing above three triangular hills, a cross sword floating in air above.* Denotes one of mystic and reformative leanings who may be impressed by invisible forces for certain work on earth, but who may not be conscious of the part he is called upon to play. He has intelligence, force, and bravery, with a strong will, and what he is willed to do he will do. He should never permit himself to be hypnotized nor entranced. nor yield his will to the power of another, in the body or out of it. It is a symbol of SERVICE

♒ 27° *A man of strong build locking securities in a great iron safe in the turret-room of an old castle.* Denotes one, forceful, strong, and aggressive, who will be the guardian of many responsibilities and who unites strength of purpose with executive ability. He defends and attacks: he is a master and a servant. Errors are always dangerous, and only from errors will regret come. It is a symbol of STEWARDSHIP.

♒ 28° *A spire on top of a pyramid, at the base of which is a horse with a manuscript in his mouth.* Denotes one born for great deeds, aspiring and energetic. His work will travel far and will be of a strong and reformative character, which will meet with the usual opposition afforded to such works amongst a certain caste. He must never stay. Ever with the symbol before his eyes must he continue his way, for victory is sure. It is a symbol of REFORMATION.

♒ 29° *Forked lightning surrounded by stars amidst storm-clouds.* Denotes one whose rise in life will be sudden and who will maintain his position with difficulty. He will enjoy the smiles of favoring fortune and suffer the frowns of envy, and is destined to wrestle with opposition and inharmonious conditions. Let him study his horoscope and steer clear of the breakers. It is a symbol of DEBATE.

♒ 30° *Wavy rays of light, in shape like a huge wheel, reflecting on a blue evening sky.* Denotes one of sober judgment and a natural leaning towards the occult arts. He has respect for such learning, in which he himself is gifted. His logical nature refuses to be led by orthodox thought or to yield to the shallow opinions of hypnotized crowds. Generally the life is fortunate. The native is slow to move, but has abundant sympathy, which his mind regulates or restrains. As he advances in earth life, his psychic eye will be opened and he will know and understand those things which he before accepted with reserve, but without scruple. It is in the latter part of his life that the gates of knowledge are opened to his soul. It is a symbol of CONTROLLING.

PISCES

♓ 1°   *A satyr sitting on a rock by a river which is running into the sea, holding a fish.* Denotes one of a peculiar disposition who is in danger of yielding to the suggestions of evil influence and being guilty of unjust actions. He may suffer sorrow from or through relatives and from secret affairs, and he may not be able to do just what he pleases. He has strong promptings towards the occult and hidden arts. It is a symbol of MISGIVING.

♓ 2°   *An old man sitting beneath a leafless tree with bread in his hand and a bag of money by his side.* Denotes one who will be no stranger to suffering. Directly or indirectly he benefits through people older than himself. No matter how important his position in life, he is limited. He feels for those whose portion of earth life is but pain and he relieves when the pained plead. It is a symbol of CLEMENCY.

♓ 3°   *The deck of a trawler on which are quantities of fish. It is night. A small cottage is on fire on the land, and this, with the shore lights, is reflected in the water.* Denotes a strong character, a leader in his sphere of life. Dangers from the elements threaten the child life. He baa the ability to grasp and utilize the ideas and suggestions of others, and his power of observation enables him to advance his interests and obtain reward. He will be successful in secret negotiations, and secret matters largely affect the life. It is a degree of SECRETIVENESS.

♓ 4°   *A lighthouse built on rocks in the midst of an angry sea. Over the sky is a rainbow.* Denotes one who will be placed in the midst of unsettled chaotic conditions and who, as complication after complication arises, allows fear to hold him. Yet he is secure against storms and firm against disaster, although not from assault. He has mediumistic power to enable him to know his inward strength, but he fears to use it. If he would but turn his eyes upwards he would see beauty above fear and ever have hope before him. It is a symbol of MISTRUST.

♓ 5° *The interior of a tent of a Roman military commander in which is a table set with abundance of food and drink in rich vessels of gold and silver.* Denotes one of good organizing and directing ability who works with a purpose in his mind and an ideal at heart. He has a love of luxury and good living, and as life advances he will be in a position to gratify his desires. He is a good, generous friend, and gains esteem. He does not allow personal comfort to affect the work he is called upon to do nor to diminish his personal courage. It is a symbol of ACCOMPLISHMENT.

♓ 6° *Pirates tying a captive to a tree by the seashore. An old sailor hidden behind the rocks and foliage watching and waiting, knife in hand, to set him free.* Denotes an adventurous nature which will attempt rash things and undertake dangerous missions. The native is in danger of restraint and attack from powerful foes seeking to put him out of action, but is fortunate in obtaining relief when he least expects it. From the twenty-seventh to the twenty-eighth, the thirty-sixth to the thirty seventh, are critical years. It is a symbol of ATTEMPTING.

♓ 7° *Two wrestlers struggling for mastery. One is dark and evil-looking, whilst the other is as an angel in manly beauty.* Denotes the dark and treacherous forces and the materialism of man combating with all that is glorious, all that is ideal and divine. To whichever the thoughts of the native incline comes victory, and many times in life he will be forced to join himself to the one or the other. May wisdom direct his choice. It is a symbol of CONTESTING.

♓ 8° *A slave merchant selling a beautiful woman in an Eastern marketplace.* Denotes one who is destined to have power over others and who may be forced by circumstances to obey the wills of stronger forces. Necessity may compel him to barter his dearest possession for external advantage, but those to whom he barters it prize it. His is a peculiar life of importance, but not one of absolute free will. It is a symbol of RESPONSIBILITIES.

♓ 9° *Venus and Cupid, metamorphosed as two fishes, swimming from agiant who stands on a rock.* Denotes one of a sensitive disposition and pure mind who understands intuitively the true meaning of love as symbolized in the planet Venus, sublime and in her dignity. His enemy is lust, which threatens to cling to him and by craft to hold the throne of his soul in the guise of love. But the native will know vice as a destroying angel only, and his knowledge will protect him and set him free. It is a symbol of TRANSMUTATION.

♓ 10° *A man sweeping together quicksilver which has fallen from a dish and has scattered in all directions.* Denotes one of an active, volatile mind, alert and restless, possessing knowledge and the power to acquire knowledge. There is, however, danger of his ideas leaving him and being scattered in parts where they are not appreciated. When he fully recognizes the gift with which he has been blessed he will by concentration draw it unto himself and bestow it on those who will hold it to advantage. It is a symbol of TEACHING.

♓ 11°   A dog running amongst some children playing on the seashore. Denotes one of sagacious mind, very faithful when trust is given, and active in the carrying out of any mission he is entrusted with. There is determination in the character, and the external appearance betrays but little the feelings and emotions. He acts with caution, craft, and confidence, and is generally friendly. It is a symbol of ALERTNESS.

♓ 12°   *An author with his head in his hands, a rejected manuscript and a lady's photograph on a table before him.* Denotes one of literary or artistic ability who attains a degree of reputation and esteem, but who is tempted by the smiles of alluring love. He will reach a stage when he will be compelled to decide between two mistresses, one as insistent as the other. It is a symbol of INTRICACY.

♓ 13°   *A man crossing a bog on an old tree which has long ago fallen.* Denotes one who meets with public favor and support whose temper will be severely tried and tested. Although possessed of radical feelings, he will find himself compelled by circumstances to obtain conservative support even though that support be grudgingly given. Still it will serve. It is a symbol of PRESERVING.

♓ 14°   *A number of stevedores loading a ship at a port.* Denotes one who sees prayer in labor and nobility in work. No matter what may be his station in life, his beliefs will be strongly democratic and just. There may be a good deal of moving about during life or a long voyage may take the native into lands remote from his place of birth. He is sincere, and can be relied on. It is a symbol of ACTIVITY.

♓ 15°   *A man standing on a high lookout, nervously scanning the horizon at high noon, a comrade fallen at his side stricken by the sun.* Denotes one gifted with keen powers of observation who gains a position of usefulness and responsibility. His life will at times be unsettled, and his advancement will be in the hands of others. He may be threatened with disfavor, illness, or accident. He should banish irritability or nervousness, for such cause trouble. Still he is always sincere. It is a symbol of TRUSTWORTHINESS.

♓ 16° *A hawk with outspread wings standing on a trumpet.* Denotes one of fearless disposition and venturesome nature who makes a big throw for fortune and who reaches a point of notoriety or fame in the face of obstacles, opposition, and envy. Favors come from authority, but dangers from falls, fire, and sword are threatened. It is a symbol of RENOWN.

♓ 17° *A gaudily dressed officer holding aloft a spear of gold.* Denotes one of magnetic force, patience, and determination who wins his way by sacrifice of self for the sake of his ambition and who will never rest until he has achieved his purpose. He is identified with a great cause or a great production, spreading knowledge or giving pleasure. It is a symbol of ANNOUNCEMENT.

♓ 18° *A spider seizing a fly caught in the web.* Denotes one who may be deceived in many important concerns of life and who should be especially careful in giving confidences and in betraying his affairs to others. He should avoid law and all forms of litigation and contention, and should not accept too lightly the opinion of others concerning his business. It is a symbol of TEMPTATION.

♓ 19° *A sick man lying at the base of a large stone cross, a greyhound running in the distance.* Denotes one of great faith which, being added to true knowledge, makes man invincible. The mind inclines to religion and charity, and is well endowed. Generally he is quick to grasp matters and to profit by his wisdom. He suffers some discomfort in life and many disappointments. Ill-health may also trouble him. Still, he has faith, and faith can truly move mountains. It is a symbol of BELIEVING.

♓ 20° *An itinerant musician playing the mandolin and singing love songs to a number of country maidens who are seated on rocks and fallen trees around him.* Denotes one who is musical, artistic, and pleasure loving who is gifted with a wealth of imagination and an engaging manner. He gives pleasure to many, and will meet with much applause. His nature is light and airy and somewhat wanting in stability. He delights to wander about, or his calling may involve much traveling. It is a symbol of ENTERTAINING.

♓ 21° *A staff adorned with colored ribbons standing in a field of violets, butterflies circling around it.* Denotes one of a fresh and beautiful mind, a lover of nature in sunshine and shower. His ideal is a life of freedom in flowered fields and woods. He inclines to people of high thoughts, children, animals, and the great things of life. He will be exposed to some dangers and will sometimes find the way blocked-the way he has to go. Still, a magical protection is over him and a defending power invisible is always near. It is a symbol of SHIELDING.

♓ 22° *A snake hidden in a bush of wild flowers near a bubbling stream.* Denotes one of wandering and inconstant nature who has cause to fear the tyranny of his senses. He will in turn be the deceived and the deceiver, and when he attempts to deceive others he deceives himself most. His nature is of the romantic tinge. He loves music and song, the theatre and the ballet, and appreciates the beautiful. If he dare, he may redeem himself. It is a symbol of ENSNARING.

♓ 23°   *A heap of broken arms and military trappings lying in a muddy pool.* Denotes one who will know the poverty of aggression and who will suffer from the effects of his actions and intentions. He will understand that what is gained by force may become a curse instead of a blessing, and why the so-called glories of ancient Rome became so many daggers at her throat when the results of her deeds brought her to earth. Let the native prove his power in a greater way than by contention. Let him clear his mind and control himself if he can. It is a symbol of MILITANCY.

♓ 24°   *A giant ape dragging a woman into the forests.* Denotes one who is in danger of becoming a slave to his desires and to sacrifice his higher self to the exhausting excesses which eat into body and soul. There is a wasting of energy and power in the pursuit of so called pleasure which deprives the native of that perfect idealistic happiness which is gained by sweet restraint and a knowledge of perfect love. It is a symbol of FALLING.

♓ 25°   *An unfurled flag on a shaft of forked lightning.* Denotes one of nervous, quick, and restless temperament, impulsive, active, and full of energy and purpose. His nature is brave and defiant, and his life will not be free of adventure of some kind. He will always be beyond want and his position will be secure. Events in his life happen abruptly and are not always expected. It is a symbol of SUDDENNESS.

♓ 26°   *A dowser with a wand of hazel in his hands, finding water on barren lands.* Denotes one who will be blessed with natural gifts of a very high order. He will be very fortunate in his undertakings, benevolent, and beneficial to the people. He is a searcher and a seeker, is rather conservative, and does not easily accept reforms and changes. It is a symbol of DISCOVERY.

♓ 27° *A horse running with flames issuing from his nostrils.* Denotes one who has special work to do and whose name will be associated with important projects. His nature is passionate, quickly receiving and recording spiritual impressions. The disposition is kindly. He is well disposed, and his sense of justice is strong. It is a symbol of DIRECTING.

♓ 28° *A black cat sitting on an old parchment-covered book.* Denotes one who, if he live beyond infancy, will rise to a position of some responsibility. Blessed with superior gifts, this native will be esteemed for his wisdom and understanding. He leans towards old things and will reflect the tendencies of his ancestors. He receives favors from old people and has fortunate dealings with others. It is a symbol of FIRMNESS.

♓ 29° *A bat flying at night in an old graveyard.* Denotes one who endures sorrow. He should strive to force himself away from lowering tendencies by mingling with cheerful and fine-minded people and by studying the true nature of thoughts, feelings, emotions, and strange happenings in one of the occult schools to which he most inclines. He should always guard against jealous feelings in himself and in others. It is a symbol of SADNESS.

♓ 30° *A man trudging along a rough road, dragging a mass of heavy chains. A strong horse in a cart standing idly near.* Denotes one who undertakes needless labor and who binds himself in chains of his own making. He has peculiar ideas, thoughts, fancies, and eccentricities, and the regulation and control of these and the cultivation of his powers of observation will lead him to the understanding of great things and open a gate which is at the beginning of the perfect way so opposed to the rough road of selfish materialism on which the majority of the world's people have been content to travel till the closing of their earth lives. It is a symbol of MISCONCEPTION.

Charubel

John Thomas (1826–1908) stands as a Welsh-American clairvoyant astrologer and seer from the late 19th century who adopted the professional moniker Charubel, aligning himself as a clairvoyant, occultist, and healer. Charubel, deeply devoted to Christianity in his childhood, transitioned to become a curative Mesmerist in his early twenties. His journey led him through herbalism, astrology, mediumship, and occultism. In 1851, he pursued studies in Calvinistic and Methodist theology, yet he diverged from the conventional path of a Methodist preacher. Instead, Thomas dedicated his life to exploring the laws of nature and life, guided by the motto 'inner and not outer.' Professing to possess second sight or precognition, he claimed a sixth sense that allowed him to perceive alarming forms termed 'Submundanes' or 'Elementals.' He was the editor of several journals, *The Seer*, *The Occultist* and *The Psychic Mirror* and of the books *The Country of the Bible* and *Psychology of Botany, Minerals and Precious Stones* (1906 - illustrated by Aubrey Beardsley). Charubel was often writing under the name Julius Balsamo.

Medium

As a Medium, Charubel communicated with the Colour Spirits, often having a close connection with them, although he faced life-threatening situations on two occasions.

Even seemingly peaceful Elementals could become violent during storms. Charubel created a set of occult symbols, first featured in Alan Leo's *Astrologer's Magazine* in 1893. He gained recognition for his healing abilities, particularly in treating rheumatism. His treatment methods often involved precipitated letters from the spirit world. He meticulously prepared numerous horoscopes on parchment and engaged in the creation of talismans.

The Celestial Brotherhood

Throughout his life, Thomas continued studying scriptures, believing that true magic facilitated a union with God. The name Charubel served as his membership designation in the occult society he founded, where he acted as the head. This esoteric order, referred to as 'The Celestial Brotherhood' or 'The British and Foreign Society of Occultists', shared similarities with the 'Order of the Golden Dawn.' Alan Leo, a member of this society, adopted the name Agorel. Despite its brief existence, the organization left an impact with its precise understanding of the spirits within our planet and the hidden forces associated with sacred names.

Zodiac degrees

After the publication in Alan Leo's *Astrologer's Magazine* in 1893, *The Degrees of the Zodiac Symbolised by 'Charubel' To which is added, The Theoretical Value of the Degrees of the*

Zodiac was first published in 1898 and later (Third Edition) extended with the degree descriptions by *La Volasfera / Sepharial*, published in London by L.N. Fowler & Co. In 1907 the book was republished as *The Degrees of the Zodiac Symbolised by Charubel, to which is added a translation of a similar series found in "La Volasfera" (translation and additional notes by Sepharial).*

■

La Volasfera / Sepharial

Possibly one of the oldest zodiac degree interpretations is believed to originate from a mysterious author known as La Volasfera. The influencial astrologer and occultist Sepharial (Walter Gorn Old, 1864-1929) claimed that La Volasfera's work was translated by a certain Antonio Borelli or Bonelli, a figure just as untraceable as La Volasfera. Sepharial's English translation of La Volasfera/Borelli was first published in1907.

Sepharial

Sepharial, also known as Walter Gornold or Walter Gorn Old (pseudonyms for Walter Richard Old) was an English author, astrologer, and Theosophist. He was born on March 20, 1864, in Handsworth (now part of Birmingham) England, and passed away on December 23, 1929, in Hove, England.

'Charubel gained recognition for his healing abilities, particularly in treating rheumatism.'

Childhood, marriage, children

Walter Richard Old, one of six children born to George († 1868) and Amelia Old († 1891), grew up in a well-off family in Handsworth, now a district of Birmingham. His father was a tailor, and after attending primary school, Old apprenticed with a pharmacist in Birmingham. His subsequent career after completing his apprenticeship remains unclear. In June 1896, he married Marie Moore, and the couple had six children.

The Theosophist

In 1887, Old initiated correspondence with Helena Blavatsky, leading to a visit to her in London, where he was captivated by her charisma. He joined the Blavatsky Lodge, quickly rising to the position of Vice President. From 1890 to 1891, he served as the General Secretary of the British Section of the Theosophical Society, succeeding Archibald Keightley. From December 1890 to July 1891, he also edited the theosophical journal *The Vahan*.

In 1892, Old traveled to India to support Henry Steel Olcott, the President of the Theosophical Society, and became embroiled in the Judge Case, a scandal involving allegedly forged Master letters by William Quan Judge. Upon returning to England in April 1894, Old handed written material related to the Judge Case to Edmund Garrett of the *Westminster Gazette*, explaining the entire situation. The ensuing publication in October 1894 portrayed the Masters of Wisdom as charlatans, casting a shadow over the Theosophical Society. Consequently, several lodges disbanded, and many members left the society. Old was expelled from the Theosophical Society during this period. Due to attacks following his disclosure of documents, he changed his name to Walter Gornold or Walter Gorn Old in 1894/95 and left London.

Esoteric interests and astrological contributions

Old had been interested in esoteric subjects, particularly astrology, numerology, and occultism, since his youth. He was largely self-taught and published his first book on astrology in 1887 at the age of twenty-three, using the pseudonym Sepharial, a name that became widely recognized. In total, he authored 58 books, including several foundational works on astrology that remain relevant to this day. Additionally, he contributed numerous articles and essays to various publications such as the *British Journal of Astrology* and *Old Moore's Almanack*.

'Old published his first book on astrology in 1887 at the age of twenty-three, using the pseudonym Sepharial, a name that became widely recognized.'

Kozminsky

Isidore Israel Kozminsky, born on October 25, 1870, came from a Prussian Jewish family that had immigrated to Australia via London a few years prior to his birth. His parents, Simon Kozminsky (born July 3, 1835, Raszkow, Prussia, died July 3, 1916, Melbourne) and Emma Esther Solomon (born 1848 in London, died November 27, 1924, Melbourne Vic), founded a jewelry shop in Melbourne under their name in 1851, which continues to exist to this day as *Kosminsky Studio*.

Kozminsky was a well-known author in the field of Jewish occult and esotericism and was reputed to be a prominent member of the *Hermetic Order of the Golden Dawn*, which has substantially influenced his writings. The Hermetic Order of the Golden Dawn was a mystical and magical organization that emerged in the late 19th century. Founded in London, England, in 1888, the Golden Dawn attracted individuals with a keen interest in esoteric knowledge, occult practices, and spiritual development. Drawing inspiration from various sources, including Hermeticism, Kabbalah, Tarot, and astrology, the Golden Dawn aimed to explore and understand the hidden mysteries of the universe. Its teachings encompassed ceremonial magic, divination, alchemy, and ritual practices. The order emphasized personal growth, self-realization, and the attainment of spiritual enlightenment. Among its notable members were renowned occultists such as Samuel Liddell MacGregor Mathers, Arthur Edward Waite, and Aleister Crowley, who later went on to make significant contributions to the field of esotericism. Although the Golden Dawn faced internal conflicts and eventually dissolved in the early 20th century, its influence and teachings continue to resonate within the realm of Western occultism, leaving a lasting legacy of magical practices and esoteric philosophy.

Kozminsky's writings exemplify his extensive knowledge of esoteric traditions and astrology. Over the course of his life, he authored numerous significant books on astrology and numerology. In 1917, following in the footsteps of Charubel and La Volasfera, he published his remarkable work on the symbolism of the zodiac degrees, titled *Zodiacal Symbology and its Planetary Power*. This enduring masterpiece continues to serve as an invaluable resource for those seeking a deeper understanding of interpreting natal charts. Kozminsky published *The Magic and Science of Jewels and Stones* in 1922, in which he republished a fraction of Charubels work *Psychology of Botany, Minerals and Precious Stones* about the spirits of stones and how to evoke them with sigils.

'Kozminsky was a well-known author in the field of Jewish occult and esotericism and was reputed to be a prominent member of the Hermetic Order of the Golden Dawn, which has substantially influenced his writings.'

February 18, 1907 Kozminsky married Eileen Watkins (1881-1952). Around 1935, Kozminsky, along with his wife and two children, relocated from Australia to London. Presumably, he made this move because London had established itself as a hub of esoteric and occult traditions by that time. Despite having a doctorate in archaeology and owning a well-established jewelry business, Kozminsky's true passion lay in the esoteric realm. At some point, possibly after his marriage, Kozminsky changed his name to Francis Coton, with the latter appearing to be his mother's maiden name. At least one of his children, Kenneth, used this name as a surname, although Kozminsky continued to publish under his original name.

There are conflicting accounts regarding his death. One version suggests that he passed away in London in 1940 at the age of 70 after an accident involving an escalator on the London Underground. Another version states that he died in London in 1944 during a V1 missile attack, possibly in a bomb shelter following pneumonia.

■

Six Axes Astrology
The zodiac in 6 axes instead
of 12 signs, or how your
opposite sign completes you
by Benjamin Adamah
100 pages, Paperback,
ISBN 9789492355607
www.vamzzz.com

You may have read about your zodiac sign, which is determined
by the position of the Sun at the time of your birth. However, what
many people don't know is that there is another important aspect
to consider. Your opposite zodiac sign represents your unconscious
self and has a significant impact on your life. The big secret is: this
opposite sign wants to be part of your game and can be of great help!
If you neglect the qualities and forces, that typify this opposite zodiac
sign, they will keep working against you – until you integrate them.

So, by simply gaining insight into your opposite sign and integrating
its qualities into your personality, decisions and actions, you avoid
a lot problems, delays, opposition, and blockages. This formula can
make your life much more stable, successful and fulfilling, and speed
up your personal development. Instead of spending a lot of money on
complex horoscope readings, try the proven formula presented in this
booklet first. Aries should integrate Libra, Taurus integrate Scorpio,
Gemini integrate Sagittarius, and so on. Don't just take the author's
word for it, try it out and see the results for yourself!

VAMzzz Publishing

PAPER BOOKS

VAMzzz Publishing is a publisher that preserves historical occult books and produces new and revised editions in various categories such as Magic & Witchcraft, Secret Rites & Societies, Demonology, Celtic & Mythology, and New Astrology.

Our books are written by highly qualified academic researchers or experts in specific fields of esoteric knowledge, craft, or practice. Many of the revised titles include a Post Scriptum with additional information about the author or subject.

Our reproductions of classic texts differ from others in two important ways. Firstly, we have chosen not to rely on OCR (Optical Character Recognition) technology, as we believe that this often results in poor quality books that are littered with typos and other errors. Secondly, in cases where the original text contains images, such as portraits, maps, or sketches, we have taken great care to preserve the quality of these illustrations, ensuring that they accurately reflect the original artefact. By preserving and sharing these works, we can gain a deeper understanding of our cultural heritage and the rich history of human thought and creativity that has come before us.

In addition to publishing books, VAMzzz Publishing also offers FREE articles on various occult topics, including Afro-American magic, folklore, and New Astrology on our blog. You are welcome to visit vamzzz.com/blog and explore these subjects further.

VAMzzz Publishing
P.O. Box 3340
1001 AC Amsterdam
The Netherlands
vamzzz@protonmail.com
www.vamzzz.com

Centaurs, Damocloids & Scattered Disc Objects
Asteroids in Astrology 1
by Benjamin Adamah, 162 pages, Hardcover
ISBN 9789492355409 (Professional literature)
Challenging the astrological status quo, this book discusses the fascinating astrological significance of no less than 85 Centaurs and Centaur related asteroids like Scattered Disc Objects (SDOs) & Detached Objects, Damocloids, retrograde Asteroids and (ex-) Comets. Centaurs are of major psychological importance, and as is the case with the first discovered Centaur Chiron, most of them are about healing and psycho-synthesis.

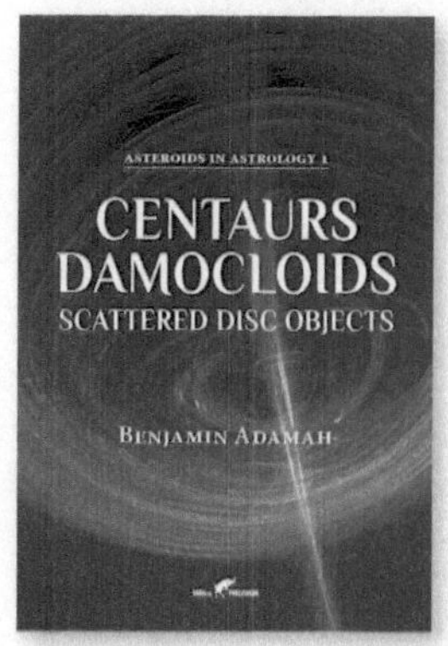

Plutinos
Asteroids in Astrology 2
by Benjamin Adamah, 126 pages, Hardcover
ISBN 9789492355522 (Professional literature)
Astrological research points out that most Plutinos, like their godfather Pluto, exert a compelling force in both personal and mundane horoscopes. They are radical, transforming, confronting, they penetrate the darkness, the blur, or daily life patterns and have a Scorpio-like preference for what you might call soul-mining. They trigger the awareness of slumbering patterns in the depths of our souls and force us to face the truth.

Cubewanos, Haumeids and other TNOs
Asteroids in Astrology 3
by Benjamin Adamah, 110 pages, Hardcover
ISBN 9789492355645 (Professional literature)
The Cubewanos get more and more attention in astrology. They form a group of asteroids and dwarf-planets in the Kuiper Belt, just beyond the orbit of Pluto. Their orbital period around the Sun is 260 to 330 years. To be classified as a Cubewano, the asteroid must be quite large (at least about 100 km in diameter). Cubewanos are complex objects, but mainly because of their versatility and less because of inherent conflicts or wounds as with Centaurs and Jupiter Trojans, or obsessive tendencies as seen with Plutinos.

www.ingramcontent.com/pod-product-compliance
Lightning Source LLC
Chambersburg PA
CBHW020313160726
47992CB00004B/1520